# LATIN AMERICAN
# WRITERS AT WORK

THE PARIS REVIEW

# LATIN AMERICAN WRITERS AT WORK

*Edited by George Plimpton*

*Introduction by Derek Walcott*

THE MODERN LIBRARY

NEW YORK

LIBRARY OF CONGRESS CATALOGING-IN-PUBLICATION DATA
Latin American writers at work / The Paris Review ; edited by
George Plimpton.
p.    cm.
Contents: Jorge Luis Borges—Pablo Neruda—Octavio Paz—Julio Cortázar—
Gabriel García Márquez—Carlos Fuentes—Guillermo Cabrera Infante—
Manuel Puig—Mario Vargas Llosa—Luisa Valenzuela.
ISBN 0-679-77349-5
1.  Authors, Spanish American—20th century—Interviews.
I.  Plimpton, George.   II.  Paris review.
PQ7081.3 .L38      2003
809'.868—dc21    2002026566
[B]

# Contents

# ACKNOWLEDGMENTS

The editor thanks the interviewers and the following staff members of *The Paris Review* for their help in preparing this volume: Tara Gallagher, James Lavino, and Sarah Lee.

# INTRODUCTION

## Derek Walcott

In Guadalajara, in the patio and the garden, I sensed a certain ferocity in the flowers, a quiet threat in the turgid mahogany furniture, a sense of usurpation in the bedroom, since there were many famous Latin American writers associated with the house—the premises of a foundation. It was an old fear, of alienation and inadequacy, because I had not read most of these writers whose names and novels you read of all the time, so my illiteracy was as much a burden in that climate as a woolen jacket and a sweater. The house had either belonged to, or was now used to commemorate, Julio Cortázar, a writer whose name I knew but whose work I have still not read, yet whose syntax I guessed from the furniture.

Even in the bright mornings, there was this sense of weight, because every object, however familiar, awaited translation, with the fear of its altering its Spanish shape. The two Indian housekeepers, sisters, knew no English and had to be addressed in emphatic mime. The wrought-iron front gate, the stairs, the tight street outside the elegant house, and of course the name of the city—the sinuous ululation of a song—strengthened the feeling that one needed to be translated into a Latin American novel, that one's gestures were being observed by García Márquez or Fuentes, that one did not violate the intricacies of a tradition, and that rituals were being encouraged by the smile of Paz.

Outside the city, on the way from the airport, the landscape was intimidating in its strangeness, its dust, its palms of a different design to those of my island, views that had to be read before they were interpreted, the sense of sorrow in its difference. You cannot love the literature without loving the landscape, and loving Guadalajara seemed hard, loving Mexico seemed like a lot of work.

To this small islander, the scale of Mexico was terrifying. The huge terra incognita of Latin America made ordinary life in so many countries inconceivable. I couldn't imagine what life in Lima was like, Buenos Aires was shrouded in my ignorance, and the little I knew of Brazil had come through its poetry like cracks of light under a door. Now these interviews are a corridor down which door after door opens, and we sit down as guests of these illuminators.

———

There was the writer, there was what he or she had written, and now there is the tape recorder, creator of the interview, a twentieth-century literary form, an intrusion on intimacy yet a form that requires journalistic, even Flaubertian, distance: a literary form in which the writer looks at his life and his work with a new impersonality, with a rhythm that should sound spontaneous in its sentences. This creates a benign beast, a double who speaks for the writer but whose stories, given the fallibility of memory, we do not completely trust. Interviews attract us because we want to devour banalities, the exactly ordinary, in other words, gossip. The old saying that no one cares "what porridge had John Keats" is a pretext. It is very important, bringing Keats up-to-date, to know if he prefers oatmeal to All-Bran, because the knowledge does not diminish but increases our astonishment at the magic of the Odes. It is like that touching confession of García Márquez's that he wanted to go back home because he had forgotten the smell of guava. We do not want our own biographies written, our sins are intolerable, yet we read the lives of other writers not as critics but as fans. That is what the greatest novels are, anyway—gossip. Joyce's voice, like a long shaggy-dog story, burbles *Ulysses* along; Flaubert, for all his nail-paring, cannot cut himself off from his fiction. From the *Odyssey* through *The Divine Comedy* to a Hemingway short story or a fable by García Márquez, what keeps fiction alive is the shared intimacy of the author whispering in our ear, as if we were the machine.

The greatest poetry has the drone of the human voice. Both *The Divine Comedy* and the *Odyssey* are, as well as being great verse, great talk. In Dante, the shifts of tone are conversational, epigram and simile rooted in the gestural vocabulary of the vulgar tongue. Of course, these interviews are respectable, without stuttering, exclamations, and obscenities, when most writers need cursing for meter and swear like sailors. Larkin was a stutterer, and Beckett was renowned for falling into chasmic silences. That meter is not represented here.

These varied individual authors "sound" general in print. Conversation democratizes identity and diffuses style, so Borges does not speak "Borges," nor does Neruda speak "Neruda" or García Márquez the prose of his novels. We want Beckett to sound like Molloy, and Borges to create, even as he answers questions, a response based on paradox and enigma; but then Shakespeare would not have replied with surges of astonishing verse. Once the subject of the interview begins to catalogue his or her actions with "I do this," then self-dramatization must assume postures of modesty or self-mockery. Sports heroes, movie stars, performers of all kinds add to their luster by showing that they are guys like us, but one is not sure that an accessible familiarity is quite what readers want. Gabo as a great guy. The fact is that there is Gabo and there is Gabriel García Márquez, and they are two different people when García Márquez is writing. We can't join in a duet with the writer, but most people who claim to love literature would prefer to have dinner or just a drink with famous writers than really read them. That was the kind of crowd that surrounded Hemingway, the cortege that grows around the famous and smothers them with adulation. Their eccentricities, their habits, their superstitions (smelling dead fruit, sharpening pencils, writing on colored paper—all talismans against failure) all reinforce the sanctity of the calling, the truth that all creation is ritual as much as it is discipline.

But sometimes in these interrogations an answer can acquire the grace of an epiphany. Here is Neruda talking about India as if he were reading from a novel with an excellent translation:

> The splendor of that unfamiliar continent overwhelmed me, and yet I felt desperate, because my life and my solitude there were so long. Sometimes I seemed locked into an unending Technicolor picture—a marvelous movie, but one I wasn't allowed to leave. I never experienced the mysticism which guided so many South Americans and other foreigners in India. People who go to India in search of a religious answer to their anxieties see things in a different way. As for me, I was profoundly moved by the sociological conditions—that immense unarmed nation, so defenseless, bound to its imperial yoke.

This is more touching than the oracular, polemical Neruda whose monody can be exhausting, whose ambition to achieve an Andean height often leaves the reader gasping. Epic and ritual are unavoidable challenges, maybe one should write "seductions," for the Latin American, that is, the New World poets. But the New World is very, very old.

The language of the conquistador and the priest, the pain of the Indian and the peon, the formalistic history of these New Spains, these remembered Portugals were as simple as the territories were incalculably immense, as everything beyond Guadalajara was to me. What poetry, what fiction could hope to contain it? This was also America, but a different one to Whitman's and the Indian presence could not be ignored.

Like the prologue to the Great Depression, the rich period that widened attention to the Latin American novel, to Carlos Fuentes, Julio Cortázar, Mario Vargas Llosa, and Gabriel García Márquez, particularly, was parenthesized by one expression (The Boom). A fecundity that had always been there was greeted with insulting astonishment, with the promise of transience and a stock market crash. First the rumblings, then the exultant gush, then the subsiding into oblivion; but many of the writers in this collection are still active. All of them are used to the prejudice that has treated the literature and art of a subcontinent (Mexico and Central America) and a continent (South America) as derivative and provincial. Caribbean colonial literature has shared that prejudice, yet it took me a long time to pay attention to writers who were virtually neighbors, sharers of a simplified history of discovery, conquest, and repression.

I came to Neruda late, probably in my late twenties, and to Paz and Borges even later, probably because I had no Spanish, but also because they were Spanish, and the British heredity of hostility to their rich, orotund, and gestural melody was natural for a poet brought up in a tradition that did not exult in but muttered its delight, that avoided yelping and surreal association. Neruda delivered me, for a long while. He was my own Boom. What happened later is not another story but the same story repeated. My early rejection of García Márquez came from this hatred of surrealism; then I saw, only on a second try, almost like an illumination, that he wrote with two narrators, his own voice and that of tribal gossip, and that they fused after the caesura into one sentence, the people of which is a masterwork, a great prose poem, *The Autumn of the Patriarch*. But the Boom?

INTERVIEWER: Do you owe your—I hate to say it—Latin American contemporaries anything?

CABRERA INFANTE: Not even money. For me there's Borges and the rest. They are the rest, a silent majority for me because I can't hear a word they're writing.

INTERVIEWER: But you are a part of the Boom of the Latin American novel of the sixties!

CABRERA INFANTE: Like hell! They were only a sonic boom, a wake. But since you press me, I confess I have a debt with Carlos Fuentes.

I have met Borges, then later Vargas Llosa, Octavio Paz, and Carlos Fuentes. Nice names to drop because affection was instantaneous, because they embraced me in brotherhood, not just shaking hands like American and British writers; because in Carlos's case, after I once dropped on my knees to the floor of an airport in greeting, he overdid it by prostrating himself, full length. All of this in joy, without solemnity. There are great and cherished faces behind their printed voices here, the basset-hound visage of Borges; Vargas Llosa, looking more like a film star than a writer; Carlos the hidalgo for whom intellect is a delight, so warm, so elegant; and then Octavio, ah, Octavio, his heavy but placid features a combination of an Indian high priest and a provincial mayor. Octavio, who spoke with an authoritative smile of such gentleness, the set of his face and the set of his lines synonymous. Carved and solid without being sullen. He looked like what he wrote, pre-Columbian; the poem became him as much as his face became his poem "Sun Stone."

"First let me say that I despise the term 'Latin America,'" says Guillermo Cabrera Infante in his interview in this collection. "Better call us Mongrelia. We are mongrels, a messy mix of white, black, and Indian. Second, aside from the elements I absorbed from the culture I grew up in I owe nothing to those 'elders' you mention, especially if they wrote in Spanish."

INTERVIEWER: What are you talking about?

CABRERA INFANTE: Well, Borges, an elder I admire, writes in Borgese, a private dialect composed of quaint and formal English that condescends to employ Spanish words with Anglo-Saxon syntax. I owe him a lot, but I owe nothing to his Spanish.

Borges's papal presence that makes a lot of his answers sound like compressed encyclicals is a great contrast to the self-mocking, satirical irreverence of Cabrera Infante, a parallel to be found in the anti-poems of Nicanor Parra versus the Marxist orthodoxies of Neruda. Borges's scholarship is astounding, the sort of authority that provokes or perhaps expects genuflection, except that in reality (whatever that meant for him), he was gentle, a sort of soft sculpture, very like his photographs (writing about him provokes imitation of his paradoxes), and genuinely curious. We had a brief conversation in which he wanted to know, out of his blindness, with startling accuracy, why I had a Dutch name. That afternoon, at a conference in New York, I had seen him attacked by a radical who accused him of arrogance and indifference—like a dog barking at an iguana—while Borges sat there, hand on the hook of his cane, containing his fear, if he had any, with that invulnerable pride that he evinces in his interview, a nearly blind and supposedly helpless man.

INTERVIEWER: Would you say that your own stories have their point of origin in a situation, not in a character?

BORGES: In a situation, right. Except for the idea of bravery, of which I'm very fond. Bravery, perhaps, because I'm not very brave myself.

English is a language that keeps its hands to its sides when it speaks. Its vehemence lies in subtleties of inflection, its emphasis in consonants rather than vowels. To read these interviews in English is more than to read them in translation, it is to hear them as the monologues of English gentlemen, without the melodic, orotundities of Latinate discourse. They are principally decent with the exception of Cabrera Infante, who parodies the idea of the interview with his delightful mischief: "Flattery will lead this interview nowhere, you know." With Infante, one feels like quoting more as one hoards the sarcastic epigrams of an irreverent friend. He describes one of his books in which a mulatto midget is "a peculiar sort of writer who has never written a line and who cannot because he cannot really speak."

INTERVIEWER: That's one paradox too many for me.

CABRERA INFANTE: The midget is very verbal and loquacious, even garrulous. But he, as one of my characters in *TTT* [ *Tres tristes tigres*] remarks, tries to turn Spanish into a dead language. He speaks in English, and because his English is not very good, he keeps on making puns and jokes. He is condemned, not to silence but to speaking gibberish.

Infante's next sentence is also excellent oral verse with English scansion.

> That is the language of Babel
> which is what Havana once was,
> Babelonia, where we spoke in tongues.

———

The influence of Hollywood on Latin American fiction is reasserted here. Many of these writers were actively involved in cinema. Cabrera Infante, Fuentes, García Márquez, and Puig wrote screenplays and reviewed movies. Borges's gaucho stories are Westerns with knives instead of guns, with the tango as their sound track. The medieval quest of a knight "pricking gently on the plain" (a long-shot of the cowboy), the smoking dragon of the railway train with the damsel lashed to the tracks, the primal fables of silent films attracted Borges as they did others, particularly Puig and García Márquez.

INTERVIEWER: Epic literature has always interested you very much, hasn't it?

BORGES: Always, yes. For example, there are many people who go to the cinema and cry. That has always happened: it has happened to me also. But I have never cried over sob stuff, or the pathetic episodes. But, for example, when I saw the first gangster films of Sternberg I remember that when there was anything epic about them—I mean Chicago gangsters dying bravely—well, I felt that my eyes were full of tears. I have felt epic poetry far more than lyric or elegy. I *always* felt that.... I think nowadays, while literary men seem to have neglected their epic duties, the epic has been saved for us, strangely enough, by the Westerns.

Cabrera Infante went to Hollywood and, to quote him, "earned more money than I had ever seen in my life." Manuel Puig wrote a novel entitled *Betrayed by Rita Hayworth* as well as *The Kiss of the Spider Woman*.

INTERVIEWER: Have you ever found that the dialogue of those 1940s films helped with fictional dialogue?

PUIG: I learned certain rules of story-telling from the films of that time. Mainly how to distribute the intrigue. But what interests me more about those films is examining the effect they had on people.

INTERVIEWER: On the people you grew up with?

PUIG: Well, yes—on my characters. My characters have all been affected by those cinematic dreams. In those days, movies were very important to people. They were their Mount Olympus. The stars were deities.

Borges's inwardly wounded gangsters were later repeated by Muni, Bogart, Cagney, Garfield, even Edward G. Robinson. They were not gringos but aliens rejected by society, their resentment easily understood by Third World audiences, not only by writers like Borges. In Westerns, the image of Mexican banditry was the same as that of the Revolution—sadistic, grinning generals with as many teeth as bullets in their crisscrossed gun belts, noble philosopher-peons, stormy-haired camp followers who are shot in the last reel to save the gringo hero from miscegenation, a fate worse than death. I enjoyed these clichés just as I did the slaughter of charging Zulus in hot boyhood cinemas, yelping at the sweep of a machine gun and at the untranslated, incomprehensible cries of my ancestral language.

Here in this collection are the voices behind the dust and the gray olive trees and the palm avenues and the congested slums and the shacks that run like wild vines or like this sentence across the hills overlooking the cities. The wind lifts them and you listen, the curtains gently stirred by their own breathing.

What these interviews achieve in their essential courtesy is the hallowing of the craft by the writers whatever their stupid quarrels, whatever their superficial cynicisms. It is this secular sacredness that, hovering on the verge of translation, of being translated myself, made me grateful for the echo of the names Cortázar, Fuentes, Paz, García Márquez, in the house in Guadalajara where the ferocity of the flowers was an ignorance that these voices dispel.

———

DEREK WALCOTT was born in 1930 in St. Lucia, Windward Islands, the West Indies. He graduated from the University of the West Indies, and in 1957 was awarded a fellowship by the Rockefeller Foundation to study the American theater. He is the founder of the Trinidad Theater Workshop and the author of five books of plays and ten books of poetry, including *The Arkansas Testament* and *Omeros*. He is an Honorary Member of the American Academy and Institute of Arts and Letters and was awarded the Nobel Prize in literature in 1992.

# LATIN AMERICAN
# WRITERS AT WORK

# JORGE LUIS BORGES

Jorge Luis Borges was born in Buenos Aires on August 24, 1899. Both of his parents spoke Spanish and English fluently, and "Georgie," as Borges was affectionately called, grew up trilingual, spending much of his childhood exploring his father's extensive library filled with books written in English, Spanish, and French.

In 1914 the Borges family moved to Europe—first to Switzerland, where young Borges and his sister Norah attended the College Calvin in Geneva, then to various cities in Spain. In Madrid, Borges began to acquaint himself with burgeoning avant-garde movements such as ultraism, and published poems in local literary magazines. In 1921 the family returned to Argentina, where Borges founded two literary magazines and published his first

*Jottings from Borges's personal notebooks.* Courtesy of the
University of Virginia Library and María Kodama.

poetry collections, *Fervor de Buenos Aires* (1923) and *Luna de Enfrente* (1925). The poems deal mainly with Borges's exuberant revisit to his hometown and his keen observations of the local color and gaucho tradition that dwelt within. In the early thirties, Borges began publishing collections of essays before he forayed into the genre for which he is perhaps best known and most praised—the short story. His first short story collections, *Historia universal de la infamia* [A Universal History of Infamy] (1935) and *Ficciones* (1944), earned him recognition as one of Argentina's greatest writers. Borges won the 1961 Prix Formentor, the International Publisher's Prize, for *Ficciones*.

From 1938 until his retirement in 1973, Borges held several jobs. The first was in a local library, a position that he described as nine years of "solid unhappiness." Not usually known for his political views, Borges began to speak out against then dictator Juan Perón; Perón retaliated by appointing Borges National Poultry Inspector. After Perón's fall, Borges was named director of the National Library of Argentina by the new government and served as professor of German, English, and North American literatures at the University of Buenos Aires. In the meantime, he wrote such notable works as *Labyrinths* (1962), *Elogie de la sombra* [In Praise of Darkness] (1969), and *El informe de Brodie* [Doctor Brodie's Report] (1970)— all collections of essays, poetry, and short stories.

During the late seventies and early eighties, at which point Borges was nearly blind, he continued to publish essays and short story collections. In April of 1986, he married his longtime secretary and collaborator María Kodama, and died later that same year of liver cancer.

———

*This interview was conducted in July 1966, in conversations I held with Borges at his office in the Biblioteca Nacional, of which he is the director. The room, recalling an older Buenos Aires, is not really an office at all, but a large, ornate, high-ceilinged chamber in the newly renovated library. On the walls—but far too high to be easily read, as if hung with diffidence—are various academic certificates and literary citations. There are also several Piranesi etchings, bringing to mind the nightmarish Piranesi ruin in*

*Borges's story "The Immortal." Over the fireplace is a large portrait; when I asked Borges's secretary, Miss Susana Quinteros, about the portrait, she responded in a fitting, if unintentional, echo of a basic Borgesian theme:* "No importa. *It's a reproduction of another painting."*

*At diagonally opposite corners of the room are two large, revolving bookcases which contain, Miss Quinteros explained, books Borges frequently consults, all arranged in a certain order and never varied so that Borges, who is nearly blind, can find them by position and size. The dictionaries, for instance, are set together, among them an old, sturdily rebacked, well-worn Anglo-Saxon dictionary. Among the other volumes, ranging from books in German and English on theology and philosophy to literature and history, are the complete* Pelican Guide to English Literature, *the Modern Library* Francis Bacon, *Hollander's* The Poetic Eddas, The Poems of Catullus, *Forsyth's* Geometry of Four Dimensions, *several volumes of* Harrap's English Classics, *Parkman's* The Conspiracy of Pontiac, *and the Chambers edition of* Beowulf. *Recently, Miss Quinteros said, Borges had been reading* The American Heritage Picture History of the Civil War, *and just the night before he had taken to his home, where his mother (who is in her nineties) reads aloud to him, Washington Irving's* Life of Mahomet. *Each day, late in the afternoon, Borges arrives at the library, where it is now his custom to dictate letters and poems which Miss Quinteros types and reads back to him. Following his revisions, she makes two or three, sometimes four copies of each poem before Borges is satisfied. Some afternoons she reads to him, and he carefully corrects her English pronunciation. Occasionally when he wants to think, Borges leaves his office and slowly circles the library's rotunda, high above the readers at the tables below. But he is not always serious, Miss Quinteros stressed, confirming what one might expect from his writing: "Always there are jokes, little practical jokes."*

*When Borges entered the library, wearing a beret and a dark grey flannel suit hanging loosely from his shoulders and sagging over his shoes, everyone stopped talking for a moment, pausing, perhaps out of respect, perhaps out of empathetic hesitation for a man who is not entirely blind. His walk is tentative, and he carries a cane which he uses like a divining rod. He is short, with hair that looks slightly unreal in the way it rises from his head. His features are vague, softened by age, partially erased by the paleness of his skin. His voice, too, is unempathetic, almost a drone, seeming, possibly because of the unfocused expression of his eyes, to come from another person behind the face, and his gestures and expressions are lethargic—characteristic is the involuntary droop of one eyelid. But when he laughs—and he laughs often—his features wrinkle into what actually resembles a wry question mark; and he is apt to make a sweeping or clearing gesture with his arm and to bring his hand down on the table. Most of his statements take the form of rhetorical questions; but in asking a genuine question, Borges displays now a looming curiosity, now a shy, almost pathetic incredulity. When he chooses, as in telling a joke, he adopts a crisp, dramatic tone, and his quotation of a line from Oscar Wilde would do justice to an Edwardian actor. His accent defies easy classification: a cosmopolitan diction emerging from a Spanish background, educated by correct English speech and influenced by American movies. (Certainly no Englishman ever pronounced* piano *as* pie-ano, *and no American says* a-nee-hilates *for* annihilates.) *The predominant quality of his articulation is the way his words slur softly into one another, allowing suffixes to dwindle so that* couldn't *and* could *are virtually indistinguishable. Slangy and informal when he wants to be, more typically he is formal and bookish in his English speech, relying, quite naturally, on phrases like "that is to say" and "wherein." Always his sentences are linked by the narrative "and then" or the logical "consequently."*

*But most of all, Borges is shy. Retiring, even self-obliterating, he avoids personal statement as much as possible and obliquely answers questions about himself by talking of other writers, using their words and even their books as emblems of his own thought.*

*In this interview, it has been attempted to preserve the colloquial quality of his English speech—an illuminating contrast to his writings and a revelation of his intimacy with a language that has figured so importantly in the development of his writing.*

INTERVIEWER: You don't object to my recording our conversations?

JORGE LUIS BORGES: No, no. You fix the gadgets. They are a hindrance, but I will try to talk as if they're not there. Now, where are you from?

INTERVIEWER: From New York.

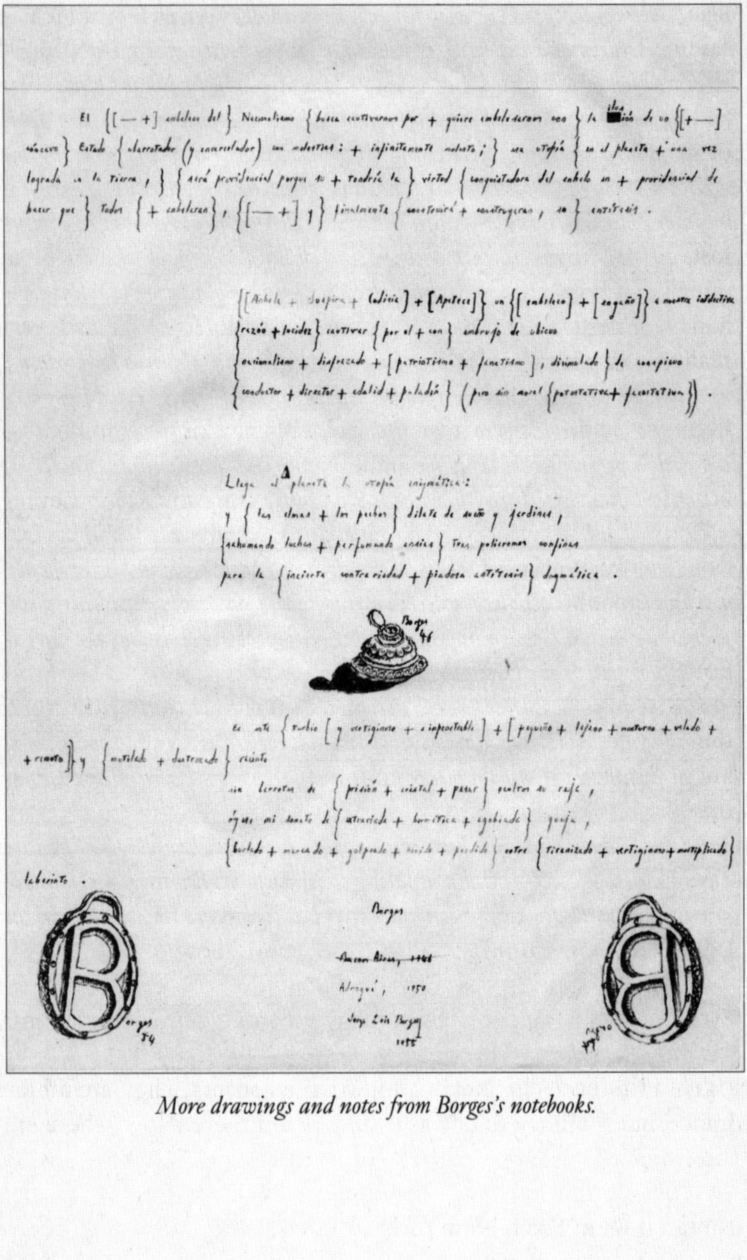


*More drawings and notes from Borges's notebooks.*

BORGES: Ah, New York. I was there and I liked it very much—I said to myself: "Well, I have made this; this is my work."

INTERVIEWER: You mean the walls of the high buildings, the maze of streets?

BORGES: Yes. I rambled about the streets—Fifth Avenue—and got lost, but the people were always kind. I remember answering many questions about my work from tall, shy young men. In Texas they had told me to be afraid of New York, but I liked it. Well, are you ready?

INTERVIEWER: Yes, the machine is already working.

BORGES: Now, before we start, what kind of questions are they?

INTERVIEWER: Mostly about your own work and about English writers you have expressed an interest in.

BORGES: Ah, that's right. Because if you ask me questions about the younger contemporary writers, I'm afraid I know very little about them. For about the last seven years I've been doing my best to know something of Old English and Old Norse. Consequently, that's a long way off in time and space from the Argentine, from Argentine writers, no? But if I have to speak to you about the *Finnsburg Fragment* or the elegies or the *Battle of Brunanburg*...

INTERVIEWER: Would you like to talk about those?

BORGES: No, not especially.

INTERVIEWER: What made you decide to study Anglo-Saxon and Old Norse?

BORGES: I began by being very interested in metaphor. And then in some book or other—I think in Andrew Lang's *History of English*

*Literature*—I read about the kennings, metaphors of Old English, and in a far more complex fashion of Old Norse poetry. Then I went in for the study of Old English. Nowadays, or rather today, after several years of study, I'm no longer interested in the metaphors, because I think that they were rather a weariness of the flesh to the poets themselves—at least to the Old English poets.

INTERVIEWER: To repeat them you mean?

BORGES: To repeat them, to use them over and over again and to keep on speaking of the *hronrad, waelrad,* or "road of the whale" instead of "the sea"—that kind of thing—and "the sea-wood," "the stallion of the sea" instead of "the ship." So I decided finally to stop using them, the metaphors that is; but in the meanwhile I had begun studying the language and I fell in love with it. Now I have formed a group—we're about six or seven students—and we study almost every day. We've been going through the highlights in *Beowulf,* the *Finnsburg Fragment* and *The Dream of the Rood.* Also, we've gotten into King Alfred's prose. Now we've begun learning Old Norse, which is rather akin to Old English. I mean the vocabularies are not really very different: Old English is a kind of halfway house between the Low German and the Scandinavian.

INTERVIEWER: Epic literature has always interested you very much, hasn't it?

BORGES: Always, yes. For example, there are many people who go to the cinema and cry. That has always happened: it has happened to me also. But I have never cried over sob stuff, or the pathetic episodes. But, for example, when I saw the first gangster films of Sternberg I remember that when there was anything epic about them—I mean Chicago gangsters dying bravely—well, I felt that my eyes were full of tears. I have felt epic poetry far more than lyric or elegy. I *always* felt that. Now that may be, perhaps, because I come from military stock. My grandfather, Colonel Borges, fought in the border warfare with the Indians and he died in a revolution;

my great-grandfather, Colonel Suárez, led a Peruvian cavalry charge in one of the last great battles against the Spaniards; another great-uncle of mine led the vanguard of San Martín's army—that kind of thing. And I had, well, one of my great-great-grandmothers was a sister of Rosas*—I'm not especially proud of that relationship, because I think of Rosas as being a kind of Perón in his day; but still all those things link me with Argentine history and also with the idea of a man's having to be brave, no?

INTERVIEWER: But the characters you pick as your epic heroes— the gangster for example—are not usually thought of as epic, are they? Yet you seem to find the epic there?

BORGES: I think there is a kind of, perhaps, low epic in him—no?

INTERVIEWER: Do you mean that since the old kind of epic is apparently no longer possible for us, we must look to this kind of character for our heroes?

BORGES: I think that as to epic poetry or as to epic literature, rather—if we except such writers as T. E. Lawrence in his *Seven Pillars of Wisdom* or some poets like Kipling, for example in "Harp Song of the Dane Women" or even in the stories—I think nowadays, while literary men seem to have neglected their epic duties, the epic has been saved for us, strangely enough, by the Westerns.

INTERVIEWER: I have heard that you have seen the film *West Side Story* many times.

BORGES: Many times, yes. Of course, *West Side Story* is not a Western.

INTERVIEWER: No, but for you it has the same epic qualities?

* Juan Manuel de Rosas (1793–1877), an Argentine military dictator.

BORGES: I think it has, yes. During this century, as I say, the epic tradition has been saved for the world by, of all places, Hollywood. When I went to Paris, I felt I wanted to shock people, and when they asked me—they knew that I was interested in the films, or that I had been, because my eyesight is very dim now—and they asked me, "What kind of film do you like?" And I said, "Candidly, what I most enjoy are the Westerns." They were all Frenchmen; they fully agreed with me. They said, "Of course we see such films as *Hiroshima, mon amour* or *L'Année dernière à Marienbad* out of a sense of duty, but when we want to amuse ourselves, when we want to enjoy ourselves, when we want, well, to get a real kick, then we see American films."

INTERVIEWER: Then it is the content, the "literary" content of the film, rather than any of the technical aspects of the movies that interests you?

BORGES: I know very little about the technical part of movies.

INTERVIEWER: If I may change the subject to your own fiction, I would like to ask about your having said that you were very timid about beginning to write stories.

BORGES: Yes, I was very timid, because when I was young I thought of myself as a poet. So I thought: "If I write a story everybody will know I'm an outsider, that I am intruding in forbidden ground." Then I had an accident. You can feel the scar. If you touch my head here, you will see. Feel all those mountains, bumps? Then I spent a fortnight in a hospital. I had nightmares and sleeplessness—insomnia. After that they told me that I had been in danger, well, of dying, that it was really a wonderful thing that the operation had been successful. I began to fear for my mental integrity—I said, "Maybe I can't write anymore." Then my life would have been practically over, because literature is very important to me. Not because I think my own stuff particularly good, but because I know that I can't get along without writing. If I don't write, I feel, well, a kind of remorse, no? Then I thought I would try my hand at writing an article or a poem. But I thought: "I have written hundreds of articles and poems. If I can't do it, then I'll know at once that I am done for, that everything is over with me." So I thought I'd try my hand at something I hadn't done: if I couldn't do it, there would be nothing strange about it, because why should I write short stories?—It would prepare me for the final overwhelming blow: knowing that I was at the end of my tether. I wrote a story called, let me see, I think, *"Hombre de la esquina rosada,"** and everyone enjoyed it very much. It was a great relief to me. If it hadn't been for that particular knock on the head I got, perhaps I would never have written short stories.

INTERVIEWER: And perhaps you would never have been translated?

BORGES: And no one would have thought of translating me. So it was a blessing in disguise. Those stories, somehow or other, made their way: they got translated into French, I won the Formentor Prize, and then I seemed to be translated into many tongues. The first translator was Ibarra. He was a close friend of mine and he translated the stories into French. I think he greatly improved upon them, no?

INTERVIEWER: Ibarra, not Caillois, was the first translator?

BORGES: He and Roger Caillois. At a ripe old age, I began to find that many people were interested in my work all over the world. It seems strange: many of my writings have been done into English, into Swedish, into French, into Italian, into German, into Portuguese, into some of the Slav languages, into Danish. And always this comes as a great surprise to me, because I remember I published a book—that must have been way back in 1932, I think—

---

* This is, perhaps, a slip of memory: the story was *"Pierre Menard, autor del Quijote,"* published in *Sur,* number 56 (May 1959).

and at the end of the year I found out that no less than thirty-seven copies had been sold!

INTERVIEWER: Was that the *Universal History of Infamy*?

BORGES: No, no. *History of Eternity*. At first I wanted to find every single one of the buyers to apologize because of the book and also to thank them for what they had done. There is an explanation for that. If you think of thirty-seven people—those people are real, I mean every one of them has a face of his own, a family, he lives on his own particular street. Why, if you sell, say two thousand copies, it is the same thing as if you had sold nothing at all, because two thousand is too vast—I mean, for the imagination to grasp. While thirty-seven people—perhaps thirty-seven are too many, perhaps seventeen would have been better or even seven—but still thirty-seven are still within the scope of one's imagination.

INTERVIEWER: Speaking of numbers, I notice in your stories that certain numbers occur repeatedly.

BORGES: Oh, yes. I'm awfully superstitious. I'm ashamed about it. I tell myself that after all, superstition is, I suppose, a slight form of madness, no?

INTERVIEWER: Or of religion?

BORGES: Well, religion, but… I suppose that if one attained one hundred and fifty years of age, one would be quite mad, no? Because all those small symptoms would have been growing. Still, I see my mother, who is ninety, and she has far fewer superstitions than I have. Now, when I was reading for the tenth time, I suppose, Boswell's *Johnson*, I found that he was full of superstition, and at the same time, that he had a great fear of madness. In the prayers he composed, one of the things he asked God was that he should not be a madman, so he must have been worried about it.

INTERVIEWER: Would you say that it is the same reason—superstition—that causes you to use the same colors—red, yellow, green—again and again?

BORGES: But do I use green?

INTERVIEWER: Not as often as the others. But you see I did a rather trivial thing, I counted the colors in ...

BORGES: No, no. That is called *estilística;* here it is studied. No, I think you'll find yellow.

INTERVIEWER: But red too, often moving, fading into rose.

BORGES: Really? Well, I never knew that.

INTERVIEWER: It's as if the world today were a cinder of yesterday's fire—that's a metaphor you use. You speak of "Red Adam," for example.

BORGES: Well, the word *Adam,* I think, in the Hebrew means "red earth." Besides it sounds well, no? *"Rojo Adán."*

INTERVIEWER: Yes it does. But that's not something you intend to show: the degeneration of the world by the metaphorical use of color?

BORGES: I don't intend to show anything. (*Laughter*) I have no intentions.

INTERVIEWER: Just to describe?

BORGES: I describe. I write. Now as for the color yellow, there is a physical explanation of that. When I began to lose my sight, the last color I saw, or the last color, rather, that stood out, because of course now I know that your coat is not the same color as this table or of the woodwork behind you—the last color to stand out was yellow, because it is the most vivid of colors. That's why you have the Yellow Cab Company in the United States. At first they thought of making the cars scarlet. Then somebody found out that at night or when there was a fog that yellow stood out in a more vivid way than scarlet. So you have yellow cabs because anybody can pick them out. Now when I began to lose my eyesight, when the world began to fade away from me, there was a time among my friends . . . well they made, they poked fun at me because I was always wearing yellow neckties. Then they thought I really liked yellow although it really was too glaring. I said, "Yes, to you, but not to me, because it is the only color I can see, practically!" I live in a grey world, rather like the silver screen world. But yellow stands out. That might account for it. I remember a joke of Oscar Wilde's: a friend of his had a tie with yellow, red, and so on in it, and Wilde said, "Oh, my dear fellow, only a deaf man could wear a tie like that!"

INTERVIEWER: He might have been talking about the yellow necktie I have on now.

BORGES: Ah, well. I remember telling that story to a lady who missed the whole point. She said, "Of course, it must be because being deaf he couldn't hear what people were saying about his necktie." That might have amused Oscar Wilde, no?

INTERVIEWER: I'd like to have heard his reply to that.

BORGES: Yes, of course. I never heard of such a case of something being so perfectly misunderstood. The perfection of stupidity. Of course, Wilde's remark is a witty translation of an idea; in Spanish as well as English you speak of a "loud color." A "loud color" is a common phrase, but then the things that are said in literature are always the same. What is important is the way they are said. Looking for metaphors, for example: when I was a young man I was always hunting for new metaphors. Then I found out that really good metaphors are always the same. I mean you compare time to a road, death to sleeping, life to dreaming, and those are the great metaphors in literature, because they correspond to something essential. If you invent metaphors, they are apt to be surprising during the fraction of a second, but they strike no deep emotion whatever. If you think of life as a dream, that is a thought, a thought that is real, or at least that most men are bound to have, no? "What oft was thought but ne'er so well expressed." I think that's better than the idea of shocking people, than finding connections between things that have never been connected before, because there is no real connection, so the whole thing is a kind of juggling.

INTERVIEWER: Juggling just words?

BORGES: Just words. I wouldn't even call them real metaphors because in a real metaphor both terms are really linked together. I have found one exception—a strange, new and beautiful metaphor from Old Norse poetry. In Old English poetry a battle is spoken of as the "play of swords" or the "encounter of spears." But in Old Norse, and I think also in Celtic poetry, a battle is called a "web of men." That is strange, no? Because in a web you have a pattern, a weaving of men, *un tejido*. I suppose in medieval battle you got a kind of web because of having the swords and spears on opposite sides and so on. So there you have, I think, a new metaphor; and, of course, with a nightmare touch about it, no? The idea of a web made of living men, of living things, and still being a web, still being a pattern. It is a strange idea, no?

INTERVIEWER: It corresponds, in a general way, to the metaphor George Eliot uses in *Middlemarch*, that society is a web and one cannot disentangle a strand without touching all the others.

BORGES: (*With great interest*) Who said that?

INTERVIEWER: George Eliot, in *Middlemarch*.

BORGES: Ah, *Middlemarch*! Yes, of course! You mean the whole universe is linked together; everything linked. Well that's one of the reasons the Stoic philosophers had for believing in omens. There's a paper, a very interesting paper, as all of his are, by De Quincey on modern superstition, and there he gives the Stoic theory. The idea is that since the whole universe is one living thing, then there is a kinship between things that seem far off. For example, if thirteen people dine together, one of them is bound to die within the year. Not merely because of Jesus Christ and the Last Supper, but also because *all* things are bound together. He said—I wonder how that sentence runs—that everything in the world is a secret glass or secret mirror of the universe.

INTERVIEWER: You have often spoken of the people who have influenced you, like De Quincey...

BORGES: De Quincey greatly, yes, and Schopenhauer in German. Yes, in fact, during the First World War, I was led by Carlyle—Carlyle: I rather dislike him: I think he invented Nazism and so on: one of the fathers or forefathers of such things—well, I was led by Carlyle to a study of German and I tried my hand at Kant's *Critique of Pure Reason*. Of course, I got bogged down as most people do—as most Germans do. Then I said, "Well, I'll try their poetry, because poetry has to be shorter because of the verse." I got hold of a copy of Heine's *Lyrisches Intermezzo* and an English-German dictionary and at the end of two or three months I found I could get on fairly well without the aid of a dictionary.

I remember the first English novel I read through was a Scottish novel called *House with the Green Shutters*.

INTERVIEWER: Who wrote that?

BORGES: A man called Douglas. Then that was plagiarized by the man who wrote *Hatter's Castle*—Cronin—there was the same plot, practically. The book was written in the Scots dialect—I mean people instead of saying *money* speak of *baubees* or instead of *children*, *bairns*—that's an Old English and Norse word also—and they say *nicht* for *night:* that's Old English.

INTERVIEWER: And how old were you when you read that?

BORGES: I must have been about—there were many things I didn't understand—I must have been about ten or eleven. Before that, of course, I had read the *Jungle Books* and I had read Stevenson's *Treasure Island,* a very fine book. But the first real novel was that novel. When I read that, I wanted to be Scotch, and then I asked my grandmother and she was very indignant about it. She said, "Thank goodness that you're not!" Of course, maybe she was wrong. She came from Northumberland; they must have had some Scottish blood in them. Perhaps even Danish blood way back.

INTERVIEWER: With this long interest in English and your great love of it…

BORGES: Look here, I'm talking to an American: there's a book I *must* speak about—nothing unexpected about it—that book is *Huckleberry Finn.* I thoroughly dislike *Tom Sawyer.* I think that Tom Sawyer spoils the last chapters of *Huckleberry Finn.* All those silly jokes. They are all pointless jokes; but I suppose Mark Twain thought it was his duty to be funny, even when he wasn't in the mood. The jokes had to be worked in somehow. According to what George Moore said, the English always thought: "Better a bad joke than no joke."

I think that Mark Twain was one of the really great writers but I think he was rather unaware of the fact. But perhaps in order to write a really great book, you *must* be rather unaware of the fact. You can slave away at it and change every adjective to some other adjective, but perhaps you can write better if you leave the mistakes. I remember what Bernard Shaw said, that as to style, a writer has as much style as his conviction will give him and not more. Shaw thought that the idea of a game of style was quite nonsensical, quite meaningless. He thought of Bunyan, for example, as a great writer because he was convinced of what he was saying. If a writer disbelieves what he is writing, then he can hardly expect his readers to believe it. In this country, though, there is a tendency to regard any kind of writing—especially the writing of poetry—as a game of style. I have known many poets here who have written well—very fine stuff—with delicate moods and so on—but if you talk with them, the only thing they tell you is smutty stories or speak of politics in the way that everybody does, so that really their writing turns out to be a kind of sideshow. They had learned writing in the way that a man might learn to play chess or to play bridge. They were not really poets or writers at all. It was a trick they had learned and they had learned it thoroughly. They had the whole thing at their finger ends. But most of them—except four or five I should say—seemed to think of life as having nothing poetic or mysterious about it. They take things for granted. They know that when they have to write, then, well, they have to suddenly become rather sad or ironic.

INTERVIEWER: To put on their writer's hat?

BORGES: Yes, put on the writer's hat and get into a right mood, and then write. Afterward, they fall back on current politics.

SUSANA QUINTEROS: (*Entering*) Excuse me. Señor Campbell is waiting.

BORGES: Ah, please ask him to wait a moment. Well, there's a Mr. Campbell waiting; the Campbells are coming.

INTERVIEWER: When you wrote your stories, did you revise a great deal?

BORGES: At first I did. Then I found out that when a man reaches a certain age he has found his real tone. Nowadays, I try to go over what I've written after a fortnight or so and of course there are many slips and repetitions to be avoided, certain favorite tricks that should not be overworked. But I think that what I write nowadays is always on a certain level and that I can't better it very much nor can I spoil it very much either. Consequently I let it go, forget all about it, and think about what I'm doing at the time. The last things I have been writing are *milongas,* popular songs.

INTERVIEWER: Yes, I saw a volume of them, a beautiful book.

BORGES: Yes, *Para seis cuerdas,* meaning, of course, the guitar. The guitar was a popular instrument when I was a boy. Then you would find people strumming the guitar, not too skillfully, at nearly every street corner of every town. Some of the best tangos were composed by people who couldn't write them nor read them. But of course they had music in their souls, as Shakespeare might have said. So they dictated them to somebody: they were played on the piano, and they got written down and they were published for the literate people. I remember I met one of them—Ernesto Poncio. He wrote "Don Juan," one of the best tangos before the tangos were spoiled by the Italians in La Boca and so on: I mean when the tangos came from the *criolla.* He once said to me: "I have been in jail many times, Señor Borges, but always for manslaughter!" What he meant to say was that he wasn't a thief or a pimp.

INTERVIEWER: In your *Antología personal* ...

BORGES: Look here, I want to say that that book is full of misprints. My eyesight is very dim, and the proofreading had to be done by somebody else.

INTERVIEWER: I see, but those are only minor errors, aren't they?

BORGES: Yes, I know, but they creep in and they worry the writer, not the reader. The reader accepts anything, no? Even the starkest nonsense.

INTERVIEWER: What was your principle of selection in that book?

BORGES: My principle of selection was simply that I felt the stuff was better than what I had left out. Of course, if I had been cleverer I would have insisted on leaving out those stories and then after my death someone would have found out that what had been left out was really good. That would have been a cleverer thing to do, no? I mean to publish all the weak stuff, then to let somebody find out that I had left out the real things.

INTERVIEWER: You like jokes very much, don't you?

BORGES: Yes, I do, yes.

INTERVIEWER: But the people who write about your books, your fiction in particular...

BORGES: No, no—they write far too seriously.

INTERVIEWER: They seldom seem to recognize that some of them are very funny.

BORGES: They are meant to be funny. Now a book will come out called *Crónicas de H. Bustos Domecq* written with Adolfo Bioy Casares. That book will be about architects, poets, novelists, sculptors and so on. All the characters are imaginary and they are all very up-to-date, very modern; they take themselves very seriously; so does the writer, but they are not actually parodies of anybody. We are simply going as far as a certain thing can be done. For example, many writers from here tell me: "We would like to have your message." You see, we have no message at all. When I write, I write because a thing has to be done. I don't think a writer should meddle too much with his own work. He should let the work write itself, no?

INTERVIEWER: You have said that a writer should never be judged by his ideas.

BORGES: No, I don't think ideas are important.

INTERVIEWER: Well then, what should he be judged by?

BORGES: He should be judged by the enjoyment he gives and by the emotions one gets. As to ideas, after all it is not very important whether a writer has some political opinion or other, because a work will come through despite them as in the case of Kipling's *Kim*. Suppose you consider the idea of the empire of the English— well, in *Kim* I think the characters one really is fond of are not the English, but many of the Indians, the Mussulmans. I think they're nicer people. And that's because he thought them—No! No! not because he thought them nicer—because he *felt* them nicer.

INTERVIEWER: What about metaphysical ideas then?

BORGES: Ah, well, metaphysical ideas, yes. They can be worked into parables and so on.

INTERVIEWER: Readers very often call your stories parables. Do you like that description?

BORGES: No, no. They're not meant to be parables. I mean if they are parables...(*long pause*)...that is, if they are parables, they have *happened* to be parables, but my intention has never been to write parables.

INTERVIEWER: Not like Kafka's parables then?

BORGES: In the case of Kafka, we know very little. We only know that he was very dissatisfied with his own work. Of course, when he told his friend, Max Brod, that he wanted his manuscripts to be burned, as Vergil did, I suppose he knew that his friend wouldn't do that. If a man wants to destroy his own work, he throws it into a fire, and there it goes. When he tells a close friend of his: "I want all the manuscripts to be destroyed," he knows that the friend will never do that, and the friend knows that he knows and that he knows that the other knows that he knows and so on and so forth.

INTERVIEWER: It's all very Jamesian.

BORGES: Yes, of course. I think that the whole world of Kafka is to be found in a far more complex way in the stories of Henry James. I think that they both thought of the world as being at the same time complex and meaningless.

INTERVIEWER: Meaningless?

BORGES: Don't you think so?

INTERVIEWER: No, I don't really think so. In the case of James...

BORGES: But in the case of James, yes. In the case of James, yes. I don't think he thought the world had any moral purpose. I think he disbelieved in God. In fact I think there's a letter written to his brother, the psychologist William James, wherein he says that the world is a diamond museum, let's say a collection of oddities, no? I suppose he meant that. Now in the case of Kafka, I think Kafka was looking for something.

INTERVIEWER: For some meaning?

BORGES: For some meaning, yes; and not finding it, perhaps. But I think that they both lived in a kind of maze, no?

INTERVIEWER: I would agree to that. A book like *The Sacred Fount* for example.

BORGES: Yes, *The Sacred Fount* and many short stories. For example, "The Abasement of the Northmores," where the whole story is a beautiful revenge, but a revenge that the reader never knows will happen or not. The woman is very sure that her husband's work, which nobody seems to have read or care about, is far better than the work of his famous friend. But maybe the whole thing is untrue.

Maybe she was just led by her love for him. One doesn't know whether those letters, when they are published, will really come to anything. Of course James was trying to write two or three stories at one time. That's the reason why he never gave any explanation. The explanation would have made the story poorer. He said: "*The Turn of the Screw* was just a pot-boiler, don't worry about it." But I don't think that was the truth. For instance, he said, "Well, if I give explanations, then the story will be poorer because the alternative explanations will be left out." I think he did that on purpose.

INTERVIEWER: I agree; people shouldn't know.

BORGES: People shouldn't know, and perhaps he didn't know himself!

INTERVIEWER: Do you like to have the same effect on your readers?

BORGES: Oh, yes. Of course I do. But I think the stories of Henry James are far above his novels. What's important in the stories of Henry James are the situations created, not the characters. *The Sacred Fount* would be far better if you could tell one character from the other. But you have to wade through some three hundred pages in order to find out who Lady So-and-so's lover was, and then at the end you may guess that it was So-and-so and not What's-his-name. You can't tell them apart; they all speak in the same way; there are no real characters. Only the American seems to stand out. If you think of Dickens, well, while the characters don't seem to stand out, they are far more important than the plot.

INTERVIEWER: Would you say that your own stories have their point of origin in a situation, not in a character?

BORGES: In a situation, right. Except for the idea of bravery, of which I'm very fond. Bravery, perhaps, because I'm not very brave myself.

INTERVIEWER: Is that why there are so many knives and swords and guns in your stories?

BORGES: Yes, that may be. Oh, but there are two causes there: first, seeing the swords at home, because of my grandfather and my great-grandfather and so on. Seeing all those swords. Then I was bred in Palermo, it all was a slum then and people always thought of themselves—I don't say that it was true, but that they always thought of themselves—as being better than the people who lived on a different side of the town—as being better fighters and that kind of thing. Of course, that may have been rubbish. I don't think they were especially brave. To call a man, or to think of him, as a coward—that was the last thing; that's the kind of thing he couldn't stand. I have even known of a case of a man coming from the southern side of the town in order to pick a quarrel with somebody who was famous as a knifer on the north side and getting killed for his pains. They had no real reason to quarrel: they had never seen each other before; there was no question of money or women or anything of the kind. I suppose it was the same thing in the West in the States. Here the thing wasn't done with guns, but with knives.

INTERVIEWER: Using the knife takes the deed back to an older form of behavior?

BORGES: An older form, yes. Also, it is a more personal idea of courage. Because you can be a good marksman and not especially brave. But if you're going to fight your man at close quarters, and you have knives...I remember I once saw a man challenging another to fight and the other caved in. But he caved in, I think, because of a trick. One was an old hand, he was seventy, and the other was a young and vigorous man, he must have been between twenty-five and thirty. Then the old man, he begged your pardon, he came back with two daggers and one was a span longer than the other. He said: "Here, choose your weapon." So he gave the other the chance of choosing the longer weapon, and having an advantage over him; but that also meant that he felt so sure of himself that he could afford that handicap. The other apologized and caved in, of course. I remember that a brave man, when I was a young man in the slums, he was always supposed to carry a *short* dagger and it was worn here. Like this, (*pointing to his armpit*) so it could be taken out at a moment's notice, and the slum word for the knife—or one of the slum words—well, one was *el fierro*, but of course that means nothing special. But one of the names, and that has been quite lost—it's a pity—was *el vaivén*, the "come and go." In the word *come-and-go* (*making gesture*) you see the flash of the knife, the sudden flash.

INTERVIEWER: It's like a gangster's holster?

BORGES: Exactly, yes, like a holster—on the left side. Then it could be taken out at a moment's notice and you scored *el vaivén*. It was spelled as one word and everyone knew it meant *knife*. *El fierro* is rather poor as a name because to call it *the iron* or *the steel* means nothing, while *el vaivén* does.

SUSANA QUINTEROS: (*Entering again*) Señor Campbell is still waiting.

BORGES: Yes, yes, we know. The Campbells are coming!

INTERVIEWER: Two writers I wanted to ask you about are Joyce and Eliot. You were one of the first readers of Joyce and you even translated part of *Ulysses* into Spanish, didn't you?

BORGES: Yes, I'm afraid I undertook a very faulty translation of the last page of *Ulysses*. Now as to Eliot, at first I thought of him as being a finer critic than a poet; now I think that sometimes he is a very fine poet, but as a critic I find that he's too apt to be always drawing fine distinctions. If you take a great critic, let's say Emerson or Coleridge, you feel that he has read a writer and that his criticism comes from his personal experience of him, while in the case of Eliot you always think—at least I always feel—that he's agreeing with some professor or slightly disagreeing with another. Consequently he's not creative. He's an intelligent man who's drawing fine distinctions, and I suppose he's right; but at the same time after reading, to take a stock example, Coleridge on Shakespeare, especially on the character of Hamlet, a new Hamlet had been created for you, or after reading Emerson on Montaigne or whoever it may be. In Eliot there are no such acts of creation. You feel that he has read many books on the subject—he's agreeing or disagreeing—sometimes making slightly nasty remarks, no?

INTERVIEWER: Yes, that he takes back later.

BORGES: Yes, yes, that he takes back later. Of course, he took those remarks back later because at first he was what might be called nowadays "an angry young man." In the end, I suppose he thought of himself as being an English classic and then he found that he had to be polite to his fellow classics, so that afterwards he took back most of the things he had said about Milton or even against Shakespeare. After all, he felt that in some ideal way they were all sharing the same academy.

INTERVIEWER: Did Eliot's work, his poetry, have any effect on your own writing?

BORGES: No, I don't think so.

INTERVIEWER: I have been struck by certain resemblances between *The Waste Land* and your story "The Immortal."

BORGES: Well, there may be something there, but in that case I'm quite unaware of it, because he's not one of the poets I love. I should rank Yeats far above him. In fact, if you don't mind my saying so, I think Frost is a finer poet than Eliot. I mean a finer *poet*. But I suppose Eliot was a far more intelligent man; however, intelligence has little to do with poetry. Poetry springs from something deeper, it's beyond intelligence. It may not even be linked with wisdom. It's a thing of its own; it has a nature of its own. Undefinable. I remember—of course I was a young man—I was even angry when Eliot spoke in a slighting way of Sandburg. I remember he said that Classicism is good—I'm not quoting his words, but the drift of them—because it enabled us to deal with such writers as Mister Carl Sandburg. When one calls a poet "Mister," (*laughter*) it's a word of haughty feelings; it means Mister So-and-so who has found his way into poetry and has no right to be there, who is really an outsider. In Spanish it's still worse because sometimes when we speak of a poet we say "El Doctor So-and-so." Then that annihilates him, that blots him out.

INTERVIEWER: You like Sandburg then?

BORGES: Yes, I do. Of course, I think Whitman is far more important than Sandburg, but when you read Whitman you think of him as a literary, perhaps a not too learned man of letters, who is doing his best to write in the vernacular and who is using slang as much as he can. In Sandburg the slang seems to come naturally. Now of course there are two Sandburgs: there is the *rough*; but there is also a very delicate Sandburg, especially when he deals with landscapes. Sometimes when he is describing the fog, for example, you are reminded of a Chinese painting. While in other poems of Sandburg you rather think of, well, gangsters, hoodlums, that kind of people. But I suppose he could be both, and I think he was equally sincere: when he was doing his best to be the poet of Chicago and when he wrote in quite a different mood. Another thing that I find strange in Sandburg is that in Whitman—but of course Whitman is Sandburg's father—Whitman is full of hope, while Sandburg writes as if he were writing in the two or three centuries to come. When he writes of the American expeditionary forces or when he writes about empire or the War or so on, he writes as if all those things were dead and gone by.

INTERVIEWER: There is an element of fantasy in his work then—which leads me to ask you about the fantastic. You use the word a great deal in your writing, and I remember that you call *Green Mansions,* for example, a fantastic novel.

BORGES: Well, it is.

INTERVIEWER: How would you define *fantastic* then?

BORGES: I wonder if you *can* define it. I think it's rather an intention in a writer. I remember a very deep remark of Joseph
Conrad—he is one of my favorite authors—I think it is in the foreword to something like *The Dark Line,* but it's not that...

INTERVIEWER: *The Shadow-Line?*

BORGES: *The Shadow-Line.* In that foreword he said that some people have thought that the story was a fantastic story because of the
captain's ghost stopping the ship. He wrote—and that struck me
because I write fantastic stories myself—that to deliberately write a
fantastic story was not to feel that the whole universe is fantastic
and mysterious; nor that it meant a lack of sensibility for a person
to sit down and write something deliberately fantastic. Conrad
thought that when one wrote, even in a realistic way, about the
world, one was writing a fantastic story, because the world itself is
fantastic and unfathomable and mysterious.

INTERVIEWER: You share this belief?

BORGES: Yes. I found that he was right. I talked to Bioy Casares,
who also writes fantastic stories—very, very fine stories—and he
said, "I think Conrad is right. Really, nobody knows whether the
world is realistic or fantastic, that is to say, whether the world is a
natural process or whether it is a kind of dream, a dream that we
may or may not share with others."

INTERVIEWER: You have often collaborated with Bioy Casares,
haven't you?

BORGES: Yes, I have always collaborated with him. Every night I
dine at his house and then after dinner we sit down and write.

INTERVIEWER: Would you describe your method of collaboration?

BORGES: Well, it's rather queer. When we write together, when we collaborate, we call ourselves H. Bustos Domecq. Bustos was a great-great-grandfather of mine and Domecq was a great-great-grandfather of his. Now, the queer thing is that when we write, and we write mostly humorous stuff—even if the stories are tragic, they are told in a humorous way or they are told as if the teller hardly understood what he was saying—when we write together what comes of the writing, if we are successful, and sometimes we are—why not? after all I'm speaking in the plural, no?—when our writing is successful, then what comes out is something quite different from Bioy Casares's stuff and my stuff, even the jokes are different. So we have created between us a kind of third person; we have somehow begotten a third person that is quite unlike us.

INTERVIEWER: A fantastic author?

BORGES: Yes, a fantastic author with his likes, his dislikes and a personal style that is meant to be ridiculous; but still, it is a style of his own, quite different from the kind of style I write when I try to create a ridiculous character. I think that's the only way of collaborating. Generally speaking, we go over the plot together before we set pen to paper—rather, I should talk about typewriters, because he has a typewriter. Before we begin writing, we discuss the whole story; then we go over the details, we change them, of course, we think of a beginning and then we think the beginning might be the end or that it might be more striking if somebody said nothing at all or said something quite outside the mark. Once the story is written, if you ask us whether this adjective or this particular sentence came from Bioy or from me, we can't tell.

INTERVIEWER: It comes from the third person.

BORGES: Yes. I think that's the only way of collaborating, because I have tried collaborating with other people. Sometimes it works out all right, but sometimes one feels that the collaborator is a kind of rival. Or, if not—as in the case of Peyrou—we began collaborating but he is timid and a very courteous, a very polite kind of person, and consequently if he says anything and you make any objections, he feels hurt and he takes it back. He says: "Oh, yes, of course, of course, yes, I was quite wrong. It was a blunder." Or if you propose anything, he says: "Oh, that's wonderful!" Now that kind of thing can't be done. In the case of me and Casares, we don't feel as if we are two rivals or even as if we were two men who play chess. There's no case of winning or losing. What we're thinking of is the story itself, the stuff itself.

INTERVIEWER: I'm sorry, I'm not familiar with the second writer you named.

BORGES: Peyrou. He began by imitating Chesterton and writing stories, detective stories, not unworthy, and even worthy of Chesterton. But now he's struck a new line of novels whose aim is to show what this country was like during Perón's time and after Perón took to flight. I don't care very much for that kind of writing. I understand that his novels are fine; but, I should say, from the historical, even the journalistic point of view. When he began writing stories after Chesterton, and then he wrote some very fine stories—one of them made me cry, but of course, perhaps it made me cry because he spoke of the quarter I was bred in, Palermo, and of hoodlums of those days—a book called *La Noche Repetida,* with very, very fine stories about gangsters, hoodlums, hold-up men, that kind of thing. And all that way back, let's say, well, at the beginning of the century. Now he has started this new kind of novel wherein he wants to show what the country was like.

INTERVIEWER: Local color, more or less?

BORGES: Local color and local politics. Then his characters are very interested, well, in graft, in loot, making money and so on. As I am less interested in those subjects, maybe it's my fault, not his, if

I prefer his early stuff. But I always think of him as a great writer, an important writer, and an old friend of mine.

INTERVIEWER: You have said that your own work has moved from, in the early times, *expression,* to, in the later times, *allusion.*

BORGES: Yes.

INTERVIEWER: What do you mean by *allusion?*

BORGES: Look, I mean to say this: when I began writing, I thought that everything should be defined by the writer. For example to say "the moon" was strictly forbidden; that one had to find an adjective, an epithet for the moon. (Of course, I'm simplifying things. I know it, because many times I have written "*la luna,*" but this is a kind of symbol of what I was doing.) Well, I thought everything had to be defined and that no common terms of phrase should be used. I would never have said "So-and-so came in and sat down," because that was far too simple and far too easy. I thought I had to find out some fancy way of saying it. Now I find out that those things are generally annoyances to the reader. But I think the whole root of the matter lies in the fact that when a writer is young he feels some- how that what he is going to say is rather silly or obvious or com- monplace, and then he tries to hide it under baroque ornament, under words taken from the seventeenth-century writers; or, if not, and he sets out to be modern, then he does the contrary: he's inventing words all the time, or alluding to airplanes, railway trains or the telegraph and telephone because he's doing his best to be modern. Then as time goes on, one feels that one's ideas, good or bad, should be plainly expressed, because if you have an idea you must try to get that idea or that feeling or that mood into the mind of the reader. If, at the same time, you are trying to be, let's say, Sir Thomas Browne or Ezra Pound, then it can't be done. So that I think a writer always begins by being too complicated: he's playing at several games at the same time. He wants to convey a peculiar mood; at the same time he must be a contemporary and if not a contemporary, then he's a reactionary and a classic. As to the vocabulary, the first thing a young writer, at least in this country, sets out to do is to show his readers that he possesses a dictionary, that he knows all the synonyms; so we get, for example, in one line, *red*, then we get *scarlet*, then we get other different words, more or less, for the same color: *purple*.

INTERVIEWER: You've worked, then, toward a kind of classical prose?

BORGES: Yes, I do my best now. Whenever I find an out-of-the-way word, that is to say, a word that may be used by the Spanish classics or a word used in the slums of Buenos Aires, I mean a word that is different from the others, then I strike it out and I use a common word. I remember that Stevenson wrote that in a well-written page all the words should look the same way. If you write an uncouth word or an astonishing or an archaic word then the rule is broken; and what is far more important, the attention of the reader is distracted by the word. One should be able to read smoothly in it, even if you're writing metaphysics or philosophy or whatever.

INTERVIEWER: Dr. Johnson said something similar to that.

BORGES: Yes, he must have said it; in any case, he must have agreed with that. Look, his own English was rather cumbersome, and the first thing you feel is that he is writing in a cumbersome English—that there are far too many Latin words in it—but if you reread what is written, you find that behind those involutions of phrase there is always a meaning, generally an interesting and a new meaning.

INTERVIEWER: A personal one?

BORGES: Yes, a personal one. So even though he wrote in a Latin style, I think he is the most English of writers. I think of him as—

this is a blasphemy, of course, but why not be blasphemous while we're about it?—I think that Johnson was a far more English writer than Shakespeare. Because if there's one thing typical of Englishmen, it's their habit of understatement. Well, in the case of Shakespeare, there are no understatements. On the contrary, he is piling on the agonies, as I think the American said. I think Johnson, who wrote a Latin kind of English, and Wordsworth, who wrote more Saxon words, and there is a third writer whose name I can't recall—well—let's say Johnson, Wordsworth and Kipling also, I think they're far more typically English than Shakespeare. I don't know why, but I always feel something Italian, something Jewish about Shakespeare, and perhaps Englishmen admire him because of that, because it's so unlike them.

INTERVIEWER: And why the French dislike him, to the extent that they do; because he's so bombastic.

BORGES: He *was* very bombastic. I remember I saw a film some days ago—not too good a film—called *Darling*. There some verses of Shakespeare are quoted. Now those verses are always better when they are quoted, because he is defining England and he calls it, for example, "This other Eden, demi-paradise... This precious stone set in the silver sea" and so on and in the end he says something like, "this realm, this England." Now when that quotation is made the reader stops there, but in the text I think the verses go on so that the whole point is lost. The real point would have been the idea of a man trying to define England, loving her very much and finding at the end that the only thing he can do is to say "England" outright—as if you said "America." But if he says "this realm, this land, this England," and then goes on "this demi-paradise" and so on, the whole point is lost, because *England* should be the last word. Well, I suppose Shakespeare always wrote in a hurry, as the player said to Ben Jonson, and so be it. You've no time to feel that that would have been the last word, the word England, summing up and blotting out all the others, saying: "Well, I've been attempting something that is impossible." But he went on with it, with his metaphors and his bombast, because he was bombastic. Even in such a famous phrase as Hamlet's last words, I think: "The rest is silence." There is something phony about it; it's meant to impress. I don't think anybody would say anything like that.

INTERVIEWER: In the context of the play, my favorite line in *Hamlet* occurs just after Claudius' praying scene when Hamlet enters his mother's chamber and says: "Now, Mother, what's the matter?"

BORGES: "What's the matter?" is the opposite of "The rest is silence." At least for me, "The rest is silence" has a hollow ring about it. One feels that Shakespeare is thinking: "Well, now Prince Hamlet of Denmark is dying: he must say something impressive." So he ekes out that phrase "The rest is silence." Now that may be impressive, but it is not true! He was working away at his job of poet and not thinking of the real character, of Hamlet the Dane.

INTERVIEWER: When you are working, what kind of reader do you imagine you are writing for, if you do imagine it? Who would be your ideal audience?

BORGES: Perhaps a few personal friends of mine. Not myself because I never reread what I've written. I'm far too afraid to feel ashamed of what I've done.

INTERVIEWER: Do you expect the many people who read your work to catch the allusions and references?

BORGES: No. Most of those allusions and references are merely put there as a kind of private joke.

INTERVIEWER: A *private* joke?

BORGES: A joke not to be shared with other people. I mean, if they share it, all the better; but if they don't, I don't care a hang about it.

INTERVIEWER: Then it's the opposite approach to allusion from, say, Eliot in *The Waste Land*.

BORGES: I think that Eliot and Joyce wanted their readers to be rather mystified and so to be worrying out the sense of what they had done.

INTERVIEWER: You seem to have read as much, if not more, non-fiction or factual material as fiction and poetry. Is that true? For example, you apparently like to read encyclopedias.

BORGES: Ah, yes. I'm very fond of that. I remember a time when I used to come here to read. I was a very young man, and I was far too timid to ask for a book. Then, I was rather, I won't say poor, but I wasn't too wealthy in those days—so I used to come every night here and pick out a volume of the *Encyclopædia Britannica*, the old edition.

INTERVIEWER: The eleventh?

BORGES: The eleventh or twelfth because those editions are far above the new ones. They were meant to be *read*. Now they are merely reference books. While in the eleventh or twelfth edition of the *Encyclopædia Britannica*, you had long articles by Macaulay, by Coleridge; no, not by Coleridge by…

INTERVIEWER: By De Quincey?

BORGES: Yes, by De Quincey and so on. So that I used to take any volume from the shelves—there was no need to ask for them: they were reference books—and then I opened the book till I found an article that interested me, for example about the Mormons or about any particular writer. I sat down and read it because those articles were really monographs, really books or short books. The same goes for the German encyclopedias—*Brockhaus* or *Meyers*.

When we got the new copy, I thought that was what they call the *Shorter Brockhaus,* but it wasn't. It was explained to me that because people live in small flats, there is no longer room for books in thirty volumes. Encyclopedias have suffered greatly; they have been packed in.

SUSANA QUINTEROS: (*Interrupting*) I'm sorry. *Está esperando el señor Campbell.*

BORGES: Ah, please ask him to wait just a moment more. Those Campbells keep coming.

INTERVIEWER: May I ask just a few more questions?

BORGES: Yes, please, of course.

INTERVIEWER: Some readers have found that your stories are cold, impersonal, rather like some of the newer French writers. Is that your intention?

BORGES: No. (*Sadly*) If that has happened, it is out of mere clumsiness. Because I have felt them very deeply. I have felt them so deeply that I have told them, well, using strange symbols so that people might not find out that they were all more or less autobiographical. The stories were about myself, my personal experiences. I suppose it's the English diffidence, no?

INTERVIEWER: Then a book like the little volume called *Everness* would be a good book for someone to read about your work?

BORGES: I think it is. Besides, the lady who wrote it is a close friend of mine. I found that word in *Roget's Thesaurus.* Then I thought that word was invented by Bishop Wilkins, who invented an artificial language.

INTERVIEWER: You've written about that.

BORGES: Yes, I wrote about Wilkins. But he also invented a wonderful word that strangely enough has never been used by English poets—an awful word really, a terrible word. *Everness*, of course, is better than *eternity* because *eternity* is rather worn now. *Ever-r-rness* is far better than the German *Ewigkeit*, the same word. But he also created a beautiful word, a word that's a poem in itself, full of hopelessness, sadness and despair: the word *neverness*. A beautiful word, no? He invented it, and I don't know why the poets left it lying about and never used it.

INTERVIEWER: Have you used it?

BORGES: No, no, never. I used *everness* but *neverness* is very beautiful. There is something hopeless about it, no? And there is no word with the same meaning in any other language, or in English. You might say *impossibility*, but that's very tame for *neverness*: the Saxon ending in *-ness*. *Neverness*. Keats used *nothingness*: "Till love and fame to nothingness do sink"; but *nothingness*, I think, is weaker than *neverness*. You have in Spanish *nadería*—many similar words—but nothing like *neverness*. So if you're a poet, you should use that word. It's a pity for that word to be lost in the pages of a dictionary. I don't think it's ever been used. It may have been used by some theologian; it might. I suppose Jonathan Edwards would have enjoyed that kind of word or Sir Thomas Browne perhaps, and Shakespeare, of course, because he was very fond of words.

INTERVIEWER: You respond to English so well, you love it so much, how is it you have written so little in English?

BORGES: Why? Why, I'm afraid. Fear. But next year, those lectures of mine that I shall deliver, I'll write them in English. I already wrote to Harvard.

INTERVIEWER: You're coming to Harvard next year?

BORGES: Yes. I'm gong to deliver a course of lectures on poetry.

And as I think that poetry is more or less untranslatable, and as I think English literature—and that includes America—is by far the richest in the world, I will take most, if not all of my examples, from English poetry. Of course, as I have my hobby, I'll try to work in some Old English verses but that's English also! In fact, according to some of my students, it's far more English than Chaucer's English!

INTERVIEWER: To get back to your own work for a moment: I have often wondered how you go about arranging works in those collections. Obviously the principle is not chronological. Is it similarity of theme?

BORGES: No, not chronology; but sometimes I find out that I've written the same parable or story twice over or that two different stories carry the same meaning, and so I try to put them alongside each other. That's the only principle. Because, for example, once it happened to me to write a poem, a not too good poem, and then to rewrite it many years afterwards. After the poem was written, some of my friends told me: "Well, that's the same poem you published some five years ago." And I said: "Well, so it is!" But I hadn't the faintest notion that it was. After all, I think that a poet has maybe five or six poems to write and not more than that. He's trying his hand at rewriting them from different angles and perhaps with different plots and in different ages and different characters, but the poems are essentially and innerly the same.

INTERVIEWER: You have written many reviews and journal articles.

BORGES: Well, I had to do it.

INTERVIEWER: Did you choose the books you wanted to review?

BORGES: Yes, I generally did.

INTERVIEWER: So the choice does express your own tastes?

BORGES: Oh yes, yes. For example, when somebody told me to write a review of a certain *History of Literature,* I found there were so many howlers and blunders, and as I greatly admire the author as a poet, I said: "No, I don't want to write about it, because if I write about it I shall write against it." I don't like to attack people, especially now—when I was a young man, yes, I was very fond of it—but as time goes on, one finds that it is no good. When people write in favor or against anybody that hardly helps or hurts them. I think that a man can be helped, well, the man can be done or undone by his *own* writing, not by what other people say of him, so that even if you brag a lot and people say that you are a genius—well, you'll be found out.

INTERVIEWER: Do you have any particular method for the naming of your characters?

BORGES: I have two methods: one of them is to work in the names of my grandfathers, great-grandfathers, and so on. To give them a kind of, well, I won't say immortality, but that's one of the methods. The other is to use names that somehow strike me. For example, in a story of mine, one of the characters who comes and goes is called Yarmolinsky because the name struck me—it's a strange word, no? Then another character is called Red Scharlach because Scharlach means *scarlet* in German and he was a murderer; he was doubly red, no? Red Scharlach: Red Scarlet.

INTERVIEWER: What about the princess with the beautiful name who occurs in two of your stories?

BORGES: Faucigny Lucinge? Well, she's a great friend of mine. She's an Argentine lady. She married a French prince and as the name is very beautiful, as most French titles are, especially if you cut out the Faucigny, as she does. She calls herself La Princesse de Lucinge. It's a beautiful word.

INTERVIEWER: What about Tlön and Uqbar?

BORGES: Oh, well, those are merely meant to be uncouth. So *u-q-b-a-r.*

INTERVIEWER: Unpronounceable in a way?

BORGES: Yes, more or less unpronounceable, and then *Tlön: t-l* is rather an uncommon combination, no? Then *ö*. The Latin *Orbis Tertius*—one can say that swimmingly, no? Perhaps in *Tlön* I may have been thinking of *Traum,* the same word as the English *dream.* But then it would have to be *Tröme,* but *Tröme* might remind the reader of a railway train: *t-l* was a queerer combination. I thought I had invented a word for imagined objects called *hrön.* Yet when I began learning Old English, I found that *hron* was one of the words for whale. There were two words, *wael* and *hron,* so the *hronrad* is the "whale road," that is to say "the sea" in Old English poetry.

INTERVIEWER: Then the word you invented to describe an object perpetrated on reality by the imagination, that word had already been invented and was, in fact, a *hrön?*

BORGES: Yes, yes, it came to me. I would like to think that it came from my ancestors of ten centuries ago—that's a probable explanation, no?

INTERVIEWER: Would you say that in your stories you have tried to hybridize the short story and the essay?

BORGES: Yes—but I have done that on purpose. The first to point that out to me was Casares. He said that I had written short stories that were really sort of halfway houses between an essay and a story.

INTERVIEWER: Was that partly to compensate for your timidity about writing narratives?

BORGES: Yes, it may have been. Yes; because nowadays, or at least today, I began writing that series of stories about hoodlums of

Buenos Aires: those are straightforward stories. There is nothing of the essay about them or even of poetry. The story is told in a straightforward way and those stories are in a sense sad, perhaps horrible. They are always understated. They are told by people who are also hoodlums and you can hardly understand them. They may be tragedies but the tragedy is not felt by them. They merely tell the story and the reader is, I suppose, made to feel that the story goes deeper than the story itself. Nothing is said of the sentiments of the characters—I got that out of the Old Norse saga—the idea that one should know a character by his words and by his deeds, but that one shouldn't get inside his skull and say what he was thinking.

INTERVIEWER: So they are non-psychological rather than impersonal?

BORGES: Yes, but there is a hidden psychology behind the story, because if not the characters would be mere puppets.

INTERVIEWER: What about the Kabbalah? When did you first get interested in that?

BORGES: I think it was through De Quincey, through his idea that the whole world was a set of symbols or that everything meant something else. Then when I lived in Geneva, I had two personal, two great friends—Maurice Abramowicz and Seymour Jichlinski—their names tell you the stock they sprang from: they were Polish Jews. I greatly admired Switzerland and the nation itself, not merely the scenery and the towns; but the Swiss are very standoffish; one can hardly have a Swiss friend, because as they have to live on foreigners, I suppose they dislike them. That would be the same case with the Mexicans. They chiefly live on Americans, on American tourists, and I don't think anybody likes to be a hotel keeper, even though there's nothing dishonorable about it. But if you are a hotel keeper, if you have to entertain many people from other countries, well, you feel that they are different from you and you may dislike them in the long run.

INTERVIEWER: Have you tried to make your own stories Kabbalistic?

BORGES: Yes, sometimes I have.

INTERVIEWER: Using traditional Kabbalistic interpretations?

BORGES: No. I read a book called *Major Trends in Jewish Mysticism*.

INTERVIEWER: The one by Scholem?

BORGES: Yes, by Scholem and another book by Trachtenberg on Jewish superstitions. Then I have read all the books of the Kabbalah I have found and all the articles in the encyclopedias and so on. But I have no Hebrew whatever. I may have Jewish ancestors, but I can't tell. My mother's name is Acevedo: Acevedo may be a name for a Portuguese Jew, but again, it may not. Now if you're called Abraham, I think there is no doubt whatever about it, but as the Jews took Italian, Spanish, Portuguese names, it does not necessarily follow that if you have one of those names you come from Jewish stock. The word *acevedo*, of course, means a kind of tree; the word is not especially Jewish, though many Jews are called Acevedo. I can't tell. I wish I had some Jewish forefathers.

INTERVIEWER: You once wrote that all men are either Platonists or Aristotelians.

BORGES: I didn't say that. Coleridge said it.

INTERVIEWER: But you quoted him.

BORGES: Yes, I quoted him.

INTERVIEWER: And which are you?

BORGES: I think I'm Aristotelian, but I wish it were the other way. I think it's the English strain that makes me think of particular things and persons being real rather than general ideas being real. But I'm afraid now that the Campbells are coming.

INTERVIEWER: Before I go would you mind signing my copy of *Labyrinths*?

BORGES: I'll be glad to. Ah yes, I know this book. There's my picture—but do I really look like that? I don't like that picture. I'm not so gloomy? so beaten down?

INTERVIEWER: Don't you think it looks pensive?

BORGES: Perhaps. But so dark? so heavy? The brow...oh, well.

INTERVIEWER: Do you like this edition of your writings?

BORGES: A good translation, no? Except that there are too many Latin words in it. For example, if I wrote, just say, *habitación oscura* (I wouldn't, of course, have written *that*, but *cuarto oscuro*, but just say that I did), then the temptation is to translate *habitación* with *habitation*, a word which sounds close to the original. But the word I want is *room*: it is more definite, simpler, better. You know, English is a beautiful language, but the older languages are even more beautiful: they had *vowels*. Vowels in modern English have lost their value, their color. My hope for English—for the English language—is America. Americans speak clearly. When I go to the movies now, I can't see much, but in the American movies, I understand every word. In the English movies I can't understand as well. Do you ever find it so?

INTERVIEWER: Sometimes, particularly in comedies. The English actors seem to speak too fast.

BORGES: Exactly! Exactly. Too fast with too little emphasis. They blur the words, the sounds. A fast blur. No, America must save the language; and, do you know, I think the same is true for Spanish? I prefer South American speech. I always have. I suppose you in America don't read Ring Lardner or Bret Harte much anymore?

INTERVIEWER: They are read, but mostly in the secondary schools.

BORGES: What about O. Henry?

INTERVIEWER: Again, mostly in the schools.

BORGES: And I suppose there mostly for the technique, the surprise ending. I don't like that trick, do you? Oh, it's all right in theory; in practice, that's something else. You can read them only once if there is just the surprise. You remember what Swift said: "the art of sinking." Now in the detective story, that's different. The surprise is there too, but there are also the characters, the scene or the landscape to satisfy us. But now I remember that the Campbells are coming, the Campbells are coming. They are supposed to be a ferocious tribe. Where are they?

—*Ronald Christ*

# PABLO NERUDA

Pablo Neruda, the most significant Latin American poet of the twentieth century, was born Ricardo Neftalí Reyes Basoalto on July 12, 1904. His mother, a schoolteacher, died of tuberculosis barely a month after her son's birth. Neruda's father soon remarried and moved the family from the small town of Parral, in southern Chile, to the frontier city of Temuco, where he began working as a railroad conductor. Neruda began writing poems as a small boy, and adopted the name Pablo Neruda while still in his early teens. Neruda's father disapproved strongly of his son's writing, and as soon as Neruda finished his secondary studies in 1921, the young man moved to the capital city of Santiago.

Neruda's breakthrough as a poet came with the publication of his early book *Veinte poemas de amor y una canción desesperada* [Twenty Love Poems and a Desperate Song] (1924), published when he was

La Carta en el camino          2 diciembre

Adiós, pero conmigo
irás, serás adentro
de una gota de sangre que circule en mis
o fuera, beso que me abrasa dedos,
o eterno cinturón en crespa el rostro,
de mi cintura.

Dulce mía, recibe
el gran amor que salió de mi vida
y que en ti no encontraba territorio,
como el explorador perdido
en las islas del pan y de la miel.

Yo te encontré después
de la tormenta,
la lluvia lavó el aire
y en el agua
tus dulces pies brillaron como peces.

Adorada, me voy a mis combates.
Arañaré la tierra para hacerte
y allí tu capitán                una cueva
te esperará con flores en el lecho.

No pienses más, mi dulce,
en el tormento
que pasó entre nosotros

*Manuscript page from "La Carta en el Camino."*
Courtesy of La Fundación Pablo Neruda.

only twenty years old. It remains his most popular work. He still had a difficult time making ends meet, and in 1927 accepted a job as a Chilean consul in Burma. He remained in Asia for five years, isolated and depressed, with few if any fellow Spanish speakers. In 1934, Neruda was assigned to Madrid, where he was accepted and praised by a generation of Spanish poets, including Federico García Lorca and Rafael Alberti. Neruda became an outspoken critic of the Fascists, helping the Republican cause in the early days of the Spanish Civil War, but his partisanship led to his recall to Chile in 1937.

He lived in Mexico from 1939 to 1943. When he returned to Chile, he became active in politics, joining the Communist party. He spent several years in exile in the late forties but resettled permanently in Chile in 1952. He continued to produce poetry at an astonishing rate. Books from this period include *Estravagario* (1958) and *Cien sonetos de amor* [One Hundred Love Sonnets] (1959).

Neruda continued to speak out for communism, and eventually stood as the official Communist candidate for Chilean president in 1970. He withdrew his candidacy before the election, however, and supported the election of his friend Salvador Allende.

In 1971, Neruda was awarded the Nobel Prize in literature. He completed his memoirs in the days immediately preceding his death, which occurred shortly after the coup that removed Allende from power.

———

*"I have never thought of my life as divided between poetry and politics," Pablo Neruda said in his September 30, 1969, acceptance speech as the Chilean Communist party candidate for presidency. "I am a Chilean who for decades has known the misfortunes and difficulties of our national existence and who has taken part in each sorrow and joy of the people. I am not a stranger to them, I come from them, I am part of the people. I come from a working class family ... I have never been in with those in power and have always felt that my vocation and my duty was to serve the Chilean people in my actions and with my poetry. I have lived singing and defending them."*

*Because of a divided left, Neruda withdrew his candidacy after four months of hard campaigning, and resigned in order to support a Popular*

Unity candidate. This interview was conducted in his home at Isla Negra in January 1970, just before his resignation.

Isla Negra (Black Island) is neither black nor an island. It is an elegant beach resort 40 kilometers south of Valparaíso and a two-hour drive from Santiago. No one knows where the name comes from; Neruda speculates about black rocks vaguely shaped like an island which he sees from his terrace. Thirty years ago, long before Isla Negra became fashionable, Neruda bought—with the royalties from his books—6,000 square meters of beachfront, which included a tiny stone house at the top of a steep slope. "Then the house started growing, like the people, like the trees."

Neruda has other houses—one on San Cristóbal Hill in Santiago and the other in Valparaíso. To decorate his houses he has scoured antique stores and junkyards for all kinds of objects. Each object reminds him of an anecdote. "Doesn't he look like Stalin?" he asks. "The antique dealer in Paris didn't want to sell it to me, but when he heard I was Chilean, he asked me if I knew Pablo Neruda. That's how I persuaded him to sell it."

It is at Isla Negra where Pablo Neruda, the "terrestrial navigator," and his third wife, Matilde Urrutia ("Patoja," as he affectionately calls her, the "muse" to whom he has written many love poems), have established their most permanent residence.

Neruda is tall, stocky, of olive complexion; his outstanding features are a prominent nose and large brown eyes with hooded eyelids. His movements are slow but firm. He speaks distinctly, without pomposity. When he goes for a walk—usually accompanied by his two chows—he wears a long poncho and carries a rustic cane.

At Isla Negra Neruda entertains a constant stream of visitors and there is always room at the table for last-minute guests. Neruda does most of his entertaining in the bar, which one enters through a small corridor from a terrace facing the beach. On the corridor floor is a Victorian bidet and an old hand organ. On the window shelves there is a collection of bottles. The bar is decorated as a ship's salon, with furniture bolted to the floor and nautical lamps and paintings. The room has glass-panel walls facing the sea. On the ceiling and on each of the wood crossbeams, a carpenter has carved, from Neruda's handwriting, names of his dead friends.

Behind the bar, on the liquor shelf, is a sign that says "No se fía" (No credit here). Neruda takes his role as bartender very seriously and likes to *make elaborate drinks for his guests, although he drinks only Scotch and wine. On a wall are two anti-Neruda posters—one he brought back from his last trip to Caracas. It shows his profile with the legend: "Neruda go home." The other is a cover from an Argentine magazine with his picture and the copy: "Neruda, why doesn't he just kill himself?" A huge poster of Twiggy stretches from the ceiling to the floor.*

*Meals at Isla Negra are typically Chilean. Neruda has mentioned some of them in his poetry: conger eel soup; fish with a delicate sauce of tomatoes and baby shrimp; meat pie. The wine is always Chilean. One of the porcelain wine pitchers, shaped like a bird, sings when wine is poured. In the summer, lunch is served on a porch facing a garden that has an antique railroad engine. "So powerful, such a corn picker, such a procreator and whistler and roarer and thunderer . . . I love it because it looks like Walt Whitman."*

*Conversations for the interview were held in short sessions. In the morning—after Neruda had his breakfast in his room—we met in the library, which is a new wing of the house. I would wait while he answered his mail, composed poems for his new book, or corrected the galleys of a new Chilean edition of* Twenty Love Poems, *which was first published in 1924, and has sold almost two million copies. Composing poetry, he writes with green ink in an ordinary composition book. He can write a fairly long poem in a very short time, after which he makes only a few corrections. The poems are then typed by his secretary and close friend of more than fifty years, Homero Arce.*

*In the afternoon, after his daily nap, we sat on a stone bench on the terrace facing the sea. Neruda would talk holding the microphone of the tape recorder, which picked up the sound of the sea as background to his voice.*

INTERVIEWER: Why did you change your name, and why did you choose "Pablo Neruda"?

PABLO NERUDA: I don't remember. I was only thirteen or fourteen years old. I remember that it bothered my father very much that I wanted to write. With the best of intentions, he thought that writing would bring destruction to the family and myself and, especially, that it would lead me to a life of complete uselessness. He had domestic reasons for thinking so, reasons which did not weigh heavily on me. It was one of the first defensive measures that I adopted—changing my name.

INTERVIEWER: Did you choose "Neruda" because of the Czech poet Jean Neruda?

NERUDA: I'd read a short story of his. I've never read his poetry, but he has a book entitled *Stories of Mala Strana* about the humble people of that neighborhood in Prague. It is possible that my new name came from there. As I say, the whole matter is so far back in my memory that I don't recall. Nevertheless, the Czechs think of me as one of them, as part of their nation, and I've had a very friendly connection with them.

INTERVIEWER: In case you are elected President of Chile, will you keep on writing?

NERUDA: For me writing is like breathing. I could not live without breathing and I could not live without writing.

INTERVIEWER: Who are the poets who have aspired to high political office and succeeded?

NERUDA: Our period is an era of governing poets: Mao Tse-tung and Ho Chi Minh. Mao Tse-tung has other qualities: as you know he is a great swimmer, something which I am not. There is also a great poet, Léopold Senghor, who is president of Senegal; another, Aimé Césaire, a surrealist poet, is the mayor of Fort-de-France in Martinique. In my country, poets have always intervened in politics, though we have never had a poet who was president of the Republic. On the other hand, there have been writers in Latin America who have been president: Rómulo Gallegos was president of Venezuela.

INTERVIEWER: How have you been running your presidential campaign?

NERUDA: A platform is set up. First there are always folk songs, and then someone in charge explains the strictly political scope of our campaign. After that, the note I strike in order to talk to the towns-people is a much freer one, much less organized; it is more poetic. I almost always finish by reading poetry. If I didn't read some poetry, the people would go away disillusioned. Of course they also want to hear my political thoughts, but I don't overwork the political or economic aspects because people also need another kind of language.

INTERVIEWER: How do the people react when you read your poems?

NERUDA: They love me in a very emotional way. I can't enter or leave some places. I have a special escort which protects me from the crowds because the people press around me. That happens everywhere.

INTERVIEWER: If you had to choose between the Presidency of Chile and the Nobel Prize, for which you have been mentioned so often—which would you choose?

NERUDA: There can be no question of a decision between such illusory things.

INTERVIEWER: But if they put the Presidency and the Nobel Prize right here on a table?

NERUDA: If they put them on the table in front of me, I'd get up and sit at another table.

INTERVIEWER: Do you think awarding the Nobel Prize to Samuel Beckett was just?

NERUDA: Yes, I believe so. Beckett writes short but exquisite things. The Nobel Prize, wherever it falls, is always an honor to literature.

I am not one of those always arguing whether the prize went to the right person or not. What is important about this prize—if it has any importance—is that it confers a title of respect on the office of writer. That is what is important.

INTERVIEWER: What are your strongest memories?

NERUDA: I don't know. The most intense memories, perhaps, are those of my life in Spain—in that great brotherhood of poets; I've never known such a fraternal group in our American world—so full of *alacraneos* (gossips) as they say in Buenos Aires. Then, afterwards, it was terrible to see that republic of friends destroyed by the Civil War, which so demonstrated the horrible reality of fascist repression. My friends were scattered: some were exterminated right there—like García Lorca and Miguel Hernández; others died in exile, and still others live on in exile. That whole phase of my life was rich in events, in profound emotions, and decisively changed the evolution of my life.

INTERVIEWER: Would they allow you to enter Spain now?

NERUDA: I'm not officially forbidden to enter. On one occasion I was invited to give some readings there by the Chilean Embassy. It is very possible that they would let me enter. But I don't want to make a point of it, because it simply may have been convenient for the Spanish government to show some democratic feeling by permitting the entry of people who had fought so hard against it. I don't know. I have been prevented from entering so many countries and I have been turned out of so many others that, truly, this is a matter which no longer causes the irritation in me that it did at first.

INTERVIEWER: In a certain way, your ode to García Lorca, which you wrote before he died, predicted his tragic end.

NERUDA: Yes, that poem is strange. Strange because he was such a happy person, such a cheerful creature. I've known very few people like him. He was the incarnation . . . well, let's not say of success, but of the love of life. He enjoyed each minute of his existence—a great spendthrift of happiness. For that reason, the crime of his execution is one of the most unpardonable crimes of fascism.

INTERVIEWER: You often mention him in your poems, as well as Miguel Hernández.

NERUDA: Hernández was like a son. As a poet, he was something of my disciple, and he almost lived in my house. He went to prison and died there because he disproved the official version of García Lorca's death. If their explanation was correct, why did the fascist government keep Miguel Hernández in prison until his death? Why did they even refuse to move him to a hospital as the Chilean Embassy proposed? The death of Miguel Hernández was an assassination too.

INTERVIEWER: What do you remember most from your years in India?

NERUDA: My stay there was an encounter I wasn't prepared for. The splendor of that unfamiliar continent overwhelmed me, and yet I felt desperate, because my life and my solitude there were so long. Sometimes I seemed locked into an unending Technicolor picture—a marvelous movie, but one I wasn't allowed to leave. I never experienced the mysticism which guided so many South Americans and other foreigners in India. People who go to India in search of a religious answer to their anxieties see things in a different way. As for me, I was profoundly moved by the sociological conditions—that immense unarmed nation, so defenseless, bound to its imperial yoke. Even the English culture, for which I had a great predilection, seemed hateful to me for being the instrument of the intellectual submission of so many Hindus at that time. I mixed with the rebellious young people of that continent; in spite of my consular post, I got to know all the revolutionaries—those in the great movement that eventually brought about independence.

INTERVIEWER: Was it in India that you wrote *Residence on Earth*?

NERUDA: Yes, though India had very little intellectual influence on my poetry.

INTERVIEWER: It was from India that you wrote those very moving letters to the Argentine, Hector Eandi?

NERUDA: Yes. Those letters were important in my life, because he, a writer I did not know personally, took it upon himself, as a good Samaritan, to send me news, to send me periodicals, to help me through my great solitude. I had become afraid of losing contact with my own language—for years I met no one to speak Spanish to. In one letter to Rafael Alberti I had to ask for a Spanish dictionary. I had been appointed to the post of consul, but it was a low-grade post and one that had no stipend. I lived in the greatest poverty and in even greater solitude. For weeks I didn't see another human being.

INTERVIEWER: While there you had a great romance with Josie Bliss, whom you mention in many poems.

NERUDA: Yes, Josie Bliss was a woman who left quite a profound imprint on my poetry. I have always remembered her, even in my most recent books.

INTERVIEWER: Your work, then, is closely linked to your personal life?

NERUDA: Naturally. The life of a poet must be reflected in his poetry. That is the law of the art and a law of life.

INTERVIEWER: Your work can be divided into stages, can't it?

NERUDA: I have quite confusing thoughts about that. I myself don't have stages; the critics discover them. If I can say anything, it is that my poetry has the quality of an organism—infantile when I was a boy, juvenile when I was young, desolate when I suffered, combative when I had to enter the social struggle. A mixture of these tendencies is present in my current poetry. I always wrote out of internal necessity and I imagine that this is what happens with all writers, poets especially.

INTERVIEWER: I've seen you writing in the car.

NERUDA: I write where I can and when I can, but I'm always writing.

INTERVIEWER: Do you always write everything in longhand?

NERUDA: Ever since I had an accident in which I broke a finger and couldn't use the typewriter for a few months, I have followed the custom of my youth and gone back to writing by hand. I discovered when my finger was better and I could type again that my poetry when written by hand was more sensitive; its plastic forms could change more easily. In an interview, Robert Graves says that in order to think one should have as little as possible around that is not handmade. He could have added that poetry ought to be written by hand. The typewriter separated me from a deeper intimacy with poetry, and my hand brought me closer to that intimacy again.

INTERVIEWER: What are your working hours?

NERUDA: I don't have a schedule, but by preference I write in the morning. Which is to say that if you weren't here making me waste my time (and wasting your own), I would be writing. I don't read many things during the day. I would rather write all day, but frequently the fullness of a thought, of an expression, of something that comes out of myself in a tumultuous way—let's label it with an antiquated term: "inspiration"—leaves me satisfied, or exhausted, or calmed, or empty. That is, I can't go on. Apart from that, I like living too much to be seated all day at a desk. I like to put myself in the goings-on of life, of my house, of politics and of nature. I am forever coming and going. But I write intensely whenever I can and wherever I am. It doesn't bother me that there may be a lot of people around.

INTERVIEWER: You cut yourself off totally from what surrounds you?

NERUDA: I cut myself off, and if everything is suddenly quiet, then that is disturbing to me.

INTERVIEWER: You have never given much consideration to prose.

NERUDA: Prose...I have felt the necessity of writing in verse all my life. Expression in prose doesn't interest me. I use prose to express a certain kind of fleeting emotion or event, really tending toward narrative. The truth is that I could give up writing in prose entirely. I only do it temporarily.

INTERVIEWER: If you had to save your works from a fire, what would you save?

NERUDA: Possibly none of them. What am I going to need them for? I would rather save a girl...or a good collection of detective stories...which would entertain me much more than my own works.

INTERVIEWER: Which of your critics has best understood your work?

NERUDA: Oh! My critics! My critics have almost shredded me to pieces, with all the love or hate in the world! In life, as in art, one can't please everybody, and that's a situation that's always with us. One is always receiving kisses and slaps, caresses and kicks, and that is the life of a poet. What bothers me is the distortion in the interpretation of poetry or the events of one's life. For example, during the P.E.N. Club Congress in New York, which brought together so many people from different places, I read my social poems, and even more of them in California—poems dedicated to Cuba in support of the Cuban Revolution. Yet the Cuban writers signed a letter and distributed millions of copies in which my opinions were doubted, and in which I was singled out as a creature protected by the North Americans; they even suggested that my entry into the United States was a kind of prize! That is perfectly stupid, if not slanderous, since many writers from socialist countries *did* come in; even the arrival of Cuban writers was expected. We did not lose our character as anti-imperialists by going to New York. Nevertheless that was suggested, either through the hastiness or bad faith of the Cuban writers. The fact that at this present moment I am my party's candidate for President of the Republic shows that I have a truly revolutionary history. It would be difficult to find *any* writers who signed that letter who could compare in dedication to revolutionary work, who could equal even one hundredth of what I have done and fought for.

INTERVIEWER: You have been criticized for the way you live, and for your economic position.

NERUDA: In general, that's all a myth. In a certain sense, we have received a rather bad legacy from Spain, which could never bear to have its people stand out or be distinguished in anything. They chained Christopher Columbus on his return to Spain. We get that from the envious *petite bourgeoisie*, who go around thinking about what others have and about what they *don't* have. In my own case, I have dedicated my life to reparations for the people, and what I have in my house—my books—is the product of my own work. I have exploited no one. It is odd. The sort of reproach *I* get is never made to writers who are rich by birthright! Instead, it is made to *me*—a writer who has fifty years of work behind him. They are always saying: "Look, look how he lives. He has a house facing the sea. He drinks good wine." What nonsense. To begin with, it's hard to drink bad wine in Chile because almost all the wine in Chile is good. It's a problem which, in a certain way, reflects the underdevelopment of our country—in sum, the mediocrity of our ways.

You yourself have told me that Norman Mailer was paid some ninety thousand dollars for three articles in a North American magazine. Here, if a Latin American writer should receive such compensation for his work, it would arouse a wave of protest from the other writers—"What an outrage! How terrible! Where is it going to stop?"—instead of everyone's being pleased that a writer can demand such fees. Well, as I say, these are the misfortunes which go by the name of cultural underdevelopment.

INTERVIEWER: Isn't this accusation more intense because you belong to the Communist Party?

NERUDA: Precisely. He who has nothing—it has been said many times—has nothing to lose but his chains. I risk, at every moment, my life, my person, all that I have—my books, my house. My house has been burned; I have been persecuted; I have been detained more than once; I have been exiled; they have declared me incommunicado; I have been sought by thousands of police. Very well then. I'm *not* comfortable with what I have. So what I have, I have put at the disposal of the people's fight, and this very house you're in has belonged for twenty years to the Communist Party to whom I have given it by public writ. I am in this house simply through the generosity of my party. All right, let those who reproach me do the same and at least leave their shoes somewhere so that they can be passed on to somebody else!

INTERVIEWER: You have donated various libraries. Aren't you now involved in the project of the writers' colony at Isla Negra?

NERUDA: I have donated more than one entire library to my country's university. I live on the income from my books. I don't have any savings. I don't have anything to dispose of, except for what I am paid each month from my books. With that income, lately, I've been acquiring a large piece of land on the coast so that writers in the future will be able to pass summers there and do their creative work in an atmosphere of extraordinary beauty. It will be the Cantalao

Foundation—with directors from the Catholic University, the University of Chile, and the Society of Writers.

INTERVIEWER: *Twenty Love Poems and a Desperate Song,* one of your first books, has been and continues to be read by thousands of admirers.

NERUDA: I had said in the prologue to the edition which celebrated the publication of one million copies of that book—soon there will be two million copies—that I really don't understand what it's all about—why this book, a book of love-sadness, of love-pain, continues to be read by so many people, by so many young people. Truly, I do not understand it. Perhaps this book represents the youthful posing of many enigmas; perhaps it represents the answers to those enigmas. It is a mournful book, but its attractiveness has not worn off.

INTERVIEWER: You are one of the most widely translated poets—into about thirty languages. Into what languages are you best translated?

NERUDA: I would say into Italian, because of the similarity between the two languages. English and French, which are the two languages I know outside of Italian, are languages which do not correspond to Spanish—neither in vocalization, or in the placement, or the color, or the weight of the words. It is not a question of interpretative equivalence; no, the sense can be right, but this correctness of translation, of meaning, can be the destruction of a poem. In many of the translations into French—I don't say in all of them—my poetry escapes, nothing remains; one cannot protest because it says the same thing that one has written. But it is obvious, that if I had been a French poet, I would not have said what I did in that poem, because the value of the words is so different. I would have written something else.

INTERVIEWER: And in English?

NERUDA: I find the English language so different from Spanish—so much more direct—that many times it expresses the meaning of my poetry, but does not convey the atmosphere of my poetry. It may be that the same thing happens when an English poet is translated into Spanish.

INTERVIEWER: You said that you are a great reader of detective stories. Who are your favorite authors?

NERUDA: A great literary work of this type of writing is Eric Ambler's *A Coffin for Dimitrios.* I've read practically all of Ambler's work since then, but none has the fundamental perfection, the extraordinary intrigue, and the mysterious atmosphere of *A Coffin for Dimitrios.* Simenon is also very important, but it's James Hadley Chase who surpasses in terror, in horror, and in the destructive spirit everything else that has been written. *No Orchids for Miss Blandish* is an old book, but it doesn't cease being a milestone of the detective story. There's a strange similarity between *No Orchids for Miss Blandish* and William Faulkner's *Sanctuary*—that very disagreeable but important book—but I've never been able to determine which was the *first* of the two. Of course, whenever the detective story is spoken of, I think of Dashiell Hammett. He is the one who changed the genre from a sub-literary phantasm and gave it a strong backbone. He is the great creator, and after him there are hundreds of others, John MacDonald among the most brilliant. All of them are prolific writers and they work extraordinarily hard. And almost all of the North American novelists of this school—the detective novel—are perhaps the most severe critics of the crumbling North American capitalist society. There is no greater denunciation than that which turns up in those detective novels about the fatigue and corruption of the politicians and the police, the influence of money in the big cities, the corruption which pops up in all parts of the North American system, in "the American way of life." It is, possibly, the most dramatic testimony to an epoch, and yet it is considered the flimsiest accusation since detective stories are not taken into account by literary critics.

INTERVIEWER: What other books do you read?

NERUDA: I am a reader of history, especially of the older chronicles of my country. Chile has an extraordinary history. Not because of monuments or ancient sculptures, which don't exist here, but rather because Chile was invented by a poet, Don Alonso de Ercilla y Zúñiga, page of Carlos V. He was a Basque aristocrat who arrived with the conquistadores—quite unusual since most of the people sent to Chile came out of the dungeons. This was the hardest place to live. The war between the Araucanians and the Spanish went on here for centuries, the longest civil war in the history of humanity. The semi-savage tribes of Araucania fought for their liberty against the Spanish invaders for three hundred years. Don Alonso de Ercilla y Zúñiga, the young humanist, came with the enslavers who wanted to dominate all America and *did* dominate it, with the exception of this bristly and savage territory we call Chile. Don Alonso wrote *The Araucana,* the longest epic in Castilian literature, in which he honored the unknown tribes of Araucania, anonymous heroes to whom he gave a name for the first time, more than his compatriots, the Castilian soldiers. *The Araucana,* published in the sixteenth century, was translated, and traveled in various versions through all of Europe. A great poem by a great poet. The history of Chile thus had this epic greatness and heroism at birth. We Chileans, quite unlike the other crossbred people of Spanish and Indian America, are not descended from the Spanish soldiers and their rapes or concubinages, but from either the voluntary or forced marriages of the Araucanians with Spanish women held captive during those long war years. We are a certain exception. Of course, then comes our bloody history of independence after 1810, a history full of tragedies, disagreements and struggles in which the names of San Martín and Bolívar, José Miguel Carrera and O'Higgins carry on through interminable pages of successes and misfortunes. All this makes me a reader of books which I unearth and dust off and which entertain me enormously as I search for the significance of this country—so remote from everybody, so cold in its latitudes, so deserted . . . its saltpeter pampas in the north, its immense Patagonias, so snowy in the Andes, so florid by the sea. And this is my country, Chile. I am one of those Chileans in perpetuity, one who, no matter how well they treat me elsewhere, must return to my country. I like the great cities of Europe: I adore the Arno Valley, and certain streets of Copenhagen and Stockholm, and naturally, Paris, Paris, Paris, and yet I still have to return to Chile.

INTERVIEWER: In an article entitled "My Contemporaries," Ernesto Montenegro criticizes the Uruguayan critic Rodríguez Monegal for expressing the vain wish that contemporary European and North American writers study their Latin American colleagues if they want to achieve the renovation of their prose. Montenegro jokes that it is like the ant saying to the elephant: "Climb on my shoulders." Then he cites Borges: "In contrast to the barbarous United States, this country (this continent) has not produced a writer of world-wide influence—an Emerson, a Whitman, a Poe... neither has it produced a great esoteric writer—a Henry James, or a Melville."

NERUDA: Why is it important if we do or don't have names like those of Whitman, Baudelaire, or Kafka on our continent? The history of literary creation is as large as humanity. We can't impose an etiquette. The United States, with an overwhelmingly literate population, and Europe, with an ancient tradition, can't be compared to our multitudes in Latin America without books or means of expressing themselves. But to pass time throwing stones at one another, to spend one's life hoping to surpass this or that continent seems a provincial sentiment to me. Besides, all this can be a matter of individual opinion.

INTERVIEWER: Would you like to comment on literary affairs in Latin America?

NERUDA: Whether a magazine is from Honduras, or New York (in Spanish) or Montevideo or from Guayaquil, we discover that almost all present the same catalogue of fashionable literature influenced by Eliot or Kafka. It's an example of cultural colonialism. We are still involved in European etiquette. Here in Chile, for example, the mistress of the house will show you anything—China plates—and tell you with a satisfied smile: "It's imported." Most of the horrible porcelain exhibited in millions of Chilean homes is imported, and it's of the worst kind, produced in the factories of Germany and France. These pieces of nonsense are accepted as top quality because they have been imported.

INTERVIEWER: Is fear of non-conformity responsible?

NERUDA: Certainly in the old days everybody was scared of revolutionary ideas, particularly writers. In this decade, and especially after the Cuban Revolution, the current fashion is just the opposite. Writers live in terror that they will *not* be taken for extreme leftists, so each of them assumes a guerrilla-like position. There are many writers who only write texts which assert that they are in the front lines of the war against imperialism. Those of us who have continually fought that war see with joy that literature is placing itself on the side of the people; but we also believe that if it's only a matter of fashion and a writer's fear of not being taken for an active leftist, well, we are not going to get very far with that kind of revolutionary. In the end, all sorts of animals fit into the literary forest. Once, when I had been offended for many years by a few pertinacious persecutors who seemed to live only to attack my poetry and my life, I said: "Let's leave them alone, there is room for all in this jungle; if there's space for the elephants, who take up such a lot of room in the jungles of Africa and Ceylon, then surely there's space for all the poets."

INTERVIEWER: Some people accuse you of being antagonistic toward Jorge Luis Borges.

NERUDA: The antagonism toward Borges may exist in an intellectual or cultural form because of our different orientation. One can fight peacefully. But I have other enemies—not writers. For me the enemy is imperialism and my enemies are the capitalists and those who drop napalm on Vietnam. But Borges is not my enemy.

INTERVIEWER: What do you think about Borges's writing?

NERUDA: He is a great writer and people who speak Spanish are very proud that Borges exists—above all, the people of Latin America. Before Borges we had very few writers who could stand in comparison with the writers of Europe. We have had great writers, but a writer of the universal type, like Borges, is not found very often in our countries. I cannot say that he has been the *greatest*, and I hope he will be surpassed many times by others, but in every way he has opened the way and attracted attention, the intellectual curiosity of Europe, toward our countries. But for me to fight with Borges, because everybody wants me to—I'll never do it. If he thinks like a dinosaur, well, that has nothing to do with my thinking. He understands nothing of what's going on in the contemporary world; he thinks that I understand nothing either. Therefore, we are in agreement.

INTERVIEWER: On Sunday we saw some young Argentines who were playing guitars and singing a *milonga* by Borges. That pleased you, didn't it?

NERUDA: Borges's *milonga* pleased me greatly—most of all because it is an example of how such a hermetic poet—let's use that term— such a sophisticated and intellectual poet can turn to a popular theme, doing it with such a true and certain touch. I liked Borges's *milonga* very much. Latin American poets ought to imitate his example.

INTERVIEWER: Have you written any Chilean folk music?

NERUDA: I've written some songs which are very well known in this country.

INTERVIEWER: Who are the Russian poets you like most?

NERUDA: The dominant figure in Russian poetry continues to be Mayakovsky. He is for the Russian Revolution what Walt Whitman was for the Industrial Revolution in North America. Mayakovsky impregnated poetry in such a way that almost all the poetry has continued being Mayakovskian.

INTERVIEWER: What do you think about the Russian writers who have left Russia?

NERUDA: People who want to leave a place ought to do so. This is really a rather individual problem. Some Soviet writers may feel themselves dissatisfied with their relationship to the literary organizations or with their own state. But I have never seen less disagreement between a state and the writers than in socialist countries. The majority of Soviet writers are proud of the socialist structure, of the great war of liberation against the Nazis, of the people's role in the revolution and in the great war, and proud of the structures created by socialism. If there are exceptions, it is a personal question and it is correspondingly necessary to examine each case individually.

INTERVIEWER: But the creative work cannot be free. It must always reflect the state's line of thought.

NERUDA: It's an exaggeration to say that. I have known many writers and painters who have absolutely no intention of eulogizing this or that in the state. There is a kind of conspiracy to suggest that this is the case. But, it's not so. Of course, every revolution needs to mobilize its forces. A revolution cannot persist without development: the very commotion provoked by the change from capitalism to socialism cannot last unless the revolution demands, and with all its power, the support of all the strata of society—including the writers, intellectuals and artists. Think about the American Revolution, or our own war of independence against imperial Spain. What would have happened if just subsequent to those events the writers dedicated themselves to subjects like the monarchy, or the restitution of English power over the United States, or the Spanish king's over former colonies? If any writer or artist had exalted colonialism he would have been persecuted. It's with even greater justification that a revolution which wants to construct a society starting from zero (after all, the step from capitalism or private property to socialism and communism has never been tried before) must by its own force mobilize the aid of intellect. Such a procedure can bring about conflicts; it is only human and political that these occur. But I hope that with time and stability the socialist societies will have less need to have their writers constantly thinking about social problems, and that they will be able to create what they most intimately desire.

INTERVIEWER: What advice would you give to young poets?

NERUDA: Oh, there is no advice to give to young poets! They ought to make their own way; they will have to encounter the obstacles to their expression and they have to overcome them. What I would never advise them to do is to begin with political poetry. Political poetry is more profoundly emotional than any other—at least as much as love poetry—and cannot be forced because it then becomes vulgar and unacceptable. It is necessary first to pass through all other poetry in order to become a political poet. The political poet must also be prepared to accept the censure which is thrown at him—betraying poetry, or betraying literature. Then too, political poetry has to arm itself with such content and substance and intellectual and emotional richness that it is able to scorn everything else. This is rarely achieved.

INTERVIEWER: You have often said that you don't believe in originality.

NERUDA: To look for originality at all costs is a modern condition. In our time, the writer wants to call attention to himself, and this superficial preoccupation takes on fetishistic characteristics. Each person tries to find a road whereby he will stand out, neither for profundity nor for discovery, but for the imposition of a special diversity. The most original artist will change phases in accord with the time, the epoch. The great example is Picasso, who begins by nourishing himself from the painting and sculpture of Africa or the primitive arts, and then goes on with such a power of transformation that his works, characterized by his splendid originality, seem to be stages in the cultural geology of the world.

INTERVIEWER: What were the literary influences on you?

NERUDA: Writers are always interchanging in some way: just as the air we breathe doesn't belong to one place. The writer is always moving from house to house: he ought to change his furniture. Some writers feel uncomfortable at this. I remember that Federico García Lorca was always asking me to read my lines, my poetry, and yet in the middle of my reading, he would say "Stop, stop! Don't go on, lest you influence me!"

INTERVIEWER: About Norman Mailer. You were one of the first writers to speak of him.

NERUDA: Shortly after Mailer's *The Naked and the Dead* came out, I found it in a bookstore in Mexico. No one knew anything about it: the bookseller didn't even know what it was about. I bought it because I had to take a trip and I wanted a new American novel. I thought that the American novel had died after the giants who began with Dreiser and finished with Hemingway, Steinbeck and Faulkner—but I discovered a writer with extraordinary verbal violence, matched with great subtlety and a marvelous power of description. I greatly admire the poetry of Pasternak, but *Dr. Zhivago* alongside *The Naked and the Dead* seems a boring novel, saved only in part by its description of nature, that is to say, by its poetry. I remember about that time I wrote the poem "Let the Rail Splitter Awake." This poem, invoking the figure of Lincoln, was dedicated to world peace. I spoke of Okinawa and of the war in

Japan, and I mentioned Norman Mailer. My poem reached Europe and was translated. I remember that Aragón said to me: "It was a great deal of trouble to find out who Norman Mailer is." In reality, nobody knew him, and I had a certain feeling of pride in having been one of the first writers to allude to him.

INTERVIEWER: Could you comment on your intense affection for nature?

NERUDA: Ever since my childhood, I've maintained an affection for birds, shells, forests and plants. I've gone to many places in search of ocean shells, and I've come to have a great collection. I wrote a book called *Art of Birds*. I wrote *Bestiary, Seaquake,* and *The Rose of Herbolario,* devoted to flowers, branches and vegetal growth. I could not live separated from nature. I like hotels for a couple of days; I like planes for an hour; but I'm happy in the woods, on the sand, or sailing, in direct contact with fire, earth, water, air.

INTERVIEWER: There are symbols in your poetry which recur and they always take the form of the sea, of fish, of birds...

NERUDA: I don't believe in symbols. They are simply material things. The sea, fish, birds exist for me in a material way. I take them into account as I have to take daylight into account. The fact that some themes stand out in my poetry—are always appearing— is a matter of material presence.

INTERVIEWER: What do the dove and guitar signify?

NERUDA: The dove signifies the dove and the guitar signifies a musical instrument called the guitar.

INTERVIEWER: You mean that those who have tried to analyze these things—

NERUDA: When I see a dove, I call it a dove. The dove, whether it is present or not, has a form for me, either subjectively or objectively—but it doesn't go beyond being a dove.

INTERVIEWER: You have said about the poems in *Residence on Earth* that "they don't help one to live. They help one to die."

NERUDA: My book *Residence on Earth* represents a dark and dangerous moment in my life. It is poetry without an exit. I almost had to be reborn in order to get out of it. I was saved from that desperation of which I still can't know the depths by the Spanish War, and by events serious enough to make me meditate. At one time I said that if I ever had the necessary power, I would forbid the reading of that book and I would arrange never to have it printed again. It exaggerates the feeling of life as a painful burden, as a mortal oppression. But I also know that it is one of my best books, in the sense that it reflects my state of mind. Still when one writes—and I don't know if this is true for other writers—one ought to think of where one's verses are going to land. Robert Frost says in one of his essays that poetry ought to have sorrow as its only orientation: "Leave sorrow alone with poetry." But I don't know what Robert Frost would have thought if a young man had committed suicide and left one of *his* books stained with blood. That happened to me—here, in this country. A boy, full of life, killed himself next to my book. I don't feel truly responsible for his death. But that page of poetry stained with blood is enough to make not only one poet think, but all poets...Of course, my opponents took advantage—as they do of almost everything I say—political advantage of the censure I gave my own book. They attributed to me the desire to write exclusively happy and optimistic poetry. They didn't know about that episode. I have never renounced the expression of loneliness, of anguish, or of melancholia. But I like to change tones, to find all the sounds, to pursue all the colors, to look for the forces of life wherever they may be—in creation or destruction.

My poetry has passed through the same stages as my life; from a solitary childhood and an adolescence cornered in distant, isolated countries, I set out to make myself a part of the great human multitude. My life matured, and that is all. It was in the style of the last century for poets to be tormented melancholiacs. But there can be poets who know life, who know its problems, and who survive by crossing through the currents. And who pass through sadness to plenitude.

—*Rita Guibert*
*Translated by Ronald Christ*

# OCTAVIO PAZ

Courtesy of Marie-José Paz.

Octavio Paz was born on March 31, 1914, in Mexico City, the son of a lawyer and the grandson of a novelist. Both figures were important to the young poet's development: he learned the value of social causes from his father—who served as counsel for the Mexican revolutionary Emiliano Zapata—and was introduced to the world of letters by his grandfather. Paz studied literature and law at the University of Mexico, but he left before earning a degree. He helped open a school for children of poor workers in Yucatán and began devoting himself to publishing the poetry he had been writing since early adolescence.

*Luna silvestre* [Savage Moon], his first book of poems, appeared in 1933 when Paz was only nineteen years old. The work establishes the themes of love and eroticism that would later become hallmarks of his work.

At the outbreak of the Spanish Civil War, Paz sided immediately with the Republican cause and in 1937 left for Spain, where he

Todas las artes, especialmente la pintura y la escultura, ~~son formas~~ al ser formas materiales,
son cosas: pueden guardarse o venderse y transformarse
en objeto de especulación monetaria. La poesía también
es cosa pero muy poca cosa: está hecha de palabras, —
una boronada de aire que no ocupa lugar en el espacio.
A la inversa del cuadro, el poema no muestra imágenes ni figuras: es un conjunto verbal que provoca en el
lector (o en el oyente) un surtidor de imágenes mentales.
La poesía se oye con los oídos pero se ve con el entendi-
miento.

   La discordia entre poesía y modernidad no es

(136)

accidental sino consustancial. La oposición entre
ambos aparece desde el comienzo de nuestra época,
con los primeros románticos. La paradoja es que esa
~~~~ incompatibilidad es uno de los atributos, —
quizá el central, de la poesía moderna. Sólo los modernos pueden ser tan total y desgarradoramente anti-
modernos como lo han sido todos nuestros grandes
poetas. La modernidad, fundada en la crítica,
secreta de un modo natural la crítica de sí
misma. La poesía ha sido una de las manifestaciones
más enérgicas y vivaces de esa crítica. Pero su crítica no
ha sido ni racional ni filosófica sino pasional y en
nombre de realidades negadas o humilladas por la Edad
Moderna. La poesía ha sido la réplica y el antídoto de
la modernidad. Así, al negarla, la ha legitimado

*Two manuscript pages from "The Other Voice," an essay on poetry by Octavio Paz.*

attended the Second International Congress of Anti-Fascist Writers. After his return to Mexico, he helped found the literary reviews *Taller* [Workshop] and *El hijo pródigo* [The Child Prodigy], out of which a new generation of Mexican writers emerged.

After spending two years traveling extensively in the United States on a Guggenheim Fellowship, Paz in 1945 entered into the Mexican diplomatic service. From 1946 until 1951, he lived in Paris, where he befriended Albert Camus, André Breton, and other French thinkers of the day. In the early 1950s, Paz's diplomatic duties took him to Japan and India. Among the many books that appeared during this period were two of his most highly acclaimed works: *El laberinto de la soledad* [The Labyrinth of Solitude] (1950), a prose study of the Mexican national character, and the book-length poem *Piedra de sol* [Sun Stone] (1957), called by J. M. Cohen "one of the last important poems to be published in the Western world."

In October 1968, Paz resigned his diplomatic post as ambassador to India to protest the Mexican government's bloody repression of student demonstrations in Mexico City. His critical work includes *Conjunciones y disjunciones* [Conjunctions and Disjunctions] (1969), and *Posdata* [The Other Mexico] (1970), as well as studies of Claude Lévi-Strauss and Marcel Duchamp.

Paz taught at numerous universities, including Cambridge and Harvard, where he received an honorary degree. Paz's later works include *El mono gramático* [The Monkey Grammarian] (1974) and *Arbol adentro* [A Tree Within] (1987). He was the recipient of numerous international prizes for poetry, including the International Grand Prix, the Jerusalem Prize, and the Nobel Prize, which he was awarded in 1990.

Paz died in 1998.

———

*Though small in stature and well into his seventies, Octavio Paz, with his deep blue eyes, gives the impression of being a much younger man. In his poetry and his prose works, which are both erudite and intensely political, he recurrently takes up such themes as the experience of Mexican history, especially as seen through its Indian past, and the overcoming of profound human loneliness through erotic love. Paz has long been considered, along with César*

*Vallejo and Pablo Neruda, to be one of the great Latin American poets of the twentieth century: indeed, three days after this interview, in 1990, he joined Neruda among the ranks of Nobel laureates in literature.*

*During this interview, which took place in front of an overflowing audience at the 92nd Street Y, under the auspices of the Poetry Center, Paz displayed the energy and power typical of him and of his poetry, which draws upon the eclectic sexual mysticism to bridge the gap between the individual and society. Appropriately, Paz seemed to welcome this opportunity to communicate with his audience.*

INTERVIEWER: Octavio, you were born in 1914, as you probably remember...

OCTAVIO PAZ: Not very well!

INTERVIEWER: ...virtually in the middle of the Mexican Revolution and right on the eve of World War I. The century you've lived through has been one of almost perpetual war. Do you have anything good to say about the twentieth century?

PAZ: Well, I have survived, and I think that's enough. History, you know, is one thing and our lives are something else. Our century has been terrible—one of the saddest in universal history—but our lives have always been more or less the same. Private lives are not historical. During the French or American revolutions, or during the wars between the Persians and the Greeks—during any great, universal event—history changes continually. But people live, work, fall in love, die, get sick, have friends, moments of illumination or sadness, and that has nothing to do with history. Or very little to do with it.

INTERVIEWER: So we are both in and out of history?

PAZ: Yes, history is our landscape or setting and we live through it. But the real drama, the real comedy also, is within us, and I think we can say the same for someone of the fifth century or for someone of a future century. Life is not historical, but something more like nature.

INTERVIEWER: In *The Privileges of Sight*, a book about your relationship with the visual arts, you say: "Neither I nor any of my friends had ever seen a Titian, a Velázquez, or a Cézanne.... Nevertheless, we were surrounded by many works of art." You talk there about Mixoac, where you lived as a boy, and the art of early-twentieth-century Mexico.

PAZ: Mixoac is now a rather ugly suburb of Mexico City, but when I was a child it was a small village. A very old village, from pre-Columbian times. The name Mixoac comes from the god Mixcoatl, the Nahuatl name for the Milky Way. It also meant "Cloud Serpent," as if the Milky Way were a serpent of clouds. We had a small pyramid, a diminutive pyramid, but a pyramid nevertheless. We also had a seventeenth-century convent. My neighborhood was called San Juan, and the parish church dated from the sixteenth century, one of the oldest in the area. There were also many eighteenth- and nineteenth-century houses, some with extensive gardens, because at the end of the nineteenth century Mixoac was a summer resort for the Mexican bourgeoisie. My family in fact had a summer house there. So when the revolution came, we were obliged, happily I think, to have to move there. We were surrounded by small memories of two pasts that remained very much alive, the pre-Columbian and the colonial.

INTERVIEWER: You talk in *The Privileges of Sight* about Mixoac's fireworks.

PAZ: I am very fond of fireworks. They were a part of my childhood. There was a part of the town where the artisans were all masters of the great art of fireworks. They were famous all over Mexico. To celebrate the feast of the Virgin of Guadalupe, other religious festivals, and at New Year's, they made the fireworks for the town. I remember how they made the church façade look like a fiery waterfall. It was marvelous. Mixoac was alive with a kind of life that doesn't exist anymore in big cities.

INTERVIEWER: You seem nostalgic for Mixoac, yet you are one of the few Mexican writers who live right in the center of Mexico City. Soon it will be the largest city in the world, a dynamic city, but, in terms of pollution, congestion and poverty, a nightmare. Is living there an inspiration or a hindrance?

PAZ: Living in the heart of Mexico City is neither an inspiration nor an obstacle. It's a challenge. And the only way to deal with challenges is to face up to them. I've lived in other towns and cities in Mexico, but no matter how agreeable they are, they seem somehow unreal. At a certain point, my wife and I decided to move into the apartment where we live now. If you live in Mexico, you've got to live in Mexico City.

INTERVIEWER: Could you tell us something about the Paz family?

PAZ: My father was Mexican, my mother Spanish. An aunt lived with us—rather eccentric as aunts are supposed to be and poetic in her own absurd way. My grandfather was a lawyer and a writer, a popular novelist. As a matter of fact, during one period we lived off the sales of one of his books, a best-seller. The Mixoac house was his.

INTERVIEWER: What about books? I suppose I'm thinking about how Borges claimed he never actually left his father's library.

PAZ: It's a curious parallel. My grandfather had a beautiful library, which was the great thing about the Mixoac house. It had about six or seven thousand books, and I had a great deal of freedom to read. I was a voracious reader when I was a child and even read "forbidden" books because no one paid attention to what I was reading. When I was very young, I read Voltaire. Perhaps that led me to lose my religious faith. I also read novels that were more or less libertine, not really pornographic, just racy.

INTERVIEWER: Did you read any children's books?

PAZ: Of course. I read a lot of books by Salgari, an Italian author very popular in Mexico. And Jules Verne. One of my great heroes was an American, Buffalo Bill. My friends and I would pass from Alexandre Dumas's *Three Musketeers* to the cowboys without the slightest remorse or sense that we were warping history.

INTERVIEWER: You said once that the first time you saw a surrealist painting—a picture where vines were twisting through the walls of a house—you took it for realism.

PAZ: That's true. The Mixoac house gradually crumbled around us. We had to abandon one room after another because the roofs and walls kept falling down.

INTERVIEWER: When you were about sixteen in 1930, you entered the National Preparatory School. What did you study, and what was the school like?

PAZ: The school was beautiful. It was built at the end of the seventeenth century, the high point of the baroque in Mexican architecture. The school was big, and there was nobility in the stones, the columns, the corridors. And there was another aesthetic attraction. During the twenties, the government had murals painted in it by Orozco and Rivera—the first mural Rivera painted was in my school.

INTERVIEWER: So you felt attracted to the work of the muralists then?

PAZ: Yes, all of us felt a rapport with the muralists' expressionist style. But there was a contradiction between the architecture and the painting. Later on I came to think that it was a pity the murals were painted in buildings that didn't belong to our century.

INTERVIEWER: What about the curriculum?

PAZ: It was a melange of the French tradition mixed with American educational theories. John Dewey, the American philosopher, was a big influence. Also the "progressive school" of education.

INTERVIEWER: So the foreign language you studied was French?

PAZ: And English. My father was a political exile during the revolution. He had to leave Mexico and take refuge in the United States. He went ahead and then we joined him in California, in Los Angeles, where we stayed for almost two years. On the first day of school, I had a fight with my American schoolmates. I couldn't speak a word of English, and they laughed because I couldn't say "spoon" during lunch hour. But when I came back to Mexico on my first day of school I had another fight. This time with my Mexican classmates and for the same reason—because I was a foreigner! I discovered I could be a foreigner in both countries.

INTERVIEWER: Were you influenced by any of your teachers in the National Preparatory School?

PAZ: Certainly. I had the chance to study with the Mexican poet Carlos Pellicer. Through him I met other poets of his generation. They opened my eyes to modern poetry. I should point out that my grandfather's library ended at the beginning of the twentieth century, so it wasn't until I was in the National Preparatory School that I learned books were published after 1910. Proust was a revelation for me. I thought no more novels had been written after Zola.

INTERVIEWER: What about poetry in Spanish?

PAZ: I found out about the Spanish poets of the Generation of 1927: García Lorca, Rafael Alberti and Jorge Guillén. I also read Antonio Machado and Juan Ramón Jiménez, who was a patriarch of poetry then. I also read Borges at that time, but remember Borges was not yet a short-story writer. During the early thirties he was a poet and an essayist. Naturally, the greatest revelation during that first period of my literary life was the poetry of Pablo Neruda.

INTERVIEWER: You went on to university, but in 1937 you made a momentous decision.

PAZ: Well, I made several. First I went to Yucatán. I finished my university work, but I left before graduating. I refused to become a lawyer. My family, like all Mexican middle-class families at that time, wanted their son to be a doctor or a lawyer. I only wanted to be a poet and also in some way a revolutionary. An opportunity came for me to go to Yucatán to work with some friends in a school for the children of workers and peasants. It was a great experience—it made me realize I was a city boy and that my experience of Mexico was that of central Mexico, the uplands.

INTERVIEWER: So you discovered geography?

PAZ: People who live in cities like New York or Paris are usually provincials with regard to the rest of the country. I discovered Yucatán, a very peculiar province of southern Mexico. It's Mexico, but it's also something very different thanks to the influence of the Mayas. I found out that Mexico has another tradition beside that of central Mexico, another set of roots—the Maya tradition. Yucatán was strangely cosmopolitan. It had links with Cuba and New Orleans. As a matter of fact, during the nineteenth century, people from the Yucatán traveled more often to the United States or Europe than they did to Mexico City. I began to see just how complex Mexico is.

INTERVIEWER: So then you returned to Mexico City and decided to go to the Spanish Civil War?

PAZ: I was invited to a congress, and since I was a great partisan of the Spanish Republic I immediately accepted. I left the Yucatán school and went to Spain, where I stayed for some months. I wanted to enroll in the Spanish Loyalist army—I was twenty-three—but I couldn't because as a volunteer I would have needed the recommendation of a political party. I wasn't a member of the Communist party or any other party, so there was no one to recommend me. I was rejected, but they told me that was not so important because I was a young writer—I was the youngest at the congress—and that I should go back to Mexico and write for the Spanish Republic. And that is what I did.

INTERVIEWER: What did that trip to Spain mean to you, above and beyond politics and the defense of the Spanish Republic?

PAZ: I discovered another part of my heritage. I was familiar, of course, with the Spanish literary tradition. I have always viewed Spanish literature as my own, but it's one thing to know books and another thing to see the people, the monuments and the landscape with your own eyes.

INTERVIEWER: So it was a geographical discovery again?

PAZ: Yes, but there was also the political or, to be more precise, the moral aspect. My political and intellectual beliefs were kindled by the idea of fraternity. We all talked a lot about it. For instance, the novels of André Malraux, which we all read, depicted the search for fraternity through revolutionary action. My Spanish experience did not strengthen my political beliefs, but it did give an unexpected twist to my idea of fraternity. One day—Stephen Spender was with me and might remember this episode—we went to the front in Madrid, which was in the university city. It was a battlefield. Sometimes in the same building the loyalists would only be separated from the fascists by a single wall. We could hear the soldiers on the other side talking. It was a strange feeling: those people facing me—I couldn't see them but only hear their voices—were my enemies. But they had human voices, like my own. They were like me.

INTERVIEWER: Did this affect your ability to hate your enemy?

PAZ: Yes. I began to think that perhaps all this fighting was an absurdity, but of course I couldn't say that to anyone. They would have thought I was a traitor, which I wasn't. I understood then, or later, when I could think seriously about that disquieting experience, I understood that real fraternity implies that you must accept the fact that your enemy is also human. I don't mean that you must be a friend to enemy. No, differences will subsist, but your enemy is also human, and the moment you understand that you can no longer accept violence. For me it was a terrible experience. It shattered many of my deepest convictions.

INTERVIEWER: Do you think that part of the horror of the situation resulted from the fact that the fascist soldiers were speaking your language?

PAZ: Yes. The soldiers on the other side of the wall were laughing and saying, "Give me a cigarette," and things like that. I said to myself, "Well, they are the same as we on this side of the wall."

INTERVIEWER: You didn't go straight back to Mexico, however.

PAZ: Of course not. It was my first trip to Europe. I had to go to Paris. Paris was a museum, it was history, it was the present. Walter Benjamin said Paris was the capital of the nineteenth century, and he was right, but I think Paris was also the capital of the twentieth century, the first part at least. Not that it was the political or economic or philosophic capital, but the artistic capital. For painting and the plastic arts in general but also for literature. Not because the best artists and writers lived in Paris but because of the great movements, right down to surrealism.

INTERVIEWER: What did you see that moved you?

PAZ: I went to the Universal Exposition and saw *Guernica*, which Picasso had just painted. I was twenty-three and had this tremendous opportunity to see the Picassos and Mirós in the Spanish pavilion. I didn't know many people in Paris, and by pure chance I went to an exhibition where I saw a painting by Max Ernst, *Europe after the Rain*, which made a deep impression on me.

INTERVIEWER: What about people?

PAZ: I met a Cuban writer who became very famous later, Alejo Carpentier. He invited me to a party at the house of the surrealist poet Robert Desnos. There was a huge crowd, many of them quite well known—but I didn't know a soul and felt lost. I was very young. Looking around the house, I found some strange objects. I asked the pretty lady of the house what they were. She smiled and told me they were Japanese erotic objects, "godemiches," and everyone laughed at my innocence. I realized just how provincial I was.

INTERVIEWER: You were back in Mexico in 1938. So were André Breton and Trotsky: did their presence mean anything to you?

PAZ: Of course. Politically, I was against Breton and Trotsky. I thought our great enemy was fascism, that Stalin was right, that we had to be united against fascism. Even though Breton and Trotsky were not agents of the Nazis, I was against them. On the other hand, I was fascinated by Trotsky. I secretly read his books, so inside myself I was a heterodox. And I admired Breton. I had read *L'amour fou*, a book that really impressed me.

INTERVIEWER: So in addition to Spanish and Spanish-American poetry you plunged into European modernism.

PAZ: Yes, I would say there were three texts that made a mark on me during this period: the first was Eliot's *Waste Land*, which I read in

Mexico in 1931. I was seventeen or so, and the poem baffled me. I couldn't understand a word. Since then I've read it countless times and still think it one of the great poems of the century. The second text was Saint-John Perse's *Anabase*, and the third was Breton's small book, which exalted free love, poetry and rebellion.

INTERVIEWER: But despite your admiration you wouldn't approach Breton?

PAZ: Once a mutual friend invited me to see him, telling me I was wrong about Breton's politics. I refused. Many years later, I met him and we became good friends. It was then—in spite of being criticized by many of my friends—I read with enthusiasm the *Manifesto for a Revolutionary Independent Art* written by Breton and Trotsky and signed by Diego Rivera. In it Trotsky renounces political control of literature. The only policy the revolutionary state can have with regard to artists and writers is to give them total freedom.

INTERVIEWER: It would seem as though your internal paradox was turning into a crisis.

PAZ: I was against Socialist Realism, and that was the beginning of my conflicts with the Communists. I was not a member of the Communist party, but I was friendly with them. Where we fought first was about the problem of art.

INTERVIEWER: So the exposition of surrealism in Mexico City in 1940 would have been a problem for you.

PAZ: I was the editor of a magazine, *Taller*. In it one of my friends published an article saying the surrealists had opened new vistas, but that they had become the academy of their own revolution. It was a mistake, especially during those years. But we published the article.

INTERVIEWER: Publish or perish.

PAZ: We must accept our mistakes. If we don't, we're lost, don't you think? This interview is in some ways an exercise in public confession—of which I am very much afraid.

INTERVIEWER: Octavio, despite the fact that you are a poet and an essayist, it seems that you have had novelistic temptations. I'm thinking of that "Diary of a Dreamer" you published in 1938 in your magazine *Taller* and *The Monkey Grammarian* of 1970.

PAZ: I wouldn't call that diary novelistic. It was a kind of notebook made up of meditations. I was probably under the spell of Rilke and his *Notebooks of Malte Laurids Brigge*. The truth is that the novel has always been a temptation for me. But perhaps I am not suited to it. The art of the novel unites two different things. It is like epic poetry, a world peopled by characters whose actions are the essence of the work. But, unlike the epic, the novel is analytical. It tells the deeds of the characters and, at the same time, criticizes them. Tom Jones, Odette de Crécy, Ivan Karamazov or Don Quixote are characters devoured by criticism. You don't find that in Homer or Virgil. Not even in Dante. The epic exalts or condemns; the novel analyzes and criticizes. The epic heroes are one-piece, solid characters; novelistic characters are ambiguous. These two poles, criticism and epic, combine in the novel.

INTERVIEWER: What about *The Monkey Grammarian*?

PAZ: I wouldn't call that a novel. It's on the frontier of the novel. If it's anything, that book is an anti-novel. Whenever I'm tempted to write a novel, I say to myself, "Poets are not novelists." Some poets, like Goethe, have written novels—rather boring ones. I think the poetic genius is synthetic. A poet creates syntheses while the novelist analyzes.

INTERVIEWER: If we could return to Mexico during the war years, I would like to ask you about your relationship with Pablo Neruda, who was sent to Mexico as Consul General of Chile in 1940.

PAZ: As I said earlier, Neruda's poetry was a revelation for me when I started to read modern poetry in the thirties. When I published my first book, I sent a copy to Neruda. He never answered me, but it was he who invited me to the congress in Spain. When I reached Paris in 1937, I knew no one. But just as I was getting off the train, a tall man ran up to me shouting, "Octavio Paz! Octavio Paz!" It was Neruda. Then he said, "Oh you are so young!" and we embraced. He found me a hotel, and we became great friends. He was one of the first to take notice of my poetry and to read it sympathetically.

INTERVIEWER: So what went wrong?

PAZ: When he came to Mexico, I saw him very often, but there were difficulties. First, there was a personal problem. Neruda was very generous, but also very domineering. Perhaps I was too rebellious and jealous of my own independence. He loved to be surrounded by a kind of court made up of people who loved him—sometimes these would be intelligent people but often they were mediocre. The second problem was politics. He became more and more Stalinist, while I became less and less enchanted with Stalin. Finally we fought—almost physically—and stopped speaking to each other. He wrote some not terribly nice things about me, including one nasty poem. I wrote some awful things about him. And that was that.

INTERVIEWER: Was there a reconciliation?

PAZ: For twenty years we didn't speak. We'd sometimes be at the same place at the same time, and I knew he would tell our mutual friends to stop seeing me because I was a "traitor." But then the Khrushchev report about the Stalinist terrors was made public and shattered his beliefs. We happened to be in London at the same poetry festival. I had just remarried, as had Pablo. I was with Marie-José, my wife, when we met Matilde Urrutia, his wife. She said, "If I'm not mistaken, you are Octavio Paz." To which I answered, "Yes, and you are Matilde." Then she said, "Do you want to see Pablo? I think he would love to see you again." We went to Pablo's room, where he was being interviewed by a journalist. As soon as the journalist left, Pablo said, "My son," and embraced me. The expression is very Chilean—"*mijito*"—and he said it with emotion. I was very moved, almost crying. We talked briefly, because he was on his way back to Chile. He sent me a book, I sent him one. And then a few years later, he died. It was sad, but it was one of the best things that has ever happened to me—the possibility to be friends again with a man I liked and admired so very much.

INTERVIEWER: The early forties were clearly difficult times for you, and yet they seem to have forced you to define your own intellectual position.

PAZ: That's true. I was having tremendous political problems, breaking with former friends—Neruda among them. I did make some new friends, like Victor Serge, a Franco-Russian writer, an old revolutionary. But I reached the conclusion that I had to leave my country, exile myself. I was fortunate because I received a Guggenheim fellowship to go to the United States. On this second visit, I went first to Berkeley and then to New York. I didn't know anyone, had no money, and was actually destitute. But I was really happy. It was one of the best periods of my life.

INTERVIEWER: Why?

PAZ: Well, I discovered the American people, and I was thrilled. It was like breathing deeply and freely while facing a vast space— a feeling of elation, lightness and confidence. I feel the same way every time I come to your country, but not with the same intensity. It was vivifying just to be in the States in those days, and, at the same time, I could step back from politics and plunge into poetry. I discovered American poetry in Conrad Aiken's *Anthology of Modern American Poetry*. I had already read Eliot, but I knew nothing about William Carlos Williams or Pound or Marianne Moore. I was slightly acquainted with Hart Crane's poetry—he lived his last years in Mexico, but he was more a legend than a body of poetry. While I was in Berkeley, I met Muriel Rukeyser, who very generously translated some of my poems. That was a great moment for me. A few years later, she sent them to *Horizon,* which Spender and Cyril Conolly were editing in London, where they were published. For me it was a kind of...

INTERVIEWER: Small apotheosis?

PAZ: A very small apotheosis. After New York, where I became a great reader of *Partisan Review,* I went on to Paris and caught up with some friends I'd met in Mexico. Benjamin Péret for example. Through him, I finally met Breton. We became friends. Surrealism was in decline, but surrealism for French literary life was something healthy, something vital and rebellious.

INTERVIEWER: What do you mean?

PAZ: The surrealists embodied something the French had forgotten: the other side of reason, love, freedom, poetry. The French have a tendency to be too rationalistic, to reduce everything to ideas and then to fight over them. When I reached Paris, Jean-Paul Sartre was the dominant figure.

INTERVIEWER: But for you existentialism would have been old hat.

PAZ: That's right. In Madrid, the Spanish philosopher Ortega y Gasset—and later his disciples in Mexico City and Buenos Aires— had published all the main texts of phenomenology and existentialism, from Husserl to Heidegger, so Sartre represented more a clever variation than an innovation. Also, I was against Sartre's politics. The one person connected to French existentialism with whom I was friendly and who was very generous to me was Albert Camus. But I must say I was nearer to the surrealist poets.

INTERVIEWER: By the end of the forties you had published two major books, the poems collected in *Freedom on Parole* (*Libertad bajo palabra*) and *The Labyrinth of Solitude*. I've always been curious about the title of *Freedom on Parole*. Does it have anything to do with the futurist poet Marinetti's "words on leave" (*parole in libertà*)?

PAZ: I'm afraid not. Marinetti wanted to free words from the chains of syntax and grammar, a kind of aesthetic nihilism. *Freedom on Parole* has more to do with morals than aesthetics. I simply wanted to say that human freedom is conditional. In English, when you are let out of jail you're "on parole," and "parole" means speech, word, word of honor. But the condition under which you are free is language, human awareness.

INTERVIEWER: So for you freedom of speech is more than the right to speak your mind?

PAZ: Absolutely. Ever since I was an adolescent I've been intrigued by the mystery of freedom. Because it is a mystery. Freedom depends on the very thing that limits or denies it, fate, God, biological or social determinism, whatever. To carry out its mission, fate counts on the complicity of our freedom, and to be free, we must overcome fate. The dialectics of freedom and fate is the theme of Greek tragedy and Shakespeare, although in Shakespeare fate appears as passion (love, jealousy, ambition, envy) and as chance. In Spanish theater—especially in Calderón and Tirso de Molina—the mystery of freedom expresses itself in the language of Christian theology: divine providence and free will. The idea of conditional freedom implies the notion of personal responsibility. Each of us, literally, either creates or destroys his own freedom. A freedom that is always precarious. And that brings up the title's poetic or aesthetic meaning: the poem—freedom—stands above an order—language.

INTERVIEWER: You wrote *Freedom on Parole* between 1935 and 1957, more than twenty years ...

PAZ: I wrote and rewrote the book many times.

INTERVIEWER: Is it an autobiography?

PAZ: Yes and no. It expresses my aesthetic and personal experiences, from my earliest youth until the beginning of my maturity. I wrote the first poems when I was twenty-one, and I finished the last when I turned forty-three. But the real protagonist of those poems is not Octavio Paz but a half-real, half-mythical figure: the poet. Although that poet was my age, spoke my language, and his vital statistics were identical with my own, he was someone else. A figure, an image derived from tradition. Every poet is the momentary incarnation of that figure.

INTERVIEWER: Doesn't *The Labyrinth of Solitude* also have an autobiographical dimension?

PAZ: Again, yes and no. I wrote *The Labyrinth of Solitude* in Paris. The idea came to me in the United States when I tried to analyze the situation of the Mexicans living in Los Angeles, the *pachucos* or Chicanos as they're called now. I suppose they were a kind of mirror for me—the autobiographical dimension you like to see. That on one side. But there is also the relationship between Mexico and the United States. If there are two countries in the world that are different, they are the United States and Mexico. But we are condemned to live together forever. So we should try to understand each other and also to know ourselves. That was how *The Labyrinth of Solitude* began.

INTERVIEWER: That book deals with ideas such as difference, resentment, the hermetic nature of Mexican man, but it doesn't touch on the life of the poet.

PAZ: True. I tried to deal with that subject in a short essay called "Poetry of Solitude and Poetry of Communion." That article in some ways is the poetic equivalent of *The Labyrinth of Solitude* because it presents my vision of man, which is very simple. There are two situations for every human being. The first is the solitude we feel when we are born. Our first situation is that of orphanhood, and it is only later that we discover the opposite, filial attachment. The second is that because we are thrown, as Heidegger says, into this world, we feel we must find what the Buddhists call "the other share." This is the thirst for community. I think philosophy and religion derive from this original situation or predicament. Every country and every individual tries to resolve it in different ways. Poetry is a bridge between solitude and communion. Communion, even for a mystic like Saint John of the Cross, can never be absolute.

INTERVIEWER: Is this why the language of mysticism is so erotic?

PAZ: Yes, because lovers, which is what the mystics are, constitute the greatest image of communion. But even between lovers solitude is never completely abolished. Conversely, solitude is never absolute. We are always with someone, even if it is only our shadow. We are never one—we are always "we." These extremes are the poles of human life.

INTERVIEWER: All in all, you spent some eight years abroad, first in the United States, then in Paris, and then in the Mexican diplomatic service. How do you view those years in the context of your career as a poet?

PAZ: Actually, I spent nine years abroad. If you count each of those years as a month, you'll find that those nine years were nine months which I lived in the womb of time. The years I lived in San Francisco, New York and Paris were a period of gestation. I was reborn, and the man who came back to Mexico at the end of 1952 was a different poet, a different writer. If I had stayed in Mexico, I probably would have drowned in journalism, bureaucracy or alcohol. I ran away from that world and also, perhaps, from myself.

INTERVIEWER: But you were hardly greeted as the prodigal son when you reappeared...

PAZ: I wasn't accepted at all, except by a few young people. I had broken with the predominant aesthetic, moral and political ideas and was instantly attacked by many people who were all too sure of their dogmas and prejudices. It was the beginning of a disagreement which has still not come to an end. It isn't simply an ideological difference of opinion. Certainly those polemics have been bitter and hard-fought, but even that does not explain the malevolence of some people, the pettiness of others, and the reticence of the majority. I've experienced despair and rage, but I've just had to shrug my shoulders and move forward. Now I see those quarrels as a blessing: if a writer is accepted, he'll soon be rejected or forgotten. I didn't set out to be a troublesome writer, but if that's what I've been, I am totally unrepentant.

INTERVIEWER: You left Mexico again in 1959.

PAZ: And I didn't come back until 1971. An absence of twelve years—another symbolic number. I returned because Mexico has always been a magnet I can't resist, a real passion, alternately happy and wretched like all passions.

INTERVIEWER: Tell me about those twelve years. First you went back to Paris, then to India as the Mexican Ambassador, and later to England and the United States.

PAZ: When I'd finished the definitive version of *Freedom on Parole*, I felt I could start over. I explored new poetic worlds, knew other countries, lived other sentiments, had other ideas. The first and greatest of my new experiences was India. Another geography, another humanity, other gods—a different kind of civilization. I lived there for just over six years. I traveled around the subcontinent quite a bit and lived for periods in Ceylon and Afghanistan—

two more geographical and cultural extremes. If I had to express my vision of India in a single image, I would say that I see an immense plain: in the distance, white, ruinous architecture, a powerful river, a huge tree and in its shade a shape (a beggar, a Buddha, a pile of stones?). Out from among the knots and forks of the tree, a woman arises . . . I fell in love and got married in India.

INTERVIEWER: When did you become seriously interested in Asian thought?

PAZ: Starting with my first trip to the East in 1952—I spent almost a year in India and Japan—I made small incursions into the philosophic and artistic traditions of those countries. I visited many places and read some of the classics of Indian thought. Most important to me were the poets and philosophers of China and Japan. During my second stay in India, between 1962 and 1968, I read many of the great philosophic and religious texts. Buddhism impressed me profoundly.

INTERVIEWER: Did you think of converting?

PAZ: No, but studying Buddhism was a mental and spiritual exercise that helped me begin to doubt the ego and its mirages. Ego worship is the greatest idolatry of modern man. Buddhism for me is a criticism of the ego and of reality. A radical criticism that does not end in negation but in acceptance. All the great Buddhist sanctuaries in India (the Hindu sanctuaries as well, but those, perhaps because they're later, are more baroque and elaborate) contain highly sensual sculptures and reliefs. A powerful but peaceful sexuality. I was shocked to find that exaltation of the body and of natural powers in a religious and philosophic tradition that disparages the world and preaches negation and emptiness. That became the central theme of a short book I wrote during those years, *Conjunctions and Disjunctions*.

INTERVIEWER: Was it hard to balance being Mexican Ambassador to India with your explorations of India?

PAZ: My ambassadorial work was not arduous. I had time, I could travel and write. And not only about India. The student movements of 1968 fascinated me. In a certain way I felt the hopes and aspirations of my own youth were being reborn. I never thought it would lead to a revolutionary transformation of society, but I did realize that I was witnessing the appearance of a new sensibility that in some fashion *rhymed* with what I had felt and thought before.

INTERVIEWER: You felt that history was repeating itself?

PAZ: In a way. The similarity between some of the attitudes of the 1968 students and the surrealist poets, for example, was clear to see. I thought William Blake would have been sympathetic to both the words and the actions of those young people. The student movement in Mexico was more ideological than in France or the United States, but it too had legitimate aspirations. The Mexican political system, born out of the Revolution, had survived but was suffering a kind of historical arteriosclerosis. On October 2, 1968, the Mexican government decided to use violence to suppress the student movement. It was a brutal action. I felt I could not go on serving the government, so I left the diplomatic corps.

INTERVIEWER: You went to Paris and then to the United States before spending that year at Cambridge.

PAZ: Yes, and during those months I reflected on the recent history of Mexico. The Revolution began in 1910 with great democratic ambitions. More than half a century later, the nation was controlled by a paternalistic, authoritarian party. So in 1969 I wrote a postscript to *The Labyrinth of Solitude,* a "critique of the pyramid," which I took to be the symbolic form of Mexican authoritarianism. I stated that the only way of getting beyond the political and historical crisis we were living through—the paralysis of the institutions created by the Revolution—was to begin democratic reform.

INTERVIEWER: But that was not necessarily what the student movement was seeking.

PAZ: No. The student leaders and the left-wing political groups favored violent social revolution. They were under the influence of the Cuban Revolution—and there are still some who defend Fidel Castro even today. My point of view put me in opposition, simultaneously, to the government and the left. The "progressive" intellectuals, almost all of whom wanted to establish a totalitarian socialist regime, attacked me vehemently. I fought back. Rather, *we* fought back: a small group of younger writers agreed with some of my opinions. We all believed in a peaceful, gradual move toward democracy. We founded *Plural,* a magazine that would combine literature, art and political criticism. There was a crisis, so we founded another, *Vuelta* ("Return"), which is still going strong and has a faithful, demanding readership. Mexico has changed, and now most of our old enemies say they are democratic. We are living through a transition to democracy, one that will have its setbacks and will seem too slow for some.

INTERVIEWER: Do you see yourself as part of a long line of Latin American statesmen-writers, one that could include Argentina's Sarmiento in the nineteenth and Neruda in the twentieth century?

PAZ: I don't think of myself as a "statesman-poet," and I'm not really comparable to Sarmiento or Neruda. Sarmiento was a real statesman and a great political figure in addition to being a great writer. Neruda was a poet, a great poet. He joined the Communist party, but for generous, semi-religious reasons. It was a real conversion. So his political militance was not that of an intellectual but of a believer. Within the Party, he seems to have been a political pragmatist, but, again, he was more like one of the faithful than a critical intellectual. As for me, well, I've never been a member of any political party, and I've never run for public office. I have been a political and social critic, but always from the marginal position of an independent writer. I'm not a joiner, although of course I've had and have my personal preferences. I'm different from Mario Vargas Llosa, who did decide to intervene directly in his country's politics. Vargas Llosa is like Havel in Czechoslovakia or Malraux in France after World War II.

INTERVIEWER: But it is almost impossible to separate politics from literature or any aspect of culture.

PAZ: Since the Enlightenment, there has been a constant confluence of literature, philosophy and politics. In the English-speaking world you have Milton as an antecedent as well as the great Romantics in the nineteenth century. In the twentieth century, there are many examples. Eliot, for instance, was never an active participant in politics, but his writing is an impassioned defense of traditional values, values that have a political dimension. I mention Eliot, whose beliefs are totally different from my own, simply because he too was an independent writer who joined no party. I consider myself a private person, although I reserve the right to have opinions and to write about matters that affect my country and my contemporaries. When I was young, I fought against Nazi totalitarianism and later on against the Soviet dictatorship. I don't regret either struggle in the slightest.

INTERVIEWER: Thinking about your time in India now and its effect on your poetry, what would you say about the influence of India?

PAZ: If I hadn't lived in India, I could not have written *Blanco* or most of the poems in *Eastern Slope*. The time I spent in Asia was a huge pause, as if time had slowed down and space had become larger. In a few rare moments, I experienced those states of being in which we are at one with the world around us, when the doors of time seem to open, if only slightly. We all live those instants in our childhood, but modern life rarely allows us to reexperience them when we're adults. As regards my poetry, that period begins with *Salamander,* culminates in *Eastern Slope,* and ends with *The Monkey Grammarian.*

INTERVIEWER: But didn't you write *The Monkey Grammarian* in 1970, the year you spent at Cambridge University?

PAZ: I did. It was my farewell to India. That year in England also changed me. Especially because of what we must necessarily refer to as English "civility," which includes the cultivation of eccentricity. That taught me not only to respect my fellow man but trees, plants, and birds as well. I also read certain poets. Thanks to Charles Tomlinson, I discovered Wordsworth. *The Prelude* became one of my favorite books. There may be echoes of it in *A Draft of Shadows.*

INTERVIEWER: Do you have a schedule for writing?

PAZ: I've never been able to maintain a fixed schedule. For years, I wrote in my few free hours. I was quite poor and from an early age had to hold down several jobs to eke out a living. I was a minor employee in the National Archive; I worked in a bank; I was a journalist; I finally found a comfortable but busy post in the diplomatic service, but none of those jobs had any real effect on my work as a poet.

INTERVIEWER: Do you have to be in any specific place in order to write?

PAZ: A novelist needs his typewriter, but you can write poetry any time, anywhere. Sometimes I mentally compose a poem on a bus or walking down the street. The rhythm of walking helps me fix the verses. Then when I get home, I write it all down. For a long time when I was younger, I wrote at night. It's quieter, more tranquil. But writing at night also magnifies the writer's solitude. Nowadays I write during the late morning and into the afternoon. It's a pleasure to finish a page when night falls.

INTERVIEWER: Your work never distracted you from your writing?

PAZ: No, but let me give you an example. Once I had a totally infernal job in the National Banking Commission (how I got it, I can't guess) which consisted in counting packets of old banknotes already sealed and ready to be burned. I had to make sure each packet contained the requisite three thousand pesos. I almost always had one banknote too many or too few—they were always fives—so I decided to give up counting them and to use those long hours to compose a series of sonnets in my head. Rhyme helped me retain the verses in my memory, but not having paper and pencil made my task much more difficult. I've always admired Milton for dictating long passages from *Paradise Lost* to his daughters. Unrhymed passages at that!

INTERVIEWER: Is it the same when you write prose?

PAZ: Prose is another matter. You have to write it in a quiet, isolated place, even if that happens to be the bathroom. But above all to write it's essential to have one or two dictionaries at hand. The telephone is the writer's devil, the dictionary his guardian angel. I used to type, but now I write everything in longhand. If it's prose, I write it out one, two or three times and then dictate it into a tape recorder. My secretary types it out, and I correct it. Poetry I write and rewrite constantly.

INTERVIEWER: What is the inspiration or starting-point for a poem? Can you give an example of how the process works?

PAZ: Each poem is different. Often the first line is a gift, I don't know if from the gods or from that mysterious faculty called inspiration. Let me use *Sun Stone* as an example: I wrote the first thirty verses as if someone were silently dictating them to me. I was surprised at the fluidity with which those hendecasyllabic lines appeared one after another. They came from far off and from nearby, from within my own chest. Suddenly the current stopped flowing. I read what I'd written: I didn't have to change a thing. But it was only a beginning, and I had no idea where those lines were going. A few days later, I tried to get started again, not in a passive way but trying to orient and direct the flow of verses. I wrote another thirty or forty lines. I stopped. I went back to it a few days later and, little by little, I began to discover the theme of the poem and where it was all heading.

INTERVIEWER: A figure began to appear in the carpet?

PAZ: It was a kind of a review of my life, a resurrection of my experiences, my concerns, my failures, my obsessions. I realized I was living the end of my youth and that the poem was simultaneously an end and a new beginning. When I reached a certain point, the verbal current stopped, and all I could do was repeat the first verses. That is the source of the poem's circular form. There was nothing arbitrary about it. *Sun Stone* is the last poem in the book that gathers together the first period of my poetry: *Freedom on Parole* (1935–1957). Even though I didn't know what I would write after that, I was sure that one period of my life and my poetry had ended, and another was beginning.

INTERVIEWER: But the title seems to allude to the cyclical Aztec concept of time.

PAZ: While I was writing the poem, I was reading an archeological essay about the Aztec calendar, and it occurred to me to call the poem *Sun Stone*. I added or cut—I don't remember which—three or four lines so that the poem would coincide with the 584 days of the conjunction of Venus with the Sun. But the time of my poem is not the ritual time of Aztec cosmogony but human, biographical time, which is linear.

INTERVIEWER: But you thought seriously enough about the numerical symbolism of 584 to limit the number of verses in the poem to that number.

PAZ: I confess that I have been and am still fond of numerological combinations. Other poems of mine are also built around certain numerical proportions. It isn't an eccentricity, but a part of the Western tradition. Dante is the best example. *Blanco*, however, was completely different from *Sun Stone*. First I had the *idea* for the poem. I made notes and even drew some diagrams which were inspired, more or less, by Tibetan mandalas. I conceived it as a spatial poem which would correspond to the four points on the compass, the four primary colors, etc. It was difficult because poetry is a temporal art. As if to prove it, the words themselves wouldn't come. I had to call them and, even though it may seem I'm exaggerating, *invoke* them. One day, I wrote the first lines. As was to be expected they were about words, how they appear and disappear. After those first ten lines, the poem began to flow with relative ease. Of course, there were, as usual, anguishing periods of sterility followed by others of fluidity. The architecture of *Blanco* is more sharply defined than that of *Sun Stone*, more complex, richer.

INTERVIEWER: So you defy Edgar Allan Poe's injunction against the long poem?

PAZ: With great relish. I've written other long poems, like *A Draft of Shadows* and *Carta de creencia*, which means "letter of faith." The first is the monologue of memory and its inventions—memory changes and re-creates the past as it revives it. In that way, it transforms the past into the present, into presence. *Carta de creencia* is a cantata where different voices converge. But, like *Sun Stone*, it's still a linear composition.

INTERVIEWER: When you write a long poem, do you see yourself as part of an ancient tradition?

PAZ: The long poem in modern times is very different from what it was in antiquity. Ancient poems, epics or allegories, contain a good deal of stuffing. The genre allowed and even demanded it. But the modern long poem tolerates neither stuffing nor transitions, for several reasons. First, with inevitable exceptions like Pound's *Cantos*, because our long poems are simply not as long as those of the ancients. Second, because our long poems contain two antithetical qualities: the *development* of the long poem and the *intensity* of the short poem. It's very difficult to manage. Actually, it's a new genre. And that's why I admire Eliot: his long poems have the same intensity and concentration as short poems.

INTERVIEWER: Is the process of writing enjoyable or frustrating?

PAZ: Writing is a painful process that requires huge effort and sleepless nights. In addition to the threat of writer's block, there is always the sensation that failure is inevitable. Nothing we write is what we wish we could write. Writing is a curse. The worst part of it is the anguish that precedes the act of writing—the hours, days or months when we search in vain for the phrase that turns the spigot that makes the water flow. Once that first phrase is written, everything changes: the process is enthralling, vital and enriching, no matter what the final result is. Writing is a blessing!

INTERVIEWER: How and why does an idea seize you? How do you decide if it is prose or poetry?

PAZ: I don't have any hard-and-fast rules for this. For prose, it would seem that the idea comes first, followed by a desire to develop the idea. Often, of course, the original idea changes, but even so the essential fact remains the same: prose is a means, an instrument. But in the case of poetry, the poet becomes the instrument. Whose? It's hard to say. Perhaps language. I don't mean automatic writing. For me, the poem is a *premeditated* act. But poetry flows from a psychic well related to language, that is, related to the culture and memory of a people. An ancient, impersonal spring intimately linked to verbal rhythm.

INTERVIEWER: But doesn't prose have a rhythm as well?

PAZ: Prose does have a rhythm, but that rhythm is not its constitutive element as it is in poetry. Let's not confuse metrics with rhythm: meter may be a manifestation of rhythm, but it is different because it has become mechanical. Which is why, as Eliot suggests, from time to time meter has to return to spoken, everyday language, which is to say, to the original rhythms every language has.

INTERVIEWER: Verse and prose are, therefore, separate entities?

PAZ: Rhythm links verse to prose: one enriches the other. The reason why Whitman was so seductive was precisely because of his surprising fusion of prose and poetry. A fusion produced by rhythm. The prose poem is another example, although its powers are more limited. Of course, being prosaic in poetry can be disastrous, as we see in so many inept poems in "free verse" every day. As to the influence of poetry on prose—just think about Chateaubriand, Nerval or Proust. In Joyce, the boundary between prose and poetry sometimes completely disappears.

INTERVIEWER: Can you always keep that boundary sharp?

PAZ: I try to keep them separate, but it doesn't always work. A prose piece, without my having to think about it, can become a poem. But I've never had a poem turn into an essay or a story. In some books—*Eagle or Sun?* and *The Monkey Grammarian*—I've tried to bring the prose right up to the border with poetry, I don't know with how much success.

INTERVIEWER: We've talked about premeditation and revision: how does inspiration relate to them?

PAZ: Inspiration and premeditation are two phases in the same process. Premeditation needs inspiration and vice-versa. It's like a river: the water can only flow between the two banks that contain it. Without premeditation, inspiration just scatters. But the role of premeditation—even in a reflexive genre like the essay—is limited. As you write, the text becomes autonomous, changes, and somehow forces you to follow it. The text always separates itself from the author.

INTERVIEWER: Then why revise?

PAZ: Insecurity. No doubt about it. Also a senseless desire for perfection. I said that all texts have their own life, independent of the author. The poem doesn't express the poet. It expresses poetry. That's why it is legitimate to revise and correct a poem. Yes, and at the same time respect the poet who wrote it. I mean the poet, not the man we were then. I was that poet, but I was also someone else—that figure we talked about earlier. The poet is at the service of his poems.

INTERVIEWER: But just how much revising do you do? Do you ever feel a work is complete, or is it abandoned?

PAZ: I revise incessantly. Some critics say too much, and they may be right. But if there's a danger in revising, there is much more danger in not revising. I believe in inspiration, but I also believe that we've got to help inspiration, restrain it and even contradict it.

INTERVIEWER: Thinking again on the relationship between inspiration and revision, did you ever attempt the kind of automatic writing the surrealists recommended in the first surrealist manifesto?

PAZ: I did experiment with "automatic writing." It's very hard to do. Actually, it's *impossible*. No one can write with his mind blank, not thinking about what he's writing. Only God could write a real automatic poem because only for God are speaking, thinking, and acting the same thing. If God says, "A horse!" a horse immediately appears. But a poet has to *reinvent* his horse, that is, his poem. He has to think it, and he has to make it. All the automatic poems I wrote during the time of my friendship with the surrealists were thought and written with a certain deliberation. I wrote those poems with my eyes open.

INTERVIEWER: Do you think Breton was serious when he advocated automatic writing?

PAZ: Perhaps he was. I was extremely fond of André Breton, really admired him. It's no exaggeration to say he was a solar figure because his friendship emitted light and heat. Shortly after I met him, he asked me for a poem for a surrealist magazine. I gave him a prose poem, "*Mariposa de obsidiana*"—it alludes to a pre-Columbian goddess. He read it over several times, liked it, and decided to publish it. But he pointed out one line that seemed weak. I reread the poem, discovered he was right, and removed the phrase. He was charmed, but I was confused. So I asked him, "What about automatic writing?" He raised his leonine head and answered without changing expression: "That line was a journalistic intromission..."

INTERVIEWER: It's curious, Octavio, how often a tension allows you to find your own special place—the United States and Mexico, the *pachuco* and Anglo-American society, solitude and communion, poetry and prose. Do you yourself see a tension between your essays and your poetry?

PAZ: If I start to write, the thing I love to write most, the thing I love most to create, is poetry. I would much rather be remembered for two or three short poems in some anthology than as an essayist. However, since I am a modern and live in a century that believes in reason and explanation, I find I am in a tradition of poets who in one way or another have written defenses of poetry. Just think of the Renaissance and then again of the Romantics—Shelley,

Wordsworth in the preface to *Lyrical Ballads*. Well, now that I'm at the end of my career, I want to do two things: to keep on writing poetry and to write another defense of poetry.

INTERVIEWER: What will it say?

PAZ: I've just written a book, *The Other Voice,* about the situation of poetry in the twentieth century. When I was young, my great idols were poets and not novelists—even though I admired novelists like Proust or Lawrence. Eliot was one of my idols, but so were Valéry and Apollinaire. But poetry today is like a secret cult whose rites are celebrated in the catacombs, on the fringes of society. Consumer society and commercial publishers pay little attention to poetry. I think this is one of society's diseases. I don't think we can have a good society if we don't also have good poetry. I'm sure of it.

INTERVIEWER: Television is being criticized as the ruination of twentieth-century life, but you have the unique opinion that television will be good for poetry as a return to the oral tradition.

PAZ: Poetry existed before writing. Essentially, it is a verbal art, that enters us not only through our eyes and understanding but through our ears as well. Poetry is something spoken and heard. It's also something we see and write. In that we see the importance in the Oriental and Asian traditions of calligraphy. In the West, in modern times, typography has also been important—the maximum example in this would be Mallarmé. In television, the aural aspect of poetry can join with the visual and with the idea of movement—something books don't have. Let me explain: this is a barely explored possibility. So I'm not saying television *will* mean poetry's return to an oral tradition but that it *could* be the beginning of a tradition in which writing, sound and images will unite. Poetry always uses all the means of communication the age offers it: musical instruments, printing, radio, records. Why shouldn't it try television? We've got to take a chance.

INTERVIEWER: Will the poet always be the permanent dissident?

PAZ: Yes. We have all won a great battle in the defeat of the Communist bureaucracies by themselves—and that's the important thing: they were defeated by themselves and not by the West. But that's not enough. We need more social justice. Free-market societies produce unjust and very stupid societies. I don't believe that the production and consumption of things can be the meaning of human life. All great religions and philosophies say that human beings are more than producers and consumers. We cannot reduce our lives to economics. If a society without social justice is not a good society, a society without poetry is a society without dreams, without words, and, most importantly, without that bridge between one person and another that poetry is. We are different from the other animals because we can talk, and the supreme form of language is poetry. If society abolishes poetry it commits spiritual suicide.

INTERVIEWER: Is your extensive critical study of the seventeenth-century Mexican nun Sor Juana Inés de la Cruz a kind of projection of the present onto the past?

PAZ: In part, but I also wanted to recover a figure I consider essential not only for Mexicans but for all of the Americas. At first, Sor Juana was buried and forgotten; then she was disinterred and mummified. I wanted to bring her back into the light of day, free her from the wax museum. She's alive and has a great deal to tell us. She was a great poet, the first in a long line of great Latin American women poets—let's not forget that Gabriela Mistral from Chile was the first Latin American writer to win the Nobel Prize. Sor Juana was also an intellectual of the first rank (which we can't say for Emily Dickinson) and a defender of women's rights. She was put on a pedestal and praised, then persecuted and humiliated. I just had to write about her.

INTERVIEWER: Finally, whither Octavio Paz? Where do you go from here?

PAZ: Where? I asked myself that question when I was twenty, again when I was thirty, again when I was forty, fifty...I could never answer it. Now I know something: I have to persist. That means live, write and face, like everyone else, the other side of every life—the unknown.

—*Alfred MacAdam*

# JULIO CORTÁZAR

Julio Cortázar was born on August 26, 1914, in Brussels, Belgium, where he lived for four years before his family returned to their native Buenos Aires. As a young boy, Cortázar was an exceptional student and avid writer, completing his first novel at age nine. He earned a teaching degree and taught high school from 1937 to 1944, publishing *Presencia,* a book of sonnets, in 1938 under the pseudonym Julio Denis. In 1944 he began teaching French literature at the Universidad de Cuyo in Mendoza but resigned the position in 1946 after he was briefly imprisoned for demonstrating against Juan Perón.

*A note from Julio Cortázar to his translator, Gregory Rabassa, and a drawing sent to Rabassa's daughter, Clara, "from the six foot four man."*

*Bestiario*, Cortázar's first short story collection, appeared in 1951 and included "*Casa tomada*" ["House Taken Over"], a story previously published in the literary journal edited by Jorge Luis Borges. That same year he received a scholarship to study in Paris, where he worked as a translator for UNESCO. In 1953 he married another translator, Aurora Bernádez, and together they collaborated on a translation of Edgar Allan Poe's prose works.

Cortázar's earlier works include three short story collections, *Final del juego* [End of the Game and Other Stories] (1956), *Todos los fuegos el fuego* [All Fires the Fire] (1966), and *Historias de cronopios y famas* [Cronopias and Famas] (1969). His stories are often marked by fantastical situations or exceptional characters, and he is known for his redefinition of the linear narrative form. His greatest work, *Rayuela* [Hopscotch], appeared in 1963 and was lauded by Carlos Fuentes as "one of the great manifestoes of Latin American modernity." Composed of 155 chapters that follow various paths to the end, *Rayuela* is about an Argentine's search for self and knowledge through the nightlife of Paris and Buenos Aires, and remains one of the greatest challenges to the conventional novel.

As the political situation in Latin America intensified through the 1970s, themes of military terror and oppression emerged in Cortázar's later works, which included two short story collections, *Alguien que anda por ahí y otros relatos* [A Change of Light and Other Stories] (1977) and *Queremos tanto a Glenda* [We Love Glenda So Much] (1980), and a novel, *Un tal Lucas* [A Certain Lucas] (1979). Throughout the 1970s, he immersed himself in the fight for political justice in Central and South America, to the detriment of his health and literary output. In 1983 he published a volume of essays with his second wife, Carol Dunlop, entitled *Nicaragua tan violentamente dulce* [Nicaragua So Violently Sweet]. When Cortázar died of cancer in 1984, the Madrid newspaper *El País* hailed him as one of Latin America's greatest writers and printed eleven full pages of tributes, reminiscences, and farewells.

—

*Throughout his expatriate years in Paris, Cortázar had lived in various neighborhoods. In the last decade, royalties from his books enabled him to buy his own apartment. The apartment, atop a building in a district of whole-salers and chinaware shops, might have been the setting for one of his stories: spacious, though crowded with books, its walls lined with paintings by friends.*

*Cortázar was a tall man, 6′4″, though thinner than his photographs revealed. The last months before this interview had been particularly diffi-cult for him, since his last wife Carol, thirty years his junior, had recently died of cancer. In addition, his extensive travels, especially to Latin America, had obviously exhausted him. He had been home barely a week and was finally relaxing in his favorite chair, smoking a pipe as we talked.*

INTERVIEWER: In some of the stories in your most recent book, *Deshoras,* the fantastic seems to encroach on the real world more than ever. Have you yourself felt as if the fantastic and the com-monplace are becoming one?

JULIO CORTÁZAR: Yes, in these recent stories I have the feeling that there is less distance between what we call the fantastic and what we call the real. In my older stories, the distance was greater because the fantastic really *was* fantastic, and sometimes it touched on the supernatural. Of course, the fantastic takes on metamor-phoses; it changes. The notion of the fantastic we had in the epoch of the gothic novels in England, for example, has absolutely noth-ing to do with our concept of it today. Now we laugh when we read Horace Walpole's *Castle of Otranto*—the ghosts dressed in white, the skeletons that walk around making noises with their chains. These days, my notion of the fantastic is closer to what we call reality. Perhaps because reality approaches the fantastic more and more.

INTERVIEWER: Much more of your time in recent years has been spent in support of various liberation struggles in Latin America. Hasn't that also helped bring the real and the fantastic closer for you, and made you more serious?

CORTÁZAR: Well, I don't like the idea of "serious," because I don't think I am serious, at least not in the sense where one speaks of a serious man or a serious woman. But in these last few years, my efforts concerning certain Latin American regimes—Argentina, Chile, Uruguay, and now above all Nicaragua—have absorbed me to such a point that I have used the fantastic in certain stories to deal with this subject—in a way that's very close to reality, in my opinion. So, I feel less free than before. That is, thirty years ago I was writing things that came into my head and I judged them only by aesthetic criteria. Now, though I continue to judge them by aesthetic criteria, first of all because I'm a writer—I'm now a writer who's tormented, very preoccupied by the situation in Latin America; consequently that often slips into my writing, in a conscious or in an unconscious way. But despite the stories with very precise references to ideological and political questions, my stories, in essence, haven't changed. They're still stories of the fantastic.

The problem for an engagé writer, as they call them now, is to continue being a writer. If what he writes becomes simply literature with a political content, it can be very mediocre. That's what has happened to a number of writers. So, the problem is one of balance. For me, what I do must always be literature, the highest I can do . . . to go beyond the possible. But, at the same time, to try to put in a mix of contemporary reality. And that's a very difficult balance. In the story in *Deshoras* about the rats, "Satarsa,"—which is an episode based on the struggle against the Argentine guerrillas—the temptation was to stick to the political level alone.

INTERVIEWER: What has been the response to such stories? Was there much difference in the response you got from literary people and that which you got from political ones?

CORTÁZAR: Of course. The bourgeois readers in Latin America who are indifferent to politics, or those who align themselves with the right wing, well, they don't worry about the problems that worry me—the problems of exploitation, of oppression, and so on. Those people regret that my stories often take a political turn. Other readers, above all the young—who share my sentiments, my need to struggle, and who love literature—love these stories. The

Cubans relish "Meeting." "Apocalypse at Solentiname" is a story that Nicaraguans read and reread with great pleasure.

INTERVIEWER: What has determined your increased political involvement?

CORTÁZAR: The military in Latin America—they're the ones who make me work harder. If they were removed, if there were a change, then I could rest a little and work on poems and stories that would be exclusively literary. But it's they who give me work to do.

INTERVIEWER: You have said at various times that, for you, literature is like a game. In what ways?

CORTÁZAR: For me, literature is a form of play. But I've always added that there are two forms of play: football, for example, which is basically a game, and then games that are very profound and serious. When children play, though they're amusing themselves, they take it very seriously. It's important. It's just as serious for them now as love will be ten years from now. I remember when I was little and my parents used to say, "Okay, you've played enough, come take a bath now." I found that completely idiotic, because, for me, the bath was a silly matter. It had no importance whatsoever, while playing with my friends was something serious. Literature is like that—it's a game, but it's a game one can put one's life into. One can do everything for that game.

INTERVIEWER: When did you become interested in the fantastic? Were you very young?

CORTÁZAR: It began in my childhood. Most of my young classmates had no sense of the fantastic. They took things as they were...this is a plant, that is an armchair. But for me, things were not that well defined. My mother, who's still alive and is a very imaginative woman, encouraged me. Instead of saying, "No, no, you should be serious," she was pleased that I was imaginative;

when I turned towards the world of the fantastic, she helped by giving me books to read. I read Edgar Allan Poe for the first time when I was only nine. I stole the book to read because my mother didn't want me to read it; she thought I was too young and she was right. The book scared me and I was ill for three months, because I believed in it... *dur comme fer* as the French say. For me, the fantastic was perfectly natural; I had no doubts at all. That's the way things were. When I gave those kinds of books to my friends, they'd say, "But no, we prefer to read cowboy stories." Cowboys were especially popular at the time. I didn't understand that. I preferred the world of the supernatural, of the fantastic.

INTERVIEWER: When you translated Poe's complete works many years later, did you discover new things for yourself from so close a reading?

CORTÁZAR: Many, many things. I explored his language, which is criticized by both the English and the Americans because they find it too baroque. Since I'm neither English nor American, I see it with another perspective. I know there are aspects which have aged a lot, that are exaggerated, but that doesn't mean anything compared to his genius. To write, in those times, "The Fall of the House of Usher," or "Ligeia," or "Berenice," or "The Black Cat," any of them, shows a true genius for the fantastic and for the supernatural. Yesterday, I visited a friend on the rue Edgar Allan Poe. There is a plaque on the street which reads, "Edgar Poe, English Writer." He wasn't English at all! We should have it changed—we'll both protest!

INTERVIEWER: In your writing, in addition to the fantastic, there is a real warmth and affection for your characters.

CORTÁZAR: When my characters are children and adolescents, I have a lot of tenderness for them. I think they are very alive in my novels and in my stories; I treat them with a lot of love. When I write a story where the character is an adolescent, I *am* the adolescent while I am writing it. With the adult characters, it's something else.

INTERVIEWER: Are many of your characters based on people that you've known?

CORTÁZAR: I wouldn't say many, but there are a few. Very often there are characters who are a mixture of two or three people. I have put together a female character, for example, from two women I have known. That gives the character in the story or the book a personality that's more complex, more difficult.

INTERVIEWER: Do you mean that when you feel the need to *thicken* a character, you combine two together?

CORTÁZAR: Things don't work like that. It's the characters who direct me. That is, I see a character, he's there, and I recognize someone I knew, or occasionally two who are a bit mixed together, but then that stops. Afterwards, the character acts on his own account. He says things … I never know *what* any of them are going to say when I'm writing dialogue. Really, it's up to them. Me, I'm just typing out what they're saying. Sometimes I burst out laughing, or I throw out a page and say, "There, there you've said silly things. Out!" And I put in another page and start over again with their dialogue.

INTERVIEWER: So it's not the characters you've known that impel you to write?

CORTÁZAR: No, not at all. Often, I have an idea for a story, but there aren't any characters yet. I'll have a strange idea: something's going to happen in a house in the country, I see … I'm very visual when I write, I see it all, I see everything. So, I see this house in the country and then, abruptly, I begin to situate the characters. At that point, one of the characters *might* be someone I knew. But it's not for sure. In the end, most of my characters are invented. Now, of course, there's myself. In *Hopscotch,* there are many autobiographical references in the character of Oliveira. It's not me, but there's a lot that derives from my early Bohemian days in Paris. Yet readers who read Oliveira *as* Cortázar in Paris would be mistaken. No, no, I was very different.

INTERVIEWER: Is this because you don't wish your writing to be autobiographical?

CORTÁZAR: I don't like autobiography. I will never write my memoirs. Autobiographies of others interest me, of course, but not my own. If I wrote my autobiography, I would have to be truthful and honest. I couldn't tell an imaginary autobiography. And so, I would be doing a historian's job, being a self-historian, and that bores me. Because I prefer to invent, to imagine. Of course, very often when I have ideas for a novel or a story, situations and moments of my life naturally place themselves in that context. In my story "Deshoras," the idea of the boy being in love with his pal's older sister is, in fact, based on an autobiographical situation. So there is a small part of it that's autobiographical, but from there on, it's the fantastic or the imaginary which dominates.

INTERVIEWER: How do you start with your stories? By any particular entry, an image?

CORTÁZAR: With me stories and novels can start anywhere. As for the writing itself, when I begin to write, the story has been turning around in me a long time, sometimes for weeks. But not in any way that's clear; it's a sort of general idea of the story. Perhaps that house where there's a red plant in one corner, and I know there's an old man who walks around in this house. That's all I know. It happens like that. And then there are the dreams. During this gestation period my dreams are full of references and allusions to what is going to be in the story. Sometimes the whole story is in a dream. One of my first and most popular stories, "House Taken Over," is a nightmare I had. I got up immediately and wrote it. But in general, what comes out of the dreams are fragments of references. That is, my subconscious is in the process of working through a story—when I am dreaming, it's being written inside there. So when I say that I begin anywhere, it's because I don't know what, at that point, is to be the beginning or the end. When I start to write, that's the beginning. I haven't decided that the story has to start like that; it simply starts there and it continues, and very often I have no clear idea about the ending—I don't know what's going to happen. It's only gradually, as the story goes on, that things become clearer and abruptly I see the ending.

INTERVIEWER: So you are discovering the story *while* you are writing it?

CORTÁZAR: That's right. It's like improvising in jazz. You don't ask a jazz musician, "But what are you going to play?" He'll laugh at you. He has a theme, a series of chords he has to respect, and then he takes up his trumpet or his saxophone and he begins. It's not a question of *idea*. He performs through a series of different internal pulsations. Sometimes it comes out well, sometimes it doesn't. It's the same with me. I'm a bit embarrassed to sign my stories sometimes. The novels, no, because the novels I work on a lot; there's a whole architecture. But my stories, it's as if they were dictated to me by something that is in me, but it's not me who's responsible. Well, since it does appear they are mine even so, I guess I should accept them!

INTERVIEWER: Are there certain aspects of writing a story that always pose a problem for you?

CORTÁZAR: In general, no, because as I was explaining, the story is already made somewhere inside me. So, it has its dimension, its structure; if it's going to be a very short story or a fairly long story, all that is as if decided in advance. But in recent years I've started to sense some problems. I reflect more in front of the page. I write more slowly. And I write in a way that's more spare. Certain critics have reproached me for that, they've told me that little by little I'm losing that suppleness in my stories. I seem to be saying what I want to with a greater economy of means. I don't know if it's for better or for worse—in any case, it's my way of writing now.

INTERVIEWER: You were saying that with the novels there is a whole architecture. Does that mean that you work very differently?

CORTÁZAR: The first thing I wrote in *Hopscotch* was a chapter that is now in the middle. It's the chapter where the characters put out a plank to cross from one window of an apartment house to another. I wrote that without knowing why I was writing it. I saw the characters, I saw the situation—it was in Buenos Aires. It was very hot, I remember, and I was next to the window with my typewriter. I saw this situation of a guy who's trying to make his wife go across the plank—because he won't go himself—to get some silly thing, some nails. I wrote all that, which was long, some forty pages, and when I'd finished I said to myself, "All right, but what have I done? Because that's not a story. What is it?" Then I understood that I was launched on a novel, but that I couldn't continue from that point. I had to stop there and go back and write the whole section in Paris which comes before, which is the whole background of Oliveira, and when I finally arrived at this chapter about walking the plank, then I went on from there.

INTERVIEWER: Do you revise much when you write?

CORTÁZAR: Very little. That comes from the fact that the thing has already been at work inside me. When I see the rough drafts of certain of my writer friends, where everything is revised, everything's changed, moved around, and there are arrows all over the place...no no no. My manuscripts are very clean.

INTERVIEWER: José Lezama Lima in *Paradiso* has Cemí saying that "the baroque...is what has real interest in Spain and Hispanic America." Why do you think that is so?

CORTÁZAR: I cannot reply as an expert. True, the baroque is greatly important in Latin America, both in the arts and in the literature as well. The baroque can offer a great richness; it lets the imagination soar in all its many spiraling directions, as in a baroque church with its decorative angels and all that, or in baroque music. But I distrust the baroque. The baroque writers, very often, let themselves go too easily in their writing. They write in five pages what one could very well write in one. I too must have fallen into the baroque because I am Latin American, but I have always had a mistrust of it. I don't like turgid, voluminous sentences, full of adjectives and descriptions, purring and purring into the reader's ear. I know it's very charming, of course. It's very beautiful but it's not me. I'm more on the side of Jorge Luis Borges. He has always been an enemy of the baroque; he tightened his writing, as if with pliers. Well, I write in a very different way than Borges, but the great lesson he taught me is one of economy. He taught me when I began to read him, being very young, that one had to try to say what one wanted to with economy, but with a beautiful economy. It's the difference, perhaps, between a plant, which would be considered baroque, with its multiplication of leaves, often very beautiful, and a precious stone, a crystal—*that* for me is more beautiful still.

INTERVIEWER: What are your writing habits? Have certain things changed?

CORTÁZAR: The one thing that hasn't changed, and never will, is the total anarchy and the disorder. I have absolutely no method. When I feel like writing a story I let everything drop; I write the story. And sometimes when I write a story, in the month or two that follows I will write two or three more. In general, the stories come in series. Writing one leaves me in a receptive state, and then I "catch" another. You see the sort of image I use, but it's like that; the story drops inside of me. But then a year can go by where I write nothing…nothing. Of course, these last few years I have spent a good deal of my time at the typewriter writing political articles. The texts I've written about Nicaragua, everything I've written about Argentina, have nothing to do with literature—they're militant things.

INTERVIEWER: You've often said that it was the Cuban revolution that awakened you to questions of Latin America and its problems.

CORTÁZAR: And I say it again.

INTERVIEWER: Do you have preferred places for writing?

CORTÁZAR: In fact, no. In the beginning, when I was younger and physically more resistant, here in Paris for example, I wrote a large part of *Hopscotch* in cafés. Because the noise didn't bother me and, on the contrary, it was a very congenial place. I worked a lot there—I read or I wrote. But with age I've become more complicated. I write when I'm sure of having some silence. I can't write if there's music, that's absolutely out. Music is one thing and writing is another. I need a certain calm; but, having said this, a hotel, an airplane sometimes, a friend's house, or here at home are places where I can write.

INTERVIEWER: What about Paris? What gave you the courage to pick up and move off to Paris when you did, more than thirty years ago?

CORTÁZAR: Courage? No, it didn't take much courage. I simply had to accept the idea that coming to Paris, and cutting the bridges with Argentina at that time, meant being very poor and having problems making a living. But that didn't worry me. I knew in one way or another I was going to manage. I came to Paris primarily because Paris, French culture on the whole, held a strong attraction for me. I had read French literature with a passion in Argentina, so I wanted to be here and get to know the streets and the places one finds in the books, in the novels. To go through the streets of Balzac or of Baudelaire... it was a very romantic voyage. I was, I *am*, very romantic. In fact, I have to be rather careful when I write, because very often I could let myself fall into...I wouldn't say bad taste, perhaps not, but a bit in the direction of an exaggerated romanticism. In my private life, I don't need to control myself. I really am very sentimental, very romantic. I'm a tender person; I have a lot of tenderness to give. What I give now to Nicaragua, it's tenderness. It is also the political conviction that the Sandinistas are right in what they're doing and that they're leading an admirable struggle; but it's not only the political impetus, it's that there's an enormous tenderness because it's a people I love, as I love the Cubans, and I love the Argentines. Well, all that makes up part of my character. In my writing I have had to watch myself, above all when I was young. I wrote things then that were tearjerkers. That was really romanticism, the *roman rose*. My mother would read them and cry.

INTERVIEWER: Nearly all your writing that people know dates from your arrival in Paris. But you were writing a lot before, weren't you? A few things had already been published.

CORTÁZAR: I've been writing since the age of nine, right up through my whole adolescence and early youth. In my early youth I was already capable of writing stories and novels, which showed me that I was on the right path. But I wasn't eager to publish. I was very severe with myself, and I continue to be. I remember that my peers, when they had written some poems or a small novel, searched for a publisher right away. I would tell myself, "No, you're not publishing, you hang onto that." I kept certain things, and others I threw out. When I did publish for the first time I was over thirty years old; it was just before my departure for France. That was my first book of stories, *Bestiario*, which came out in '51, the same month that I took the boat to come here. Before that, I had published a little text called *Los Reyes*, which is a dialogue. A friend who had a lot of money, who did small editions for himself and his friends, had done a private edition. And that's all. No, there's another thing—a sin of youth—a book of sonnets. I published it myself, but with a pseudonym.

INTERVIEWER: You are the lyricist of a recent album of tangos, *Trottoirs de Buenos Aires*. What got you started writing tangos?

CORTÁZAR: Well, I am a good Argentine and above all a *porteño*—that is, a resident of Buenos Aires, because it's the port. The tango was our music, and I grew up in an atmosphere of tangos. We listened to them on the radio, because the radio started when I was little, and right away it was tango after tango. There were people in my family, my mother and an aunt, who played tangos on the piano and sang them. Through the radio, we began to listen to Carlos Gardel and the great singers of the time. The tango became like a part of my consciousness and it's the music that sends me back to my youth again and to Buenos Aires. So, I'm quite caught up in the tango, all the while being very critical, because I'm not one of those Argentines who believes that the tango is the wonder of wonders. I think that the tango on the whole, especially next to jazz, is a very poor music. It is poor but it is beautiful. It's like those plants that are very simple, that one can't compare to an orchid or a rosebush, but which have an extraordinary beauty in themselves. In recent years, friends of mine have played tangos here; the Cuarteto Cedrón are great friends, and a fine *bandoneón* player named Juan José Mosalini—so we've listened to tangos, talked about tangos. Then one day a poem came to me like that, which I thought perhaps could be set to music, I didn't really know. And then, looking among unpublished poems (most of my poems are unpublished), I found some short poems which those fellows could set to music, and they did. Also, we've done the opposite as well. Cedrón gave me a musical theme to which I wrote the words. So I've done it both ways.

INTERVIEWER: In the biographical notes in your books, it says you are also an amateur trumpet player. Have you ever played with any groups?

CORTÁZAR: No. That's a bit of a legend that was invented by my very dear friend Paul Blackburn, who died quite young unfortunately. He knew that I played the trumpet a little, mainly for myself at home. So he would always tell me, "But you should meet some musicians to play with." I'd say, "No, as the Americans say, 'I haven't got what it takes.'" I didn't have the talent; I was just playing for myself. I would put on a Jelly Roll Morton record, or Armstrong, or early Ellington—where the melody is easier to follow, especially the blues, which has a given scheme. And I would have fun hearing them play and adding my trumpet. I played along with them...but it certainly wasn't *with* them! I never dared approach jazz musicians; now my trumpet is lost somewhere in the other room there. Blackburn put that in one of the blurbs. And because there is a photo of me playing the trumpet, people thought I really could play well. As I never wanted to publish before being sure, it was the same with the trumpet—I never wanted to play before being sure. And that day has never arrived.

INTERVIEWER: Have you worked on any novels since *A Manual for Manuel*?

CORTÁZAR: Alas no, for reasons that are very clear. It's due to political work. For me, a novel requires a concentration and a quantity of time, at least a year, to work tranquilly and not to abandon it. And now, I cannot. A week ago I didn't know I would be leaving for Nicaragua in three days. When I return I won't know what's going to happen next. But this novel is already written. It's there, it's in my dreams. I dream all the time of this novel. I don't know what happens in the novel, but I have an idea. As in the stories, I know it will be something fairly long, with some elements of the fantastic, but not too many. It will be in the genre of *A Manual for Manuel*, where the fantastic elements are mixed in; but it won't be a political book. It will be a book of pure literature. I hope that life will give me a sort of desert island, even if the desert island is this room...and a year, I ask for a year. But when these bastards—the Hondurans, the Somocistas and Reagan—are in the act of destroying Nicaragua, I don't have my island. I couldn't begin to write, because I would be obsessed constantly by that problem. It demands top priority.

INTERVIEWER: And it can be difficult enough as it is balancing life and literature.

CORTÁZAR: Yes and no. It depends on the kind of priorities. If the priorities are, like those I just mentioned, touching on the moral responsibility of an individual, I would agree. But I know many people who are always complaining, "Oh, I'd like to write my novel, but I have to sell the house, and then there are the taxes, what am I going to do?" Reasons like, "I work in the office all day, how do you expect me to write?" Me, I worked all day at UNESCO and then I came home and wrote *Hopscotch*. When one wants to write, one writes. If one is condemned to write, one writes.

INTERVIEWER: Do you work anymore as a translator or interpreter?

CORTÁZAR: No, that's over. I lead a very simple life. I don't need much money to buy the things I like: records, books, tobacco. So now I can live from my royalties. They've translated me into so many languages that I receive enough money to live on. I have to be a little careful; I can't go out and buy myself a yacht, but since I have absolutely no intention of buying a yacht...

INTERVIEWER: Have fame and success been pleasurable?

CORTÁZAR: Ah, listen, I'll say something I shouldn't say because no one will believe it, but success isn't a pleasure for me. I'm glad to be able to live from what I write, so I have to put up with the popular and critical side of success. But I was happier as a man when I was unknown. Much happier. Now I can't go to Latin America or to Spain without being recognized every ten yards, and the autographs, the embraces.... It's very moving, because they're readers who are frequently quite young. I'm happy that they like what I do, but it's terribly distressing for me on the level of privacy. I can't go to a beach in Europe; in five minutes there's a photographer. I have a physical appearance that I can't disguise; if I were small I could shave and put on sunglasses, but with my height, my long arms and all that, they discover me from afar. On the other hand, there are very beautiful things: I was in Barcelona a month ago, walking around the Gothic Quarter one evening; and there was an American girl, very pretty, playing the guitar very well and singing. She was seated on the ground singing to earn her living. She sang a bit like Joan Baez, a very pure, clear voice. There was a group of young people from Barcelona listening. I stopped to listen to her, but I stayed in the shadows. At one point, one of these young men who was about twenty, very young, very handsome, approached me. He had a cake in his hand. He said, "Julio, take a piece." So I took a piece and I ate it, and I told him, "Thanks a lot for coming up and giving that to me." He said to me, "But, listen, I give you so little next to what you've given me." I said, "Don't say that, don't say that," and we embraced and he went away. Well, things like that, that's the best recompense for my work as a writer. That a boy or a girl comes up to speak to you and to offer you a piece of cake, it's wonderful. It's worth the trouble of having written.

—*Jason Weiss*

# GABRIEL GARCÍA MÁRQUEZ

© Wilson Daza

Gabriel García Márquez was born on March 6, 1928, in the small Colombian town of Aracataca. Surrounded by banana plantations, its neighboring village is called Macondo, which he would later transform into the setting for *One Hundred Years of Solitude*. García Márquez spent much of his childhood with his grandparents, whom he recalls with special fondness as magical storytellers and the early inspiration for many of his novels and short stories. Although he believes his initial literary influences were poetical and mythical, his first published writings were journalistic, appearing in the Colombian newspaper *El Espectador*, where he was a reporter and a

callejero que por cinco centavos recitaba los versos del olvidado poeta Rubén Darío y había vuelto feliz con una morrocota legítima con que le habían premiado un recital que hizo sólo para él, aunque no lo había visto por supuesto, no porque fuera ciego sino porque ningún mortal lo había visto desde los tiempos del vómito negro, pero sabíamos que él estaba ahí, puesto que el mundo seguía, la vida seguía, el correo llegaba, la banda municipal tocaba la retreta de valses bobos bajo las palmeras polvorientas y los faroles pálidos de la Plaza de Armas, y otros músicos viejos reemplazaban en la banda a los músicos muertos. En los últimos años, cuando no se volvieron a oír ruidos humanos ni cantos de pájaros en el interior y se cerraron para siempre los portones blindados, sabíamos que había alguien en la casa presidencial porque de noche se veían luces que parecían de navegación a través de las ventanas del lado del mar, y quienes se atrevieron a acercarse oyeron desastres de pezuñas y suspiros de animal grande detrás de las paredes fortificadas, y una tarde de enero habíamos visto una vaca contemplando el crepúsculo desde el balcón presidencial, imagínese, una vaca en el balcón de la patria, qué cosa más inicua, qué país de mierda, pero se hicieron tantas conjeturas de cómo era posible que una vaca llegara hasta un balcón si todo el mundo sabía que las vacas no se trepaban por las escaleras, y menos si eran de piedra, y mucho menos si estaban alfombradas, que al final no supimos si en realidad la vimos o si era que pasamos una tarde por la Plaza de Armas y habíamos soñado caminando que habíamos visto una vaca en el balcón presidencial, y desde entonces nada se volvió a ver ni nada se volvió a oír en muchos años, sólo la bandada densa de gallinazos que vinieron de donde estaban siempre adormilados en la cornisa del hospital de pobres, vinieron más de tierra adentro, vinieron en oleadas sucesivas desde el horizonte del mar de polvo donde estuvo el mar, volaron todo un día en círculos lentos sobre la casa del poder hasta que un rey con plumas de novia y golilla encarnada impartió una orden silenciosa y empezó aquel estropicio de vidrios, aquel viento de muerto grande, aquel entrar y salir de gallinazos por las ventanas como sólo era concebible en una casa sin autoridad, de modo que subimos hasta la colina y encontramos en el interior desierto los escombros de la grandeza, el cuerpo picoteado, las manos lisas de doncella con el anillo del poder en el hueso anular, y tenía todo el cuerpo retoñado de líquenes minúsculos y animales parasitarios de fondo de mar, sobre todo en las axilas y en las ingles, y tenía el braguero de lona en el testículo herniado que era lo único que habían eludido los gallinazos a pesar de ser tan grande como un riñón de buey, pero ni siquiera entonces nos atrevimos a creer en su muerte porque era la segunda vez que lo encontraban en aquella oficina, solo y vestido, y muerto al parecer de muerte natural durante el sueño, como estaba anunciado desde hacía muchos años en las aguas premonitorias de los lebrillos de las pitonisas. La primera vez que lo encontraron, en el principio de su otoño, la nación estaba todavía bastante viva como para que él se sintiera amenazado

*A corrected galley from* The Autumn of the Patriarch.

film critic; for a few years in the mid-1950s he worked as a foreign correspondent based in Rome and Paris.

García Márquez's first short stories were written at night after the other journalists had left the office, but it took a few years and the prodding of a few close friends before they were published. Today his fiction has been translated into more than twenty languages and includes *La hojarasca* [Leaf Storm] (1955), *El coronel no tiene quien le escriba* [No One Writes to the Colonel] (1961), and *La mala hora* [In Evil Hour] (1962). It wasn't until 1967, however, when *Cien años de soledad* [One Hundred Years of Solitude], a book he had been struggling to write for many years, was published, that he achieved international recognition. Immediately hailed as a masterpiece, the novel won the best foreign book prize in 1969 from the Académie Française. In 1975, *El otoño del patriarca* [The Autumn of the Patriarch]—a continuation of his fictional investigation of solitude and its relationship to power—was greeted with equivalently high praise.

In 1982 García Márquez was awarded the Nobel Prize.

Later books include *El amor en los tiempos del cólera* [Love in the Time of Cholera] (1985) and *El general en su laberinto* [The General in His Labyrinth] (1989), a fictional account of Venezuelan revolutionary Simón Bolívar's last days.

García Márquez recently made a series of well-received films for Spanish television and, in 1995, started the Foundation for a New Ibero-American Journalism.

———

*Gabriel García Márquez was interviewed in his studio/office located just behind his house in San Angel Inn, an old and lovely section of Mexico City, full of spectacularly colorful flowers. The studio is a short walk from the main house. A low elongated building, it appears to have been designed originally as a guest house. Within, at one end, are a couch, two easy chairs, and a makeshift bar—a small white refrigerator with a supply of* agua mineral *on top.*

*The most striking feature of the room is a large blown-up photograph above the sofa of García Márquez alone, wearing a stylish cape and standing on some windswept vista, looking somewhat like Anthony Quinn.*

*García Márquez was sitting at his desk at the far end of the studio. He came to greet me, walking briskly with a light step. He is a solidly built man, only about five feet eight or nine in height, who looks like a good middleweight fighter—broad-chested, but perhaps a bit thin in the legs. He was dressed casually, in corduroy slacks with a light turtleneck sweater and black leather boots. His hair is dark and curly brown and he wears a full mustache.*

*The interview took place over the course of three late afternoon meetings of roughly two hours each. Although his English is quite good, García Márquez spoke mostly in Spanish and his two teenage sons, who have attended British schools in Mexico and Spain for many years, shared the translating. When García Márquez speaks, his body often rocks back and forth. His hands too are often in motion making small but decisive gestures to emphasize a point, or to indicate a shift of direction in his thinking. He alternates between leaning forward toward his listener, and sitting far back with his legs crossed when speaking reflectively.*

INTERVIEWER: How do you feel about using the tape recorder?

GABRIEL GARCÍA MÁRQUEZ: The problem is that the moment you know the interview is being taped, your attitude changes. In my case I immediately take a defensive attitude. As a journalist, I feel that we still haven't learned how to use a tape recorder to do an interview. The best way, I feel, is to have a long conversation without the journalist taking any notes. Then afterward he should reminisce about the conversation and write it down as an impression of what he felt, not necessarily using the exact words expressed. Another useful method is to take notes and then interpret them with a certain loyalty to the person interviewed. What ticks you off about the tape recording everything is that it is not loyal to the person who is being interviewed, because it even records and remembers when you make an ass of yourself. That's why when there is a tape recorder, I am conscious that I'm being interviewed; when there isn't a tape recorder, I talk in an unconscious and completely natural way.

INTERVIEWER: Well, you make me feel a little guilty using it, but I think for this kind of an interview we probably need it.

GARCÍA MÁRQUEZ: Anyway, the whole purpose of what I just said was to put you on the defensive.

INTERVIEWER: So you have never used a tape recorder yourself for an interview?

GARCÍA MÁRQUEZ: As a journalist, I never use it. I have a very good tape recorder, but I just use it to listen to music. But then as a journalist I've never done an interview. I've done reports, but never an interview with questions and answers.

INTERVIEWER: I heard about one famous interview with a sailor who had been shipwrecked.

GARCÍA MÁRQUEZ: It wasn't questions and answers. The sailor would just tell me his adventures and I would rewrite them trying to use his own words and in the first person, as if he were the one who was writing. When the work was published as a serial in a newspaper, one part each day for two weeks, it was signed by the sailor, not by me. It wasn't until twenty years later that it was published and people found out I had written it. No editor realized that it was good until after I had written *One Hundred Years of Solitude*.

INTERVIEWER: Since we've started talking about journalism, how does it feel being a journalist again, after having written novels for so long? Do you do it with a different feel or a different eye?

GARCÍA MÁRQUEZ: I've always been convinced that my true profession is that of a journalist. What I didn't like about journalism before were the working conditions. Besides, I had to condition my thoughts and ideas to the interests of the newspaper. Now, after having worked as a novelist, and having achieved financial independence as a novelist, I can really choose the themes that interest me and correspond to my ideas. In any case, I always very much enjoy the chance of doing a great piece of journalism.

INTERVIEWER: What is a great piece of journalism for you?

GARCÍA MÁRQUEZ: *Hiroshima* by John Hersey was an exceptional piece.

INTERVIEWER: Is there a story today that you would especially like to do?

GARCÍA MÁRQUEZ: There are many, and several I have in fact written. I have written about Portugal, Cuba, Angola and Vietnam. I would very much like to write on Poland. I think if I could describe exactly what is now going on, it would be a very important story. But it's too cold now in Poland; I'm a journalist who likes his comforts.

INTERVIEWER: Do you think the novel can do certain things that journalism can't?

GARCÍA MÁRQUEZ: Nothing. I don't think there is any difference. The sources are the same, the material is the same, the resources and the language are the same. *The Journal of the Plague Year* by Daniel Defoe is a great novel and *Hiroshima* is a great work of journalism.

INTERVIEWER: Do the journalist and the novelist have different responsibilities in balancing truth versus the imagination?

GARCÍA MÁRQUEZ: In journalism just one fact that is false prejudices the entire work. In contrast, in fiction one single fact that is true gives legitimacy to the entire work. That's the only difference and it lies in the commitment of the writer. A novelist can do anything he wants so long as he makes people believe in it.

INTERVIEWER: In interviews a few years ago, you seemed to look back on being a journalist with awe at how much faster you were then.

GARCÍA MÁRQUEZ: I do find it harder to write now than before, both novels and journalism. When I worked for newspapers, I wasn't very conscious of every word I wrote, whereas now I am. When I was working for *El Espectador* in Bogotá, I used to do at least three stories a week, two or three editorial notes every day, and I did movie reviews. Then at night, after everyone had gone home, I would stay behind writing my novels. I liked the noise of the Linotype machines, which sounded like rain. If they stopped, and I was left in silence, I wouldn't be able to work. Now, the output is comparatively small. On a good working day, working from nine o'clock in the morning to two or three in the afternoon, the most I can write is a short paragraph of four or five lines, which I usually tear up the next day.

INTERVIEWER: Does this change come from your works being so highly praised or from some kind of political commitment?

GARCÍA MÁRQUEZ: It's from both. I think that the idea that I'm writing for many more people than I ever imagined has created a certain general responsibility that is literary and political. There's even pride involved, in not wanting to fall short of what I did before.

INTERVIEWER: How did you start writing?

GARCÍA MÁRQUEZ: By drawing. By drawing cartoons. Before I could read or write I used to draw comics at school and at home. The funny thing is that I now realize that when I was in high school I had the reputation of being a writer though I never in fact wrote anything. If there was a pamphlet to be written or a letter of petition, I was the one to do it because I was supposedly the writer. When I entered college I happened to have a very good literary background in general, considerably above the average of my friends. At the university in Bogotá, I started making new friends and acquaintances, who introduced me to contemporary writers. One night a friend lent me a book of short stories by Franz Kafka. I went back to the pension where I was staying and began to read *The Metamorphosis*. The first line almost knocked me off the bed. I was so surprised. The first line reads, "As Gregor Samsa awoke that morning from uneasy dreams, he found himself transformed in his bed into a gigantic insect...." When I read the line I thought to myself that I didn't know anyone was allowed to write things like that. If I had known, I would have started writing a long time ago. So I immediately started writing short stories. They are totally intellectual short stories because I was writing them on the basis of my literary experience and had not yet found the link between literature and life. The stories were published in the literary supplement of the newspaper *El Espectador* in Bogotá and they did have a certain success at the time—probably because nobody in Colombia was writing intellectual short stories. What was being written then was mostly about life in the countryside and social life. When I wrote my first short stories I was told they had Joycean influences.

INTERVIEWER: Had you read Joyce at that time?

GARCÍA MÁRQUEZ: I had never read Joyce, so I started reading *Ulysses*. I read it in the only Spanish edition available. Since then, after having read *Ulysses* in English as well as a very good French translation, I can see that the original Spanish translation was very bad. But I did learn something that was to be very useful to me in my future writing—the technique of the interior monologue. I later found this in Virginia Woolf and I like the way she uses it better than Joyce. Although I later realized that the person who invented this interior monologue was the anonymous writer of the *Lazarillo de Tormes*.

INTERVIEWER: Can you name some of your early influences?

GARCÍA MÁRQUEZ: The people who really helped me to get rid of my intellectual attitude towards the short story were the writers of the American Lost Generation. I realized that their literature had a relationship with life that my short stories didn't. And then an event took place which was very important with respect to this attitude. It was the Bogotazo, on the ninth of April, 1948, when a political leader, Gaitán, was shot and the people of Bogotá went raving mad in the streets. I was in my pension ready to have lunch when I heard the news. I ran towards the place, but Gaitán had just been put into a taxi and was being taken to a hospital. On my way back to the pension, the people had already taken to the streets and they were demonstrating, looting stores and burning buildings. I joined them. That afternoon and evening, I became aware of the kind of country I was living in, and how little my short stories had to do with any of that. When I was later forced to go back to Barranquilla on the Caribbean, where I had spent my childhood, I realized that that was the type of life I had lived, knew, and wanted to write about.

Around 1950 or '51 another event happened that influenced my literary tendencies. My mother asked me to accompany her to Aracataca, where I was born, and to sell the house where I spent my first years. When I got there it was at first quite shocking because I was now twenty-two and hadn't been there since the age of eight. Nothing had really changed, but I felt that I wasn't really looking at the village, but I was *experiencing* it as if I were reading it. It was as if everything I saw had already been written, and all I had to do was to sit down and copy what was already there and what I was just reading. For all practical purposes everything had evolved into literature: the houses, the people, and the memories. I'm not sure whether I had already read Faulkner or not, but I know now that only a technique like Faulkner's could have enabled me to write down what I was seeing. The atmosphere, the decadence, the heat in the village were roughly the same as what I had felt in Faulkner. It was a banana plantation region inhabited by a lot of Americans from the fruit companies which gave it the same sort of atmosphere I had found in the writers of the Deep South. Critics have spoken of the literary influence of Faulkner but I see it as a coincidence: I had simply found material that had to be dealt with in the same way that Faulkner had treated similar material.

From that trip to the village I came back to write *Leaf Storm,* my first novel. What really happened to me in that trip to Aracataca was that I realized that everything that had occurred in my childhood had a literary value that I was only now appreciating. From the moment I wrote *Leaf Storm* I realized I wanted to be a writer and that nobody could stop me and that the only thing left for me to do was to try to be the best writer in the world. That was in 1953, but it wasn't until 1967 that I got my first royalties after having written five of my eight books.

INTERVIEWER: Do you think that it's common for young writers to deny the worth of their own childhoods and experiences and to intellectualize as you did initially?

GARCÍA MÁRQUEZ: No, the process usually takes place the other way around, but if I had to give a young writer some advice I would say to write about something that has happened to him; it's always easy to tell whether a writer is writing about something that has happened to him or something he has read or been told. Pablo Neruda has a line in a poem that says "God help me from inventing when I sing." It always amuses me that the biggest praise for my work comes for the imagination while the truth is that there's not a single line in all my work that does not have a basis in reality. The problem is that Caribbean reality resembles the wildest imagination.

INTERVIEWER: Whom were you writing for at this point? Who was your audience?

GARCÍA MÁRQUEZ: *Leaf Storm* was written for my friends who were helping me and lending me their books and were very enthusiastic about my work. In general I think you usually do write for some-one. When I'm writing I'm always aware that this friend is going to like this, or that another friend is going to like that paragraph or chapter, always thinking of specific people. In the end all books are written for your friends. The problem after writing *One Hundred Years of Solitude* was that now I no longer know whom of the millions of readers I am writing for; this upsets and inhibits me. It's like a million eyes are looking at you and you don't really know what they think.

INTERVIEWER: What about the influence of journalism on your fiction?

GARCÍA MÁRQUEZ: I think the influence is reciprocal. Fiction has helped my journalism because it has given it literary value. Journalism has helped my fiction because it has kept me in a close relationship with reality.

INTERVIEWER: How would you describe the search for a style that you went through after *Leaf Storm* and before you were able to write *One Hundred Years of Solitude*?

GARCÍA MÁRQUEZ: After having written *Leaf Storm,* I decided that writing about the village and my childhood was really an escape from having to face and write about the political reality of the country. I had the false impression that I was hiding myself behind this kind of nostalgia instead of confronting the political things that were going on. This was the time when the relationship between literature and politics was very much discussed. I kept trying to close the gap between the two. My influence had been Faulkner; now it was Hemingway. I wrote *No One Writes to the Colonel, In Evil Hour,* and *The Funeral of the Great Matriarch,* which were all written at more or less the same time and have many things in common. These stories take place in a different village from the one in which *Leaf Storm* and *One Hundred Years of Solitude* occur. It is a village in which there is no magic. It is a journalistic literature. But when I finished *In Evil Hour,* I saw that all my views were wrong again. I came to see that in fact my writings about my childhood were *more* political and had more to do with the reality of my country than I had thought. After *In Evil Hour* I did not write anything for five years. I had an idea of what I always wanted to do, but there was something missing and I was not sure what it was until one day I discovered the right tone—the tone that I eventually used in *One Hundred Years of Solitude*. It was based on the way my grandmother used to tell her stories. She told things that sounded supernatural and fantastic, but she told them with complete naturalness. When I finally discovered the tone I had to use, I sat down for eighteen months and worked every day.

INTERVIEWER: How did she express the "fantastic" so naturally?

GARCÍA MÁRQUEZ: What was most important was the expression she had on her face. She did not change her expression at all when telling her stories and everyone was surprised. In previous attempts to write *One Hundred Years of Solitude,* I tried to tell the story without believing in it. I discovered that what I had to do was believe in them myself and write them with the same expression with which my grandmother told them: with a brick face.

INTERVIEWER: There also seems to be a journalistic quality to that technique or tone. You describe seemingly fantastic events in such minute detail that it gives them their own reality. Is this something you have picked up from journalism?

GARCÍA MÁRQUEZ: That's a journalistic trick which you can also apply to literature. For example, if you say that there are elephants flying in the sky, people are not going to believe you. But if you say that there are four hundred and twenty-five elephants in the sky, people will probably believe you. *One Hundred Years of Solitude* is full of that sort of thing. That's exactly the technique my grandmother used. I remember particularly the story about the character who is surrounded by yellow butterflies. When I was very small there was an electrician who came to the house. I became very curious because he carried a belt with which he used to suspend himself from the electrical posts. My grandmother used to say that every time this man came around, he would leave the house full of butterflies. But when I was writing this, I discovered that if I didn't say the butterflies were yellow, people would not believe it. When I was writing the episode of Remedios the Beauty going to heaven it took me a long time to make it credible. One day I went out to the garden and saw a woman who used to come to the house to do the wash and she was putting out the sheets to dry and there was a lot of wind. She was arguing with the wind not to blow the sheets away. I discovered that if I used the sheets for Remedios the Beauty, she would ascend. That's how I did it, to make it credible. The problem for every writer is credibility. Anybody can write anything so long as it's believed.

INTERVIEWER: What was the origin of the insomnia plague in *One Hundred Years of Solitude?*

GARCÍA MÁRQUEZ: Beginning with Oedipus, I've always been interested in plagues. I have studied a lot about medieval plagues. One of my favorite books is *The Journal of the Plague Year* by Daniel Defoe, among other reasons because Defoe is a journalist who sounds like what he is saying is pure fantasy. For many years I thought Defoe had written about the London plague as he observed it. But then I discovered it was a novel, because Defoe was less than seven years old when the plague occurred in London. Plagues have always been one of my recurrent themes— and in different forms. In *In Evil Hour,* the pamphlets are plagues. For many years I thought that the political violence in Colombia had the same metaphysics as the plague. Before *One Hundred Years of Solitude,* I had used a plague to kill all the birds in a story called "The Day After Saturday." In *One Hundred Years of Solitude* I used the insomnia plague as something of a literary trick since it's the opposite of the sleeping plague. Ultimately, literature is nothing but carpentry.

INTERVIEWER: Can you explain that analogy a little more?

GARCÍA MÁRQUEZ: Both are very hard work. Writing something is almost as hard as making a table. With both you are working with reality, a material just as hard as wood. Both are full of tricks and techniques. Basically very little magic and a lot of hard work are involved. And as Proust, I think, said, it takes ten percent inspiration and ninety percent perspiration. I never have done any carpentry but it's the job I admire most, especially because you can never find anyone to do it for you.

INTERVIEWER: What about the banana fever in *One Hundred Years of Solitude*? How much of that is based on what the United Fruit Company did?

GARCÍA MÁRQUEZ: The banana fever is modeled closely on reality. Of course, I've used literary tricks on things which have not been proved historically. For example, the massacre in the square is completely true but while I wrote it on the basis of testimony and documents, it was never known exactly how many people were killed. I used the figure three thousand, which is obviously an exaggeration. But one of my childhood memories was watching a very, very long train leave the plantation supposedly full of bananas. There could have been three thousand dead on it, eventually to be dumped in the sea. What's really surprising is that now they speak very naturally in the Congress and the newspapers about the "three thousand dead." I suspect that half of all our history is made in this fashion. In *The Autumn of the Patriarch*, the dictator says it doesn't matter if it's not true now, because sometime in the future it will be true. Sooner or later people believe writers rather than the government.

INTERVIEWER: That makes the writer pretty powerful, doesn't it?

GARCÍA MÁRQUEZ: Yes, and I can feel it too. It gives me a great sense of responsibility. What I would really like to do is a piece of journalism which is completely true and real, but which sounds as fantastic as *One Hundred Years of Solitude*. The more I live and remember things from the past the more I think that literature and journalism are closely related.

INTERVIEWER: What about a country giving up its sea for its foreign debt as in *The Autumn of the Patriarch*?

GARCÍA MÁRQUEZ: Yes, but that actually happened. It's happened and will happen many times more. *The Autumn of the Patriarch* is a completely historical book. To find probabilities out of real facts is the work of the journalist and the novelist, and it is also the work of the prophet. The trouble is that many people believe that I'm a writer of fantastic fiction, when actually I'm a very realistic person and write what I believe is the true socialist realism.

INTERVIEWER: Is it utopian?

GARCÍA MÁRQUEZ: I'm not sure if the word *utopian* means the real or the ideal. But I think it's the real.

INTERVIEWER: Are the characters in *The Autumn of the Patriarch,* the dictators, for example, modeled after real people? There seem to be similarities with Franco, Perón and Trujillo.

GARCÍA MÁRQUEZ: In every novel, the character is a collage: a collage of different characters that you've known, or heard about or read about. I read everything that I could find about Latin American dictators of the last century, and the beginning of this one. I also talked to a lot of people who had lived under dictatorships. I did that for at least ten years. And when I had a clear idea of what the character was going to be like, I made an effort to forget everything I had read and heard, so that I could invent, without using any situation that had occurred in real life. I realized at one point that I myself had not lived for any period of time under a dictatorship, so I thought if I wrote the book in Spain, I could see what the atmosphere was like living in an established dictatorship. But I found that the atmosphere was very different in Spain under

Franco from that of a Caribbean dictatorship. So the book was kind of blocked for about a year. There was something missing and I wasn't sure what it was. Then overnight, I decided that the best thing was that we come back to the Caribbean. So we all moved back to Barranquilla in Colombia. I made a statement to the journalists which they thought was a joke. I said that I was coming back because I had forgotten what a guava smelled like. In truth, it was what I really needed to finish my book. I took a trip through the Caribbean. As I went from island to island, I found the elements which were the ones that had been lacking from my novel.

INTERVIEWER: You often use the theme of the solitude of power.

GARCÍA MÁRQUEZ: The more power you have, the harder it is to know who is lying to you and who is not. When you reach absolute power, there is no contact with reality, and that's the worst kind of solitude there can be. A very powerful person, a dictator, is surrounded by interests and people whose final aim is to isolate him from reality; everything is in concert to isolate him.

INTERVIEWER: What about the solitude of the writer? Is this different?

GARCÍA MÁRQUEZ: It has a lot to do with the solitude of power. The writer's very attempt to portray reality often leads him to a distorted view of it. In trying to transpose reality he can end up losing contact with it, in an ivory tower, as they say. Journalism is a very good guard against that. That's why I have always tried to keep on doing journalism because it keeps me in contact with the real world, particularly political journalism and politics. The solitude that threatened me after *One Hundred Years of Solitude* wasn't the solitude of the writer; it was the solitude of fame, which resembles the solitude of power much more. My friends defended me from that one, my friends who are always there.

INTERVIEWER: How?

GARCÍA MÁRQUEZ: Because I have managed to keep the same friends all my life. I mean I don't break or cut myself off from my old friends and they're the ones who bring me back to earth; they always keep their feet on the ground and they're not famous.

INTERVIEWER: How do things start? One of the recurring images in *The Autumn of the Patriarch* is the cows in the palace. Was this one of the original images?

GARCÍA MÁRQUEZ: I've got a photography book that I'm going to show you. I've said on various occasions that in the genesis of all my books there's always an image. The first image I had of *The Autumn of the Patriarch* was a very old man in a very luxurious palace into which cows come and eat the curtains. But that image didn't concretize until I saw the photograph. In Rome I went into a bookshop where I started looking at photography books, which I like to collect. I saw this photograph and it was just perfect. I just saw that was how it was going to be. Since I'm not a big intellectual, I can find my antecedents in everyday things, in life, and not in the great masterpieces.

INTERVIEWER: Do your novels ever take unexpected twists?

GARCÍA MÁRQUEZ: That used to happen to me in the beginning. In the first stories I wrote I had a general idea of the mood, but I would let myself be taken by chance. The best advice I was given early on was that it was all right to work that way when I was young because I had a torrent of inspiration. But I was told that if I didn't learn technique, I would be in trouble later on when the inspiration had gone and the technique was needed to compensate. If I hadn't learned that in time, I would not now be able to outline a structure in advance. Structure is a purely technical problem and if you don't learn it early on you'll never learn it.

INTERVIEWER: Discipline then is quite important to you?

GARCÍA MÁRQUEZ: I don't think you can write a book that's worth anything without extraordinary discipline.

INTERVIEWER: What about artificial stimulants?

GARCÍA MÁRQUEZ: One thing that Hemingway wrote that greatly impressed me was that writing for him was like boxing. He took care of his health and his well-being. Faulkner had a reputation of being a drunkard, but in every interview that he gave me he said that it was impossible to write one line when drunk. Hemingway said this too. Bad readers have asked me if I was drugged when I wrote some of my works. But that illustrates that they don't know anything about literature or drugs. To be a good writer you have to be absolutely lucid at every moment of writing and in good health. I'm very much against the romantic concept of writing which maintains that the act of writing is a sacrifice and that the worse the economic conditions or the emotional state, the better the writing. I think you have to be in a very good emotional and physical state. Literary creation for me requires good health, and the Lost Generation understood this. They were people who loved life.

INTERVIEWER: Blaise Cendrars said that writing is a privilege compared to most work and that writers exaggerate their suffering. What do you think?

GARCÍA MÁRQUEZ: I think that writing is very difficult, but so is any job carefully executed. What is a privilege, however, is to do a job to your own satisfaction. I think that I'm excessively demanding of myself and others because I cannot tolerate errors; I think that it is a privilege to do anything to a perfect degree. It is true though that writers are often megalomaniacs and they consider themselves to be the center of the universe and society's conscience. But what I most admire is something well done. I'm always very happy when I'm traveling to know that the pilots are better pilots than I am a writer.

INTERVIEWER: When do you work best now? Do you have a work schedule?

GARCÍA MÁRQUEZ: When I became a professional writer the biggest problem I had was my schedule. Being a journalist meant working at night. When I started writing full-time I was forty years old, my schedule was basically from nine o'clock in the morning until two in the afternoon, when my sons came back from school. Since I was so used to hard work, I felt guilty that I was only working in the morning; so I tried to work in the afternoons, but I discovered that what I did in the afternoon had to be done over again the next morning. So I decided that I would just work from nine until two-thirty and not do anything else. In the afternoons I have appointments and interviews and anything else that might come up. I have another problem in that I can only work in surroundings that are familiar and have already been warmed up with my work. I cannot write in hotels or borrowed rooms or on borrowed typewriters. This creates problems because when I travel I can't work. Of course, you're always trying to find a pretext to work less. That's why the conditions you impose on yourself are more difficult all the time. You hope for inspiration whatever the circumstances. That's a word the romantics exploited a lot. My Marxist comrades have a lot of difficulty accepting the word, but whatever you call it, I'm convinced that there is a special state of mind in which you can write with great ease and things just flow. All the pretexts—such as the one where you can only write at home—disappear. That moment and that state of mind seem to come when you have found the right theme and the right ways of treating it. And it has to be something you really like too, because there is no worse job than doing something you don't like.

One of the most difficult things is the first paragraph. I have spent many months on a first paragraph and once I get it, the rest just comes out very easily. In the first paragraph you solve most of the problems with your book. The theme is defined, the style, the tone. At least in my case, the first paragraph is a kind of sample of what the rest of the book is going to be. That's why writing a book of short stories is much more difficult than writing a novel. Every time you write a short story, you have to begin all over again.

INTERVIEWER: Are dreams ever important as a source of inspiration?

GARCÍA MÁRQUEZ: In the very beginning I paid a good deal of attention to them. But then I realized that life itself is the greatest source of inspiration and that dreams are only a very small part of that torrent that is life. What is very true about my writing is that I'm quite interested in different concepts of dreams and interpretations of them. I see dreams as part of life in general, but reality is much richer. But maybe I just have very poor dreams.

INTERVIEWER: Can you distinguish between inspiration and intuition?

GARCÍA MÁRQUEZ: Inspiration is when you find the right theme, one which you really like; that makes the work much easier. Intuition, which is also fundamental to writing fiction, is a special quality which helps you to decipher what is real without needing scientific knowledge, or any other special kind of learning. The laws of gravity can be figured out much more easily with intuition than anything else. It's a way of having experience without having to struggle through it. For a novelist intuition is essential. Basically it's contrary to intellectualism, which is probably the thing that I detest most in the world—in the sense that the real world is turned into a kind of immovable theory. Intuition has the advantage that either it is, or it isn't. You don't struggle to try to put a round peg into a square hole.

INTERVIEWER: Is it the theorists that you dislike?

GARCÍA MÁRQUEZ: Exactly. Chiefly because I cannot really understand them. That's mainly why I have to explain most things through anecdotes, because I don't have any capacity for abstractions. That's why many critics say that I'm not a cultured person. I don't quote enough.

INTERVIEWER: Do you think that critics type you or categorize you too neatly?

GARCÍA MÁRQUEZ: Critics for me are the biggest example of what intellectualism is. First of all, they have a theory of what a writer should be. They try to get the writer to fit their model and if he doesn't fit they still try to get him in by force. I'm only answering this because you've asked. I really have no interest in what critics think of me; nor have I read critics in many years. They have claimed for themselves the task of being intermediaries between the author and the reader. I've always tried to be a very clear and precise writer trying to reach the reader directly without having to go through the critic.

INTERVIEWER: How do you regard translators?

GARCÍA MÁRQUEZ: I have great admiration for translators except for the ones who use footnotes. They are always trying to explain to the reader something which the author probably did not mean; since it's there the reader has to put up with it. Translating is a very difficult job, not at all rewarding, and very badly paid. A good translation is always a re-creation in another language. That's why I have such great admiration for Gregory Rabassa. My books have been translated into twenty-one languages and Rabassa is the only translator who has never asked for something to be clarified so he can put a footnote in. I think that my work has been completely re-created in English. There are parts of the book which are very difficult to follow literally. The impression one gets is that the translator read the book and then rewrote it from his recollections. That's why I have such admiration for translators. They are intuitive rather than intellectual. Not only is what publishers pay them completely miserable, but they don't see their work as literary creation. There are some books I would have liked to translate into Spanish, but they would have involved as much work as writing my own books and I wouldn't have made enough money to eat.

INTERVIEWER: What would you have liked to translate?

GARCÍA MÁRQUEZ: All Malraux. I would have liked to translate Conrad, and Saint Exupéry. When I'm reading I sometimes get the feeling that I would like to translate this book. Excluding the great masterpieces, I prefer reading a mediocre translation of a book than trying to get through it in the original language. I never feel comfortable reading in another language, because the only language I really feel inside is Spanish. However, I speak Italian and French, and I know English well enough to have poisoned myself with *Time* magazine every week for twenty years.

INTERVIEWER: Does Mexico seem like home to you now? Do you feel part of any larger community of writers?

GARCÍA MÁRQUEZ: In general, I'm not a friend of writers or artists just because they are writers or artists. I have many friends of different professions, amongst them writers and artists. In general terms, I feel that I'm a native of any country in Latin America but not elsewhere. Latin Americans feel that Spain is the only country in which we are treated well, but I personally don't feel as though I'm from there. In Latin America I don't have a sense of frontiers or borders. I'm conscious of the differences that exist from one country to another, but in my mind and heart it is all the same. Where I really feel at home is the Caribbean, whether it is the French, Dutch, or English Caribbean. I was always impressed that when I got on a plane in Barranquilla, a black lady with a blue dress would stamp my passport, and when I got off the plane in Jamaica, a black lady with a blue dress would stamp my passport, but in English. I don't believe that the language makes all that much difference. But anywhere else in the world, I feel like a foreigner, a feeling that robs me of a sense of security. It's a personal feeling, but I always have it when I travel. I have a minority conscience.

INTERVIEWER: Do you think that it's an important thing for Latin American writers to live in Europe for a while?

GARCÍA MÁRQUEZ: Perhaps to have a real perspective from outside. The book of short stories I'm thinking of writing is about Latin Americans going to Europe. I've been thinking about it for twenty years. If you could draw a final conclusion out of these short stories it would be that Latin Americans hardly ever get to Europe, especially Mexicans, and certainly not to stay. All the Mexicans I've ever met in Europe always leave the following Wednesday.

INTERVIEWER: What effects do you think the Cuban Revolution has had on Latin American literature?

GARCÍA MÁRQUEZ: Up until now it has been negative. Many writers who think of themselves as being politically committed feel obligated to write stories not about what they want, but about what they think they should want. That makes for a certain type of calculated literature that doesn't have anything to do with experience or intuition. The main reason for this is that the cultural influence of Cuba on Latin America has been very much fought against. In Cuba itself, the process hasn't developed to the point where a new type of literature or art has been created. That is something that needs time. The great cultural importance of Cuba in Latin America has been to serve as a kind of bridge to transmit a type of literature which had existed in Latin America for many years. In a sense, the boom in Latin American literature in the United States has been caused by the Cuban Revolution. Every Latin American writer of that generation had been writing for twenty years but the European and American publishers had very little interest in them. When the Cuban Revolution started there was suddenly a great interest about Cuba and Latin America. The revolution turned into an article of consumption. Latin America came into fashion. It was discovered that Latin American novels existed which were good enough to be translated and considered with all other world literature. What was really sad is that cultural colonialism is so bad in Latin America that it was impossible to convince the Latin Americans themselves that their own novels were good until people outside *told* them they were.

INTERVIEWER: Are there some lesser-known Latin American writers you especially admire?

GARCÍA MÁRQUEZ: I doubt there are any now. One of the best side effects of the boom in Latin American writing is that publishers are always on the lookout to make sure that they're not going to miss the new Cortázar. Unfortunately many young writers are more concerned with fame than with their own work. There's a French professor at the University of Toulouse who writes about Latin American literature; many young authors wrote to him telling him not to write so much about me because I didn't need it anymore and other people did. But what they forget is that when I was their age the critics weren't writing about me, but rather about Miguel Angel Asturias. The point I'm trying to make is that these young writers are wasting their time writing to critics rather than working on their own writing. It's much more important to write than to be written about. One thing that I think was very important about my literary career was that until I was forty years old, I never got one cent of author's royalties though I'd had five books published.

INTERVIEWER: Do you think that fame or success coming too early in a writer's career is bad?

GARCÍA MÁRQUEZ: At any age it's bad. As I've said before, I would have liked for my books to have been recognized posthumously, at least in capitalist countries, where you turn into a kind of merchandise.

INTERVIEWER: Aside from your favorites, what do you read today?

GARCÍA MÁRQUEZ: I read the weirdest things. I was reading Muhammad Ali's memoirs the other day. Bram Stoker's *Dracula* is a great book and one I probably would not have read many years ago because I would have thought it was a waste of time. But I never really get involved with a book unless it's recommended by some-body I trust. I don't read any more fiction. I read many memoirs and documents, even if they are forged documents. And I reread my favorites. The advantage of rereading is that you can open at any page and read the part that you really like. I've lost this sacred notion of reading only "literature." I will read anything. I try to keep up to date. I read almost all the really important magazines from all over the world every week. I've always been on the look-out for news since the habit of reading the teletype machines. But after I've read all the serious and important newspapers from all over, my wife always comes around and tells me of news I hadn't heard. When I ask her where she read it, she will say that she read it in a magazine at the beauty parlor. So I read fashion magazines and all kinds of magazines for women and gossip magazines. And I learn many things that I could only learn from reading them. That keeps me very busy.

INTERVIEWER: Why do you think fame is so destructive for a writer?

GARCÍA MÁRQUEZ: Primarily because it invades your private life. It takes away from the time that you spend with friends, and the time that you can work. It tends to isolate you from the real world. A famous writer who wants to continue writing has to be constantly defending himself against fame. I don't really like to say this because it never sounds sincere, but I would really have liked for my books to have been published after my death, so I wouldn't have to go through all this business of fame and being a great writer. In my case, the only advantage in fame is that I have been able to give it a political use. Otherwise, it is quite uncomfortable. The problem is that you're famous for twenty-four hours a day and you can't say, "Okay, I won't be famous until tomorrow," or press a button and say, "I won't be famous here or now."

INTERVIEWER: Did you anticipate the extraordinary success of *One Hundred Years of Solitude*?

GARCÍA MÁRQUEZ: I knew that it would be a book that would please my friends more than my others had. But when my Spanish publisher told me he was going to print eight thousand copies I was stunned because my other books had never sold more than seven hundred. I asked him why not start slowly, but he said he was convinced that it was a good book and that all eight thousand copies would be sold between May and December. Actually they were all sold within one week in Buenos Aires.

INTERVIEWER: Why do you think *One Hundred Years of Solitude* clicked so?

GARCÍA MÁRQUEZ: I don't have the faintest idea because I'm a very bad critic of my own works. One of the most frequent explanations that I've heard is that it is a book about the private lives of the people of Latin America, a book that was written from the inside. That explanation surprises me because in my first attempt to write it the title of the book was going to be *The House*. I wanted the whole development of the novel to take place inside the house and anything external would be just in terms of its impact on the house. I later abandoned the title *The House*, but once the book goes into the town of Macondo it never goes any further. Another explanation I've heard is that every reader can make of the characters in the book what he wants and make them his own. I don't want it to become a film since the film viewer sees a face that he may not have imagined.

INTERVIEWER: Was there any interest in making it into a film?

GARCÍA MÁRQUEZ: Yes, my agent put it up for one million dollars to discourage offers and as they approximated that offer she raised it to around three million. But I have no interest in a film, and as long as I can prevent it from happening, it won't. I prefer that it remain a private relationship between the reader and the book.

INTERVIEWER: Do you think any books can be translated into films successfully?

GARCÍA MÁRQUEZ: I can't think of any one film that improved on a good novel but I can think of many good films that came from very bad novels.

INTERVIEWER: Have you ever thought of making films yourself?

GARCÍA MÁRQUEZ: There was a time when I wanted to be a film director. I studied directing in Rome. I felt that cinema was a medium which had no limitations and in which everything was possible. I came to Mexico because I wanted to work in film not as a director but as a screenplay writer. But there's a big limitation in cinema in that it's an industrial art, a whole industry. It's very difficult to express in cinema what you really want to say. I still think of it, but it now seems like a luxury which I would like to do with friends but without any hope of really expressing myself. So I've moved farther and farther away from the cinema. My relation with it is like that of a couple who can't live separated, but who can't live together either. Between having a film company or a journal, though, I'd choose a journal.

INTERVIEWER: How would you describe the book on Cuba that you're working on now?

GARCÍA MÁRQUEZ: Actually, the book is like a long newspaper article about what life in Cuban homes is like, how they have managed to survive the shortages. What has struck me during the many trips that I've made to Cuba in the last two years is that the blockade has created in Cuba a kind of "culture of necessity," a social situation in which people have to get along without certain things. The aspect that really interests me is how the blockade has contributed to changing the mentality of the people. We have a clash between an anti-consumer society and the most consumption-oriented society in the world. The book is now at a stage where after thinking that it would be just an easy, fairly short piece of journalism, it is now turning into a very long and complicated book. But that doesn't really matter because all of my books have been like that. And besides, the book will prove with historical facts that the real world in the Caribbean is just as fantastic as in the stories of *One Hundred Years of Solitude.*

INTERVIEWER: Do you have any long-range ambitions or regrets as a writer?

GARCÍA MÁRQUEZ: I think my answer is the same as the one I gave you about fame. I was asked the other day if I would be interested in the Nobel Prize, but I think that for me it would be an absolute catastrophe. I would certainly be interested in deserving it, but to receive it would be terrible. It would just complicate even more the problems of fame. The only thing I really regret in life is not having a daughter.

INTERVIEWER: Are there any projects now underway you can discuss?

GARCÍA MÁRQUEZ: I'm absolutely convinced that I'm going to write the greatest book of my life, but I don't know which one it will be or when. When I feel something like this—which I have been feeling now for a while—I stay very quiet so that if it passes by I can capture it.

—*Peter H. Stone*

# THREE DAYS WITH GABO

*Silvana Paternostro*

Distressed by what he saw happening to Latin American journalism, Gabriel García Márquez, the Nobel laureate author of *One Hundred Years of Solitude* and a former newspaper reporter himself, started in March 1995 what he describes as "a school without walls"—the Foundation for a New Ibero-American Journalism. Its purpose is to rejuvenate, through traveling workshops, journalism in the region. He insists that what is being taught and practiced needs urgent renovation and complains that today's journalists are more interested in chasing after breaking news and in the perks and privileges of a press pass than they are in creativity and ethics. They pride themselves on being able to read a secret document upside down, he says, but their work is full of grammatical and spelling mistakes and it lacks depth. "They are not moved by the basis that the best story is not the one that is filed first but the one that is told best," he wrote in his inaugural remarks.

García Márquez is critical of the way universities and newspaper publishers in Latin America are treating the profession—which he considers the best job in the world. Disagreeing with the professional schools' stance that journalists are not artists, García

Márquez considers that print journalism is "a literary form." He would also like to convince newspapers to invest less in technology and more in training personnel.

With the support of UNESCO, García Márquez's foundation, based in Barranquilla, Colombia, has organized, in less than two years, twenty-eight workshops attended by three hundred and twenty journalists from eleven countries. The themes of the workshops have ranged from teaching the narrative techniques of reportage in print, radio, and television, to discussions of ethics, freedom of the press, reporting under dangerous circumstances, and the challenges of new technology for the profession. The workshops are taught by established professionals and are intended for the younger generation of journalists, preferably under thirty, who have at least three years of experience. Although based in Colombia, the workshops have also been conducted in Ecuador, Venezuela, Mexico, and Spain. The centerpiece of the foundation's curriculum is the three-day workshop taught by García Márquez on reportage.

As a freelance journalist who has been writing about Latin America in English, I applied and was accepted for his fifth workshop. I was so excited to meet him that I, who am late for everything, was the first to arrive at the Spanish Cultural Center in Cartagena, a beautifully renovated two-story house with red begonias and a fountain in the courtyard, owned by the Spanish government. The setting could not be more appropriate. Cartagena is home to García Márquez, and many of the characters from his fiction walked the narrow cobblestones of the city's colonial center. A few blocks away from the Cultural Center, at the Cathedral's Square, Florentino Ariza noticed Fermina Daza's walk was no longer that of a schoolgirl. Sierva María de Todos los Angeles, the twelve-year-old girl whose hair continued to grow long after she died, lived in the Convent of Santa Clara nearby. Adjacent to the walls that kept Cartagena safe from English pirates, García Márquez's house here is so close to the convent—now a five-star hotel—that guests have an unimpeded view right into the author's home. "It was embarrassing," one guest at the hotel told me. "I could see him having breakfast every morning. Finally, I closed the curtains."

MONDAY, APRIL 8, 1996
9:00 A.M.

I am one of twelve journalists sitting around a large wooden oval table. We are very quiet, like disciplined students in a Jesuit school waiting for class to begin. Gabriel García Márquez opens the door and comes in, looking at us mischievously, as if he knows how nervous we are. García Márquez—Gabo as everyone knows him—is dressed in white. Here on the Caribbean coast of Colombia, men often wear white, white all the way down to their shoes. He says good morning and, just for a second, it feels as if we might stand, bow or curtsy and answer in unison: "*Buenos días, profesor.*"

The two empty seats in the room face the windows with their backs to the door. Gabo picks out César Romero, the Mexican journalist sitting next to me—we are facing the door—and asks him for his seat.

"I've seen too many cowboy movies," he says; "I never sit with my back to the door. Plus, I'm sure I have more enemies than you do."

"Don Gabriel," says César Romero, "of course."

As Gabo walks over, I remember my conversation with a Cuban friend who recently graduated from the film school that García Márquez founded outside of Havana and where he sometimes teaches. "You'll have a great time," Juan Carlos said. "He always pays more attention to the women than the men in the class. He says women bring him luck." I look around the table. Out of the twelve participants, Andrea Varela and I are the only women.

Gabo sits down to my left, and I am nervous. My hands start to sweat. I dry them against my pants. I cross my arms. He crosses his legs. I look down at the floor. His pointy, well-polished shoes are white. I look up. His watchband is also white. I focus on his *guayabera*, those shirts favored by Latin men, worn outside the pants, that rest on the hips, have four pockets, and sometimes embroidery and ruffles. I have always identified them with grandfathers, cabinet members and landowners—men who usually smell of cologne and sometimes of scotch. His shirt is simple, no ruffles, no smell, and made of such fine linen it is almost see-through. His seersucker pants make a funny, unexpected contrast.

He places on the table a black leather purse, the kind men started carrying around in the seventies. With his glasses on, he takes out the list of class participants from a black folder—where he also has the articles we had been asked to submit, a piece of reportage for Gabo to criticize and edit during the three days he will work with us. The only sound is the rumbling of the air conditioner. No one really looks at him, yet all of us, bona fide reporters, have been in situations much harder to handle than this one. Rubén Valencia, from Cali, traveled by himself to Urabá, Colombia's most violent zone, where drug traffickers, guerrillas, and paramilitary groups massacre each other. Wilson Daza spent twenty days roaming downtown Medellín with drug pushers, prostitutes and gang members. César Romero covered the Zapatista insurrection in Chiapas. Edgar Téllez investigated President Samper's alleged link with drug cartels.

But ever since Gabo won the Nobel Prize in 1982, he has gone from being the writer of *One Hundred Years of Solitude* to being a celebrity and an important political actor. In Latin America, especially in Colombia and in Mexico, where he spends most of his time, not even presidents have his stature. Here his stardom compares only to that of soccer stars and beauty queens. People stop him on the street for autographs, even those who have not read his books. Presidents, ministers, politicians, newspaper publishers, guerrilla leaders consult him, write him letters, want him around. Whatever he says, on whatever subject, makes the headlines. Last year a guerrilla group in Colombia kidnapped the brother of a former president. Their demand was that García Márquez accept the presidency. In their request they wrote: "Nobel, please save the Fatherland."

For us Colombians, to refer to García Márquez by his nickname *Gabo* is to bring his success closer to us and, like a proud family, make his greatness our own. In a region consumed by violence, poverty, drug trafficking and corruption, he is the son the family shows off—even those who disapprove of his friendship with Fidel Castro. In Barranquilla, my hometown, where he worked as a reporter in 1950 and where he met his wife Mercedes, *su mujer de siempre,* he has been completely embraced. He is not even Gabo but Gabito—the affectionate diminutive by which parents, spouses and friends call their dear ones.

His name comes up in our beauty pageants as often as the Pope's. The contestants' answers have become repetitive: Who is your favorite author? García Márquez. Whom do you admire the most? My father, the Pope and García Márquez. Whom would you like to meet? García Márquez and the Pope. If the same questions were posed to a Latin American journalist, the answers would probably be the same—perhaps leaving out the Pope. For us, Latin American journalists in the early stages of our careers, he is a role model. We like to say that before he was a novelist he was a reporter. He says he has never stopped being one.

Gabo reads our names off the list and adds a comment—always curious, always warm—to each. Rubén Valencia and a few others call him *maestro,* which to me sounds a little too respectful. I've called him Gabo many times when talking about him, but once in his presence that feels a little too forward. He is friendliest with Andrea, who has already been in a workshop with him. "You spend more time here at the workshops than at work," he jokes, calling her Andreita. "We're going to call your boss and ask her to send your bed over." Andrea is shy, and Gabo's warmth makes her blush.

The door opens in a rush and a young man—out of breath, a light blue shirt glued to his chest and a newspaper tucked under his arm—brings in the heat and the chaos of downtown Cartagena.

"*Permiso,*" he apologizes, and sits quickly next to César Romero.

"And who are you?"

"Tadeo Martínez."

Tadeo is nervous, and Gabo knows it.

"Tadeo Martínez. *El Periódico de Cartagena,*" he says, reading from his list. "Your colleagues are here from, let's see, Caracas,

Bogotá, Cali, Medellín, San José, Mexico, New York and Miami but you, coming from around the corner, are the last one to arrive."

We all feel bad for him, but then Gabo shakes his head and smiles.

10:00 A.M.

Gabo starts by talking about his book on Simón Bolívar—our George Washington, Thomas Jefferson, Benjamin Franklin, all of the Founding Fathers wrapped up in one—who liberated five countries from Spanish rule and envisioned a unified Latin America, an empire running from California all the way down to Tierra del Fuego. *El Libertador,* as depicted in portraits on every public office wall, is always dressed in a starched military uniform, ready for battle or riding his white horse.

"But no one ever said in Bolívar's biographies that he sang or that he was constipated," says Gabo. He adds that he believes the world is divided into two groups: "Those who shit well and those who don't; it makes for very different characters. But historians don't say these things because they think they are not important." His dissatisfaction with the cardboard image that official historians have given to his hero explains why he decided to write *The General in His Labyrinth,* whose pages contain the complete story of the figure who has been such an important influence on his political thought. He tells us he wrote it in the form of a *reportaje,* reportage.

"Reportage is the complete story, the complete reconstruction of an event. Every little detail counts. This is the basis of the credibility and the strength of a story. In *The General in His Labyrinth* each verifiable fact, no matter how simple, can strengthen the whole work. For example, I placed a full moon—that full moon which is so easy to insert—on the night that Simón Bolívar slept in Guaduas on May 10, 1830. I wanted to find out if there was a full moon that night, so I called the Academy of Science in Mexico and they found out that there actually was one. If there wasn't, well, I would just cross out the full moon and that's that. The moon is a detail that no one notices. But if there is one false fact in a reporting piece, then everything else is false. In fiction, if there is a fact that can be verified—that there was a full moon that night in Guaduas—then the readers are going to believe everything else."

Someone asks about fiction techniques in reportage. Gabo replies that he admires the work of Gay Talese, Norman Mailer, and Truman Capote, all of whom have practiced New Journalism. "The only literary aspect of New Journalism is its narrative style. Literary license is allowed as long as it is believable and stays true to all the verifiable facts."

As he says this, I recall the piece Gabo wrote about Caracas in a terrible drought and about a man who had taken to shaving with peach juice—a fact that is definitely credible, and verifiable, but one that reeks of literary license. It has been said that Gabo is too creative to be a good journalist. After all, he is the same writer who in his novels, with a straight face, had Remedios the Beauty levitating to the skies and the smell of Santiago Nasar after his well-announced death penetrating the entire town.

As if reading my mind he says, "The strange episodes in my novels are all real, or they have a starting point, a basis in reality. Real life is always much more interesting than what we can invent." He says that the ascension of Remedios the Beauty was inspired by a woman he saw spreading clean white sheets with her arms stretched out to the sun. He has also said that "to move between the magical and the incredible, one has to become a journalist."

He tells us about *Story of a Shipwrecked Sailor,* which was originally written as a series of stories when he was working as a staff reporter for *El Espectador* in Bogotá. He had been assigned to write the adventures of a sailor lost at sea but the story was of no interest to him. "Every newspaper had written about it." But then he relented. In those days, the fifties—as in the days when Charles Dickens's novels appeared in the London broadsheets—serialization was a common marketing tool. Gabo's job was to interview the sailor and write his story in segments. After the first two parts were published, Don Guillermo Cano, the paper's editor (assassinated by drug cartels in 1986), walked up to his desk. " '*Oiga,* Gabrielito, those things you are writing—are they fiction or are they true?' I told him, 'It is a novel and it is true.' Then he asked me, 'And how many more parts are you thinking of submitting?'

" 'Two more,' I said.

" 'No way, sales are up threefold. Give me a hundred.'

"I wrote fourteen.

"I knew the sailor had spent fourteen days lost at sea," Gabo tells us, "so I decided to write fourteen chapters, one for each day at sea. I sat down with the guy again and started slicing his days thinner. I began by asking him what he did every day, then what he did every hour, and then every minute. I asked him what time the sharks arrived; what time he ate."

NOON

It is almost lunchtime. Gabo began talking at nine sharp and he has not stopped. More than teaching, Gabo chats, tells stories. For more than three hours, the twelve of us have sat, saying little. I have not had breakfast but I am not feeling hungry. He doesn't drink coffee but many of us do. It is the perfect accompaniment to his stories.

Storytellers, he says, are born, not made: "Like singers, to be a storyteller is something life gives you. It cannot be learned. Technique, yes, that can be learned, but to be able to tell a story is something with which you are born. It is easy to tell a good storyteller from a bad one: ask someone to tell you about the last movie they've seen."

Then he emphasizes, "The difficult thing is to realize that you are not a storyteller and then have the courage to move on and do something else." César Romero later tells me that of all Gabo's statements this is the one that struck him the most.

He gives an example. Soon after he received the Nobel Prize, a young journalist in Madrid approached Gabo as he was leaving his hotel and asked for an interview. Gabo, who dislikes being asked for interviews, refused to give one, but invited her to accompany him and his wife throughout the day. "She spent the whole day with us. We shopped, my wife bargained, we went to lunch, we walked, we talked; she came with us everywhere." When they returned to the hotel and Gabo was ready to say good-bye, she asked him for an interview. "I told her she should change jobs," says Gabo. "She had the complete story, she had the reportage."

He went on to talk about the difference between an interview and reportage—a confusion, he says, journalists are constantly making. "An interview in print journalism is always a dialogue between the journalist and someone who has something to say or think *about* an event. Reportage is the meticulous and truthful reconstruction *of* an event.

"Tape recorders are nefarious because one falls into the trap of believing that the tape recorder thinks, and so we disconnect our brains the moment we plug in the cord. A tape recorder is a digital parrot, it has ears but it doesn't have a heart. It does not pick up details so our job is to listen beyond the words, pick up on what is not said and then write the complete story." He looks down at the pile of papers in front of him—our articles! "Writing is a hypnotic act," he says. "If successful the writer has hypnotized the reader. Wherever there is a stumble the reader wakes up, comes out of the hypnosis and stops reading. If the prose limps, the reader abandons you. One must keep the reader hypnotized by tending to every detail, every word. It is a continuous act where you poison the reader with credibility and with rhythm." He pauses, then taps on the papers. "Now I must tell you that I read the articles you've all sent and I was *fully awake* the whole time."

I gasp, some giggle, and others move around uncomfortably in their chairs.

1:00 P.M.

"Let's see what's in the paper today." He reaches across the table for Tadeo Martínez's newspaper. "Is there a story we could go out and cover?" he asks. He studies the front page and shakes his head in disapproval. "Incredible," he says. "This is a local paper and not one story about Cartagena on the front page. Tell your boss, Tadeo, that a local paper should have local front-page news.

"Nothing here," he mumbles as he turns the pages. "Let's see, something here. *Stove for sale, unused, unassembled stove. Must sell. Call*

*Gloria Bedoya, 660-1127, extension 113.* This could be a story. Should we call? I bet there's something here. Why is this woman selling a stove, why is the stove unassembled? What do we know from this about this woman? Could be interesting." He pauses, waiting for us to get excited. But no one seems to be interested in finding out why a woman is selling an unassembled stove, especially when we can keep listening to him.

Gabo sees stories everywhere. During the next three days he says "*eso es un reportaje*" (that's a story) constantly. I realize that Gabo is full of nostalgia. He misses being a reporter. "Journalism is not a job, it's a gland," he says.

It is not a coincidence that his new book, *News of a Kidnapping,* is a work of nonfiction. It allowed him—during the three years it took him to write it—to be a reporter once again. It is the story of nine kidnappings engineered between 1989 and 1991 by Pablo Escobar, the head of the violent Medellín drug cartel, who wanted to avoid at any cost Colombia signing an extradition treaty with the United States. In keeping with his motto ("Better a grave in Colombia than a cell in the United States"), Escobar pressured the government by bombing buildings, killing presidential candidates, ministers, judges, police officers and ultimately kidnapping nine people, eight of whom were journalists.

Vividly and eerily, Gabo reconstructs the six months of captivity—recording the impatience and anxiety not only of the kidnapped and their families but also that of the kidnappers, members of Escobar's cartel, and of the government officials involved in the negotiating process. Of course, as García Márquez, he had the kind of access any journalist would desire. He was able to meet with the families, with government officials, including three former presidents. He talked with the teenagers who kept guard, who listened to Guns n' Roses and watched *Lethal Weapon* on video repeatedly, high on crack with their machine guns cocked next to them—kids who kill for the cartels in order to buy refrigerators for their mothers. When Gabo started writing the book, Pablo Escobar was already dead—shot by police forces in 1993. But he had access to the drug lord's principal partners, the Ochoa brothers, who received him in jail. Escobar's lawyers showed him handwritten letters. "Every single detail in this book is real; as much as it was humanly possible to verify the facts, they were verified. If Pablo Escobar himself could not revise the text, it was because he was dead. I know he would have agreed to meet with me."

The fact he can meet anyone he chooses makes Gabo miss the days when he was a faceless journalist, one who could pick up a pad and go find out why the stove is unassembled. "It is difficult for me now to write a reporting piece. I wanted to write about that village whose bread supply had been poisoned but I knew that if I went there the news would be distorted; *I* would become the news." He is referring to an incident which occurred outside of Bogotá a few years ago—a whole town poisoned.

Apart from allowing him to go back to journalism, *News of a Kidnapping* served another purpose. "I wanted to see if I was still able to write like a journalist," he tells us. "It has been the most difficult book I've written. It is much easier to write fiction, where I am the master. I control it all. But this was written as if for the newspapers. I wrote this book without using a literary adjective or a metaphor. It was a useful exercise because it is important for me not to repeat myself. The challenge of writing *Autumn of the Patriarch* after writing *One Hundred Years of Solitude* was self-imposed. I could have written three hundred *One Hundred*s. I knew how to do that, so I decided I would write *Autumn* in a very different style. *Autumn* was not successful when it came out. If I had written another *One Hundred* it would have been better received." He smiles and tells us that one of his most satisfying moments was seeing in the United States an edition of *One Hundred Years* with a gray stripe down one side which read: From the author of *Love in the Time of Cholera*. "This was the victory over *One Hundred Years*," he says.

"As writers we also have to defend ourselves from those authors we like. It is easy to fall into a trap and start imitating them. For example, people like to say I imitated Faulkner, but during my trip to the American South, when I went with Mercedes, a son still in arms and twenty dollars to our name, I realized I was identifying not so much with his writing but with a reality, which is that the American South is like Aracataca."

Aracataca is the small town in the Caribbean region of Colombia where he was born, about two hundred miles from where my grandfather grew up. Something has felt familiar ever since Gabo walked into the room, sat next to me and started talking. He has said many times that he retells the stories his grandmother told him. Listening to Gabo makes me feel as if I am listening to my grandfather—if only my grandfather could write!

Gabo leans back in his chair, touches his white mustache and warns us, "You are not writing well if you feel happy when the phone rings and you answer it; or if there is a power blackout and that makes you happy. But if you are on track and the phone rings, you won't answer it; you will damn the lights if they shut off." His example about the electricity must seem farfetched to some, but to us Latin American journalists, blackouts and the loss of the text on our computers are always in the backs of our minds. Gabo, who once lost a whole text, now has his own emergency generator.

He begins to read paragraphs out loud from some of our articles; he offers light copyediting. Some of the sentences are too long and Gabo pretends to be choking as he reads along. "We have to use breathing commas," he says. "If not, the hypnotic act does not work. Remember, wherever there is a stumble, the reader wakes up and escapes. And one of the things that will make the reader wake up from hypnosis is to feel out of breath."

We have spent almost the entire morning listening to Gabo teach by telling stories. Our job, I've realized, is to kick back and enjoy him—as if we are on an extended coffee break or drinking at the nearest bar. "I know journalism cannot be taught, it must be lived, but I can transmit to you some of my experience. There are no theories. Reality has no theories, reality narrates. From it we have to learn."

AFTER LUNCH

The light in the room was so dim that it took a moment for their eyes to adjust. It was a space no longer than two by three meters, with one boarded-up window. Two men were sitting on a single mattress that had been placed on the floor: they wore hoods, like the men in the first house, and were absorbed in watching television. Everything was dismal and oppressive. In the corner to the left of the door, on a narrow bed with iron posts, sat a spectral woman with limp white hair, dazed eyes and skin that adhered to her bones. She gave no sign of having heard them come in; not a glance, not a breath. Nothing, a corpse could not have seemed so dead. Maruja had to restrain her shock when she realized who it was.

Gabo is reading a chapter from *News of a Kidnapping*. I am willing to surrender to his words, except his white shoes are impossible to ignore. I close my eyes to give myself entirely to his "poison."

At night the silence was total and the solitude immense, interrupted only by a demented rooster with no sense of time who crowed whenever he felt like it. Barking dogs could be heard on the horizon, and there was one very close by that sounded to them like a trained guard dog. Maruja got off to a bad start. She curled up in the mattress, closed her eyes, and for several days did not open them again except when she had to, trying to attain the privacy she needed to think with more clarity. Not that she slept for eight hours at a time: she would doze off for half an hour and wake again to the same reality, the same agony waiting to ambush her. It was a permanent dread: the constant physical sensation in her stomach of something hard, coiled and ready to explode into panic. Maruja ran the complete film of her life in an effort to hold on to good memories, but disagreeable ones always intervened...

He reads the entire chapter. I feel Marina Montoya's panic as she dressed in the pink sweat suit and men's brown socks and said goodbye to her two roommates. I am transported to the cramped room where the guards are telling Marina she is going to be freed. But everyone knows that the high heels she wears with the sweats are taking her to her execution.

"Any comments? Anything I should change?"

No one says a word.

"It is an investigation of three years," he says with pride. "The research was crucial. Every fact that could be verified was verified. I give credit in the book to my research assistant."

Gabo is talking, but my head is still heavy. I haven't come out of my hypnosis. I feel groggy and can still see Marina's body, dressed in pink, lying dead on the grass that divides the only road to Bogotá's airport, the same one I take every time I visit my parents.

"A good piece of advice is first to write the beginning and the ending. Begin with an anecdote and close with a resonant ending. Then fill in the in-between. You have to fence in your story, almost as if with cattle. If not, you keep researching, and that could take you anywhere. You have to enclose the story, you have to learn how to end the circle of information. Details are the key. You must hold on to a thread in the narrative. If not you get swamped. Even Cervantes lost a donkey, and we must avoid losing as many donkeys as possible," he says.

"One of the big problems about writing is worrying too much. If you could just write it as you speak it, that is the dream of a writer, to be able to write as one speaks. It's not done, because when one tries, one realizes how difficult it is to do. In Mexico I used to write with my windows open, so I would hear the birds or the rain, and I would include them in the text I was working on. Not anymore. That thing about only being able to write in a particular space, in a particular way, is a novelist's mania. Now I can write anywhere just as I used to do when I was a reporter. I just plug in my PowerBook in any hotel room. But I am used to writing on the long screen. I save as I write and transfer to a floppy disk right away. Each chapter is a file."

He tells us he is hooked on writing on screens shaped like pages. But they aren't manufactured anymore. "I buy all the ones I can find. I have eleven," he says. "I believe one needs to buy anything that makes our job easier. Computers are extraordinary. I can prove it. I started writing on a computer with *Love in the Time of Cholera*. I went from writing one page to writing ten a day, from writing a book every seven years to writing a book every three. Still, writing never stops being difficult. Staring at a blank page, one gets the same anxiety as with sex, always anticipating if it's going to work or not. There's always the anguish. As Borges used to say: what God is the God behind the God who moves the pieces of chess?"

He tells us he knows that the worst moment for a writer, or for a journalist, is facing the blank page and shares what for him has been one of the most useful tips, what Ernest Hemingway told *The Paris Review* in 1958: "You read what you have written and, as you always stop when you know what is going to happen next, you go on from there. You write until you come to a place where you still have your juice and know what will happen next and you stop and try to live through until the next day when you hit it again."

"I write from eight-thirty in the morning to about two or three in the afternoon," Gabo says. "From those long years at the chair I've developed a bad back; that's why I play tennis every day. Sometimes after I finish, my back pain is such that I just have to throw myself to the floor." It is a little before seven when he looks at his white watch. "You guys are not going to make me miss my tennis," he says. He gets up and walks out.

TUESDAY, APRIL 9
9:00 A.M.

Almost fifty years ago today Gabo lost his first typewriter—the one he used to write "The Third Resignation," his first published short story. He was an unhappy law student living in an inexpensive hostel in downtown Bogotá. He missed the heat of the Caribbean coast. He rarely went to classes: law, which his family expected him to study, had never interested him. At lunchtime on April 9, 1948, Gabo was about to sit down to eat when he overheard that Jorge Eliecer Gaitán, a popular young presidential candidate who was shaking Colombia's traditional political structure, had been shot.

Gabo tells us that he got to the square only to find "people were already soaking their handkerchiefs in Gaitán's blood." The streets of Bogotá burned and Gabo's typewriter went up in the conflagration. Colombia was paralyzed. Universities shut down. It was a few months later, here in Cartagena, that Gabo, at the age of nineteen, started his life as a journalist by writing editorials.

"I was walking around one day and Zavala, the editor of *El Universal*, was sitting at his typewriter outside on the square. He tells me, 'I know you.' He says, 'You are the guy with the short stories in *El Espectador*. Why don't you sit down and help me with this editorial I'm finishing?' I wrote something. Zavala took out his pencil and crossed some things out. The next time I wrote an editorial, he scratched out only a few things. By the third day I was writing without editing. I had become a journalist."

He is not sitting next to me today. He is not wearing a white *guayabera* but a turquoise short-sleeved silk shirt. The shoes are still white. My connection with him feels distant but I'm still drawn to his tales. "I started making money from writing when I was forty-three years old," he tells us. "I bought my first house, the one in Cuernavaca, in 1970, twenty-five years after my first story was published. I calculated that to take my sons to the movies back then I had to write twelve pages, and to take them to the movies and buy them ice cream I had to write twenty. When I lived in Paris, I didn't keep constant hours and wrote mostly at night. During the day, I had to worry about feeding myself. Now I know it is better to write during the day, on a computer, with a full stomach and with air-conditioning."

COFFEE BREAK

Jaime Abello, the foundation's director, has hired a photographer and calls us together for a group picture. The foundation issues no certificates: "Life, in its due course, will decide who is capable and who is not," Gabo has said. "At least, you can all go back with a souvenir," Jaime says. "Come and sit on the stairs."

Gabo is complacent and sits in the middle. The photographer from *El Universal* orders us to smile at the camera.

"Wait," shouts the woman who runs the Center. "I want a picture with Gabo." She climbs over us and sits next to him.

1:00 P.M.

It was inevitable. Fidel Castro had to come up. We were, or I should say I was, waiting for the right moment. Gabo wants to talk about ethics: should a reporter read a document left unattended, one that has the potential for a scoop?

His question gives me a chance. "I had an experience like that," I say. In 1991 I attended the opening ceremony of the first Ibero-American presidential summit, held in Guadalajara. Castro was told that all the dignitaries had to limit their speeches to seven minutes. Everyone waited apprehensively for Castro's turn since he is known for his long speeches. We all wondered if Castro, who the day after the triumph of the Revolution in 1959 ad-libbed for seven hours, would keep to his instructions. He spoke for exactly seven minutes. President Balaguer of the Dominican Republic spoke for forty-five.

During the break, the pool of journalists, including myself, surrounded Fidel. In person he looms larger than life, even if his military uniform seemed a little faded and the collar of his shirt too frayed. As he walked outside, the crowd followed him. He seemed to love it.

"*Comandante,* I cut cane in the Venceremos Brigade," a journalist yelled.

He stopped and looked for the voice. "Where?"

A woman extended a black-and-white photograph over the crowd—a picture of the two of them together when his beard was dark. "Can you sign it, *Comandante?*"

"Was it hard to speak for seven minutes?" someone else called out.

"I was tricked," said Fidel. "They told me that if I spoke for longer than seven minutes all of the bells in Guadalajara would toll."

I had noticed a small, crumpled piece of paper next to a yellow pad where he had been sitting. As the crowd moved out with him, I returned to his seat and picked up the ball of paper. I opened it and read his small and cramped handwriting: "*Por cuánto tiempo habré hablado?*" (How long have I spoken?) On the bigger pad, Fidel had made a list of the presidents and the amount of time, to the exact second, that each had spoken. I walked away leaving the note behind. I've regretted it ever since.

"I would definitely have grabbed it," says Gabo. "Believe me, if he thought it was so important, he would have never left it there. Yes, I would have kept it as a souvenir."

As I had hoped, Gabo begins to speak about Fidel Castro. He talks about Cuba openly, with concern and passion, like a university student who keeps a poster of Che Guevara on the wall. But about Fidel, he speaks without really saying anything negative, compromising or even revelatory. "I speak about Fidel more from sentiment than from a place of judgment. He is one of the people I love most in the world."

"A dictator," someone says.

"To have elections is not the only way to be democratic."

The American journalist in the group keeps after him. Gabo starts to answer, but sees we are taking notes. His voice turns stern: "This is not an interview. If I want to express my opinion on Fidel, I'll write it myself and believe me, I'll do a better job."

Perhaps feeling somewhat guilty for snapping at us, he describes a profile he wrote about Fidel. "I gave it to him to read. In it, I was critical. I spoke about the situation of the free press. But he said nothing about that. What really irked him about my article was that I mentioned he had eaten eighteen scoops of ice cream after lunch one day. 'Did I really eat eighteen scoops?' he asked me repeatedly."

AFTER LUNCH

"Tell us about your trip to Chigorodó." Gabo is calling on Rubén Valencia.

Chigorodó is a village in Urabá, Colombia's most dangerous region—which is saying a lot coming from a country that has been described as the most violent in the world. The Gulf of Urabá, on the western coast of Colombia, is a geographical Molotov cocktail. It has the country's most fertile land; it is a point of entry for arms and a port of exit for drugs; it has poor peasants and rich landowners; it has guerrilla groups, military forces and death squads. Last year, one thousand people were killed, victims of political violence. According to a newspaper report, a twenty-year-old hitman has already killed eighty-three people. In August of 1995, eighteen people were killed inside a dance hall. Massacres like this are frequent.

Rubén is the last person I would have expected to visit Chigorodó. He is a scrawny young man with square glasses too big for his face, with so much prescription in his lenses that his eyes seem tiny. "I went there," he says, "to write about the effect that violence was having on the lives of the people in the area, to find the human face of the story."

The piece he published is the one he submitted to the workshop. Gabo is holding it in his hand. "Tell us what happened from the moment you arrived. Who was the first person you talked to?" he asks.

"The town was desolate, *maestro*. I found a twelve-year-old kid, I asked him if he knew where the dance hall was and he took me there. After the massacre, there was an exodus; all the peasants left in fear." Valencia tells us that he walked around looking for someone to talk to, but fear and silence were all he found. A woman stopped on a motorcycle and offered him a ride to Apartadó, about a half-hour ride in the rain, where he could get more information. He checked into the Hotel Las Molas. On his third day there, a visitor was waiting for him in the lobby.

"Are you the person who is investigating the massacres?" the stranger asked him. "Let's go out and have a drink. I think you want to talk to me."

"Sorry," replied Valencia. "It's too late. I don't go out after dark. Do you want to come up to my room?"

Once in the room, the man asked, "What have you found out? What do you want to know?"

"I'm a journalist, I'm trying to find the human face to this conflict."

"Ah, ya."

"Who are you?" Valencia finally asked him.

"I am an angel," said the man.

"What kind of an angel?"

"An angel with a white wing and a black wing."

"And with what wing will you be talking to me?"

"That depends."

"On what?"

As Valencia speaks, we are all silent, immersed in his story. I am feeling somewhat envious, what a story!

"But that is not what I read here," says Gabo, raising the article. "Why didn't you write that story? Why didn't you write that just the way you just told it to us? That's the story I would have written.

"Describe that man," says Gabo, looking at him.

Rubén remains silent.

"Can you remember his face?"

"Yes."

"What animal did he remind you of?"

"An iguana."

"That's it, you need nothing more," says Gabo. "You lost the trip, my boy. We are not sociologists, we are tale-tellers, we tell the stories of people. Reporting with a human voice is what makes journalists big. Where is that story?"

Rubén, who insists on calling García Márquez *maestro,* responds: "It's not easy. When I propose to write that story, my editor tells me, 'Valencia, you are not García Márquez. Stick to the facts!' "


3:00 P.M.

"Daza, why don't you read us one of your pieces?" Gabo asks. I am feeling impatient. The day is almost over. The workshop is almost over, and Gabo has not said a word about my piece. Because I had written about Cuba I thought he would show a particular interest. But he has not even acknowledged reading it.

Daza has written about one of Medellín's underground characters—a profile of a man who prefers the company of animals to
humans. He shares his daily *buñuelo*, a fried dough, his only meal,
with a pet rat. He carries a chicken on a leash and keeps fleas in his
room. Daza reads it to us. The piece is touching, the writing lyrical,
maybe even too lyrical. It is not traditional reportage.

"I will not touch Daza's writing," says Gabo. "He might be
inventing a new form here, one I know nothing about."

If he thought it was good or bad, we do not know.

Daza is not only daring in his writing style. He is the only one
who has shown some disdain: "Gabo is a little full of himself."

Daza had been sent to cover the Ibero-American presidential
summit, which in 1994 was held in Cartagena. Reporters were furi-
ous because dignitaries were impossible to interview. Gabo, being
an important political actor, was there as a guest in a delegation. He
was reported as saying that, instead of complaining, journalists
need to go out on the street looking for stories, and not expect news
to be handed to them on silver platters. If the presidents were
unavailable, a good journalist would find a story nonetheless.

Refuting him, Daza says, "It was easy for you to say that. I wrote
a story about how unfair I thought that comment was, especially
coming from you. I mean you were there, behind doors, with all of
the presidents."

"I was not there as a working journalist."

Daza admits that Gabo's reprimand was useful. He gives an
illustration: when he then was sent to cover the summit of the
Group of the Non-Aligned Countries held in Cartagena last year,
he didn't go to the convention center where the leaders were meeting. To write about Yassir Arafat, who was attending, and about the
Israel-Palestine conflict, he went to one of Cartagena's many poor
slums instead—to one that is actually called Palestina. He wrote a
story comparing Arafat's situation with that of a girl living in
Palestina, marginalized in the outskirts of a rich, tourist-filled city.

"You learned the lesson," says Gabo.

"You were also at that meeting." Daza is unrelenting. "You were
there with the Cuban delegation."

"I was there," Gabo says impatiently. "I was there because there were rumors that there was going to be an assassination attempt on Fidel. And the Cuban security wasn't going to let Fidel be part of the procession so I proposed to go on the horse-drawn carriage with him. I told them that here in Colombia if I'm on board, no one will shoot. So five of us squeezed into the carriage, tight, joking. While I was telling Fidel that I was sure nothing was going to happen, the horse actually tripped."

## DINNER

He is having dinner with us at La Vitrola, Cartagena's most cosmopolitan restaurant. The decor is more British colonial than Spanish, but the group of Cuban musicians dressed in white sings traditional *sones*. It is where Colombia's upper class eats when they are vacationing, where the president stops by for a drink. Soap-opera stars, small but flashy drug dealers, young rich kids on their first date, the few local yuppies all come too. The menu resembles that of a New York restaurant. The vinaigrette is made with balsamic vinegar, the mozzarella is fresh and the wine, for Colombia, is good.

We sit and wait in a small room sipping fruit punches. Gabo arrives wearing a dark blue jumpsuit, zipped from his navel to his chest. Caribbean man by day, by night he seems as though he has just jumped off the cover of a record—funk or disco. His shoes are exactly the same model as this morning's but this time they are gray. He asks the waiter for a whiskey. We go to the private room next to the entrance. He sits between Andrea and me.

The menu is fixed: fried zucchini followed by a choice of shrimp in coconut sauce or red snapper in cream.

"That's too heavy for me to eat at night," Gabo complains.

The host comes over. "I can give you the snapper, grilled with no sauce? Or a pasta?"

"What kind?"

"How would *you* want it?"

"Simple."

"How about *pasta in brodo?*"

"Perfect. Bring me that."

I ask if I can have the same; I have felt feverish all day.

"Two of those," Gabo tells him.

When the wine is served, he declines and keeps drinking his whisky.

The restaurant is filling up. Our table is in plain view. Everyone notices Gabo. He requests that the doors be closed, and I ask the waiter to do so. A reporter from *Newsweek* who has come from Buenos Aires to interview Gabo is sitting at my left. I speak to him for a while but I really only want to talk to Gabo, whisper to him, not share him with the rest of my colleagues.

I turn to him. We converse about many things. He wants to know why and where I live in New York. I tell him I live in the Village and I ask him if he likes New York. He does very much, but not when it's too cold because he likes doing nothing better than walking through the streets. I tell him I will take him around the Village, and he promises to call. We talk about Cuba, about Barranquilla, about Bill Clinton, *The New Yorker* and Sunday magazines. He tells me in intricate detail about a short story he wants to write and about a yellow silk shirt he has, one he wears when he feels in love. His glass is empty so he sips from mine. "I like being around women. I know them better than I know men. I feel more comfortable around them; I grew up with women around me."

The waiter walks over and hands Gabo a white napkin, folded. He opens it and reads what's on it. He tells the waiter to say nothing. It must be difficult to have everyone want something from him all the time. He has told us about a friend running for the assembly who called him up. "Gabo, can you write something about me, say something about me, even if it's just to insult me."

The door opens and a man peeks in. Gabo looks up, stands up and, with his arms extended, walks over. "*Ah, mon ami, quelle coincidence.*" I suppose it is the man who had sent him the note on the napkin. As he sits back again he whispers in my ear, "I just want to escape out that window."

(*Standing*) Manuel Bermudez (*left*), Jaime Abello;
(*kneeling*) Juan Manuel Buelvas (Abello's assistant);
(*seated, near banister, from top*) Oscar Becerra, Tadeo Martínez, director for
the Spanish Cultural Center, César Romero;
(*seated, middle row, from top*) Wilson Daza, Alejandro Manrique, Gabriel
García Márquez, Rubén Valencia, Silvana Paternostro;
(*seated, near wall, from top*) Elias Garía, Tim Johnson, Andrea Varela,
Edgar Téllez.

WEDNESDAY, APRIL 10
9:30 A.M.

Gabo is sitting at the head of the table again, reading from what appears to be a manuscript, waiting for everyone to arrive. He knows the class went out after dinner last night. He looks amused at the last ones arriving late, perhaps with a hint of nostalgia. Everyone looks sleepy, unshowered and irritable with pounding headaches from too much anisette. He looks sparkling clean in his white outfit.

I sit at the other end of the table and I wonder if he has not mentioned my piece to keep me on tenterhooks. Time is ticking, an hour left, and Tadeo's story about a convicted Spanish woman in Cartagena who was not allowed to serve her prison sentence because she was HIV-positive is still being discussed. "You have the best story here," says Gabo, "but you got lost telling it; this makes no sense."

He finally looks at me. I am less nervous than when he first sat next to me but nonetheless my heart races.

"Silvana has good taste in music," Gabo says. "Like me, she likes Van Morrison."

My piece is about the difficulties young rock musicians have in Cuba, where the state does not support them and private initiatives are impossible. I wrote about a struggling troubador with a stringless guitar whose voice I described as like Van Morrison's.

"Silvana has written a good piece, well-structured. I wouldn't change anything," Gabo says. But he disagrees with some of my descriptions: "Is it necessary to say that a television is broken, that it is black-and-white and that there is no money to fix it? There are many homes right here in Cartagena where money is short and TVs are not in color. Would you write that if it weren't about Cuba?"

We go back and forth on the subject of culture control in the Cuban government. "I've talked to them many times," he says as if frustrated that they haven't listened to him. Then he gets up, walks over to me and hands me my piece. He has not done that with anyone else.

He walks back to his seat. My feet are not touching the ground. I feel like Remedios the Beauty—I'm levitating.

Gabo has a last comment to make: "I see you all—and in your fears, in your clumsiness, in your questioning, I am reminded of the way I felt when I was your age. Telling you about my experiences has also allowed me to look at myself. After all, it will be fifty years since I started writing—every day of my life. If you don't like your job, resign. The only thing you die from is from doing something you don't like. If you like your work, you have longevity and happiness assured."

Everyone makes a queue toward him. Copies of *One Hundred Years of Solitude*, *Chronicle of a Death Foretold*, *No One Writes to the Colonel* all need to be signed. He inscribes all, and shakes everyone's hand. Rubén Valencia hands him a copy of *Autumn of the Patriarch*. Curious to know what Gabo would write to someone who has been so respectful and so adoring, I ask Valencia to show me the inscription. It reads: "From the patriarch of the workshop." César Romero wants his book signed for his newborn son. Gabo writes: "For Rodrigo when you were beginning."

I have not brought a book for him to sign. I wait next to the door. As he sees me, he smiles the same smile of mischief he had when he entered the room the first time. "And you, Silvana, aren't you sad it's over? Aren't you going to cry?"

# CARLOS FUENTES

© Thomas Victor

Carlos Fuentes was born in Panama City on November 11, 1928, to a well-to-do family. His father, an ambassador for Mexico, traveled extensively, and Fuentes attended schools in America, Argentina, Chile, and Switzerland before finally receiving a law degree from the University of Mexico. Following in the footsteps of his father, he became involved in international politics, working in 1950 for the United Nations Information Center.

Like that of his countryman Octavio Paz, Fuentes's work shows an intense interest in Mexican history and the Mexican national character. His first published novel, *La región más transparente* [Where the Air Is Clear] (1958), was a caustic analysis of Mexico after the 1910–1920 Revolution. This was followed by *Las buenas conciencias* [The Good Conscience] (1959), a short bildungsroman that describes the education of Jaime Ceballos and his ultimate absorption into the Mexican establishment. Fuentes earned international critical acclaim with *La muerte de Artemio Cruz* [The Death of Artemio Cruz] (1962), a metaphorical novel inspired in part by Orson Welles's *Citizen Kane.*

Fuentes was instrumental in garnering international attention toward Latin American writers. In *La nueva novela hispanoamericana* [The New Latin American Novel] (1969), Fuentes introduced the work of authors like Mario Vargas Llosa, Julio Cortázar, and Gabriel García Márquez to a worldwide audience.

In his magnum opus, *Terra nostra* (1975), Fuentes investigates the Mediterranean roots of Hispanic culture in order to discover where that culture "went wrong." He finds its fatal sin in Philip II's maniacal search for purity and orthodoxy, and his ruthless extirpation of the heterodox (Jewish and Arabian) elements of Spanish culture. *Terra nostra,* along with Fuentes's essays on Cervantes, marked a new epoch in pan-Hispanic studies, a new way to find unity in the fragmented Hispanic world.

From 1975 to 1977, Fuentes served as Mexican ambassador to France. He found it impossible to write during that time but after leaving the post composed *The Hydra Head* (1979), which marked a return to contemporary Mexico as the setting. *El gringo viejo* [The Old Gringo] (1985), a highly acclaimed fictional account of the mysterious fate of Ambrose Bierce, who disappeared in Mexico in 1913, was the first novel by a Mexican to appear on *The New York Times* best-seller list.

Fuentes has received honorary degrees from almost a dozen colleges and universities, including Harvard and Cambridge. He was admitted to the French Legion of Honor in 1992.

———

*Carlos Fuentes was interviewed on a snowy December day at his home in Princeton, New Jersey—a large Victorian house in the old residential section. He is a tall, heavyset man, dressed on that winter's day in a turtleneck sweater and jacket. The tree stood in the drawing room. His two young children were out ice-skating with Mrs. Fuentes. A considerable art collection was on display in the room—Oriental bronzes, pre-Columbian ceramics, and Spanish colonial santos—reflecting Fuentes's cultural background and his*

CAPITULO

saber. Diez años después del cuento de las naranjas, peras e higos

los Four Jodiditos están tocando rockazteck en la disco flotante de

Ada Ching frente a la Califurnace Beach en Old Akapulkey y mis padres

aprovechan la circuncisión, como quien dice, para pedirle al tío Homero

que los invite a pasar navidad y año nuevo en su casa amurallada de

Peachy Tongue Beach.

—Cómo se llamaba cuando tú eras niño? pregunta mi madre y mi

padre ríe, oye si no fue hace tanto, recuerdas? insiste ella, sí, se

llamaba Pichilingue pero todo se ha modernizado insensiblemente, y el

tío Homero siempre ha sabido acomodarse al cambio sin sacrificar lo

permanente, así dice el y si no fuera tan inmensamente gordo que todo

diminutivo le es extraño y su persona acabaría por agigantarse, lo

llamaríamos el Tío Jarrito donde todo cabe sabiéndolo acomodar, pero

ahora en México todo es corrupción verbal hasta Jarrito de Harry como

en Jarrito Homovero, el Trigésimo Tercer Presidente de los USA (Errare

Trumanum Est) y el propio tío Homero, para mantener con el mundo editorial

anglo las excelentes relaciones que debe mantener en su calidad de Presi-

dente de la Academia Mexicana de la Lengua correspondiente de la Real

Academia de Madrid, admite el kiprokó, Chabela de los Angeles, de que

su dirección privada sea Mel O'Field Road aunque el procer liberal

don Melchor Ocampo dé de tumbos en su michoacana tumba y que su oficina

esté en la Frank Wood Avenue por más que le pese a don Panchito Madero

en la suya y además, quién se acuerda ya de ellos?, están muertos, dice

mi mami tubi, verdaderamente muertos, Angel, porque ya nadie los recuerda,

eso es estar muerto, nada más, tú no crees?

Cuando escucha estas cosas el tío don Homero Fagoaga finge un sollozo

*A manuscript page from Carlos Fuentes's* Cristóbal Nonato.

*various diplomatic assignments. On the walls were paintings and prints by Picabia, Miró, Matta, Vasarely, among others—most of them gifts given him by artist friends.*

*The interview was conducted in the library in front of a blazing fire with a hot pot of coffee available. The walls were lined with books. It is at a simple desk in this room that Carlos Fuentes does his work—in front of a window that on this December day looked out on ice-laden shrubbery and trees barely visible in the snow flurries.*

*The interview began with Fuentes's description of his return to writing after he left his ambassadorial post.*

CARLOS FUENTES: I left my post as ambassador to France on the first of April, 1977, and immediately rented a house on the outskirts of Paris where I could begin to write again. I had not written a word for two years, being a conscientious diplomat. The house I rented, as it turned out, had belonged to Gustave Doré, and it brought back all my yearnings for form and terror. Doré's illustrations for "Little Red Riding Hood" for example: they're so incredibly erotic! The little girl in bed with the wolf! Those were the signs under which my latest novel, *Distant Relations,* was born.

INTERVIEWER: Why did you find it impossible to write while you were ambassador?

FUENTES: Diplomacy in a sense is the opposite of writing. You have to disperse yourself so much: the lady who comes in crying because she's had a fight with the secretary; exports and imports; students in trouble; thumbtacks for the embassy. Writing requires the concentration of the writer, demands that nothing else be done except that. So I have all this pent-up energy which is flowing out right now. I'm writing a great deal these days. Besides, I have learned how to write. I didn't know how to write before and I guess I learned by being a bureaucrat. You have so much mental time on your hands when you are a bureaucrat: you have time to think and to learn how to write in your head. When I was a young man I suffered a great deal because I faced the challenge of Mallarmé's blank page every day without knowing exactly what I was going to say. I fought the page and paid for it with ulcers. I made up for it with sheer vigor, because you have vigor when you are writing in your twenties and thirties. Then later on you have to use your energy wisely. When I look back on it, I think perhaps it was the fact that I was behind an official desk for two years that left my mind free to write within itself, to prepare what I was going to write once I left that post. So now I can write before I sit down to write, I can use the blank page in a way I couldn't before.

INTERVIEWER: Tell us how the process of writing takes place within you.

FUENTES: I am a morning writer; I am writing at eight-thirty in longhand and I keep at it until twelve-thirty, when I go for a swim. Then I come back, have lunch, and read in the afternoon until I take my walk for the next day's writing. I must write the book out in my head now, before I sit down. I always follow a triangular pattern on my walks here in Princeton: I go to Einstein's house on Mercer Street, then down to Thomas Mann's house on Stockton Street, then over to Herman Broch's house on Evelyn Place. After visiting those three places, I return home, and by that time I have mentally written tomorrow's six or seven pages.

INTERVIEWER: You write in longhand?

FUENTES: First I write it out in longhand and then when I feel I "have" it, I let it rest. Then I correct the manuscript and type it out myself, correcting it until the last moment.

INTERVIEWER: Is the rewriting extensive or is most of the rewriting taken into account during the mental writing?

FUENTES: By the time I get it on paper, it is practically finished: there are no missed sections or scenes. I know basically how things are going and I have it more or less fixed, but at the same time I am sacrificing the element of surprise in myself. Everyone who writes a novel knows he is involved in the Proustian problem of in some way knowing what he is going to write and at the same time being amazed at what is actually coming out. Proust only wrote when he had lived what he was going to write, and yet he had to write as though he knew nothing about it—which is extraordinary. In a way we are all involved in the same adventure: to know what you are going to say, to have control over your material, and at the same time to have that margin of freedom which is discovery, amazement, and a precondition of the freedom of the reader.

INTERVIEWER: It's possible in England and the United States to write a history of editors and their influence on literature. Would such a history be possible in the Hispanic world?

FUENTES: Impossible, because the dignity of Spanish *hidalgos* would never allow a menial laborer to come and tell us what to do with our own work. It comes from the fact that we are caught in a terrible kind of schizophrenia made up of extreme pride, and extreme individualism which we inherited from Spain. The *hidalgo* expects everyone else to respect him, just as he kowtows to superior power. If you were to try to edit anyone's text in Latin America, even a hack, he would resign immediately, accusing you of censoring or insulting him.

INTERVIEWER: You would say then that your relationship to your society is rather different from that of an American writer? That, for example, the *hidalgo* image suggests the greater dignity of writing in your culture?

FUENTES: My situation as a Mexican writer is like that of writers from Eastern Europe. We have the privilege of speech in societies where it is rare to have that privilege. We speak for others, which is very important in Latin America, as it is in Central Europe. Of course you have to pay for that power: either you serve the community or you fall flat on your face.

INTERVIEWER: Does that mean that you see yourself as the official representative of your culture?

FUENTES: No, I hope not. Because I always remember that remark by the French surrealist Jacques Vaché, "Nothing kills a man as much as having to represent his country." So I hope it isn't true.

INTERVIEWER: Do you see a difference between the social roles of American and Latin American writers?

FUENTES: We have to do more things in our culture than American writers do in theirs. They can have more time for themselves and for their writing, whereas we have social demands. Pablo Neruda used to say that every Latin American writer goes around dragging a heavy body, the body of his people, of his past, of his national history. We have to assimilate the enormous weight of our past so we will not forget what gives us life. If you forget your past, you die. You fulfill certain functions for the collectivity because they are obligations you have as a citizen, not as a writer. Despite that, you reserve your esthetic freedom and your esthetic privileges. This creates a tension, but I think it is better to have the tension than to have no tension at all, as sometimes happens in the United States.

INTERVIEWER: In your earlier works you focus on the life of Mexico after the 1910–1920 Revolution. That is your Mexico and I can see you in those works as a Mexican writer. But after you became so popular internationally, say with *The Death of Artemio Cruz,* I wonder if your concept of your role changed.

FUENTES: No. I think all writers live off of obsessions. Some of these come from history, others are purely individual, and still others belong to the realm of the purely obsessive, which is the most universal thing a writer has in his soul. My obsessions are in all my books: they have to do with fear. All of my books are about fear— the universal sensation of fear about who might be coming through the door, about who desires me, whom do I desire and how can I achieve my desire. Is the object of my desire the subject of my desire in the mirror I am watching? These obsessions are in all my works along with the more general, historical context I deal with, but both in history and individuality, my theme is being incomplete because we fear the world and ourselves.

INTERVIEWER: You spoke of writing in your head while you were ambassador and continuing to do so now that you are writing again. I wonder if at some point—especially since you are away from your country and speaking a different language—writing first in your head and editing mentally has changed the nature of your writing.

FUENTES: You must understand that I am a peculiar case in Mexican literature because I grew up far from Mexico, because Mexico is an imaginary space for me, and has never ceased to be so, I might add. My Mexico and my Mexican history take place in my mind. Its history is something I have dreamed, imagined, and is not the actual history of the country. When as a young man I finally went to live in Mexico, of course I had to compare my dreams, my fears of that country with reality. This created a profound tension, the result of which was *Where the Air Is Clear,* a book nobody else could have written in Mexico. Nobody had written a novel about the post-Revolutionary era as it was reflected in the city, in the social structure, in the survival of so many ancient strands of our imaginary and historical life. This came, I say, out of my discovering Mexico with a sense of fear and enchantment when I was fifteen years old. Being outside of Mexico has always helped me enormously.

INTERVIEWER: Are you saying that seeing Mexico from both a physical and a mental distance enables you to see it more clearly than you could if you were there?

FUENTES: Yes, I have a perspective on Mexico which is renewed, you see, by surprise. Quevedo, the great Spanish baroque poet, expresses this when he says, "Nothing astonishes me because the world has bewitched me." I am still bewitched by Mexico. As you say, I live using a different language, but this helps me enormously with the Spanish language. I grew up with American English and yet I was able to maintain my Spanish. Spanish became something I had to maintain and re-create. When I am outside of Mexico, the same sensation of being alone with the language and wrestling with it becomes extremely powerful, whereas when I am in Mexico, it is immediately debased into asking for coffee, answering the phone, and whatnot. For me Spanish becomes an extraordinary experience when I am outside of Mexico. I feel I have to maintain it for myself. It becomes a very demanding fact of my life.

INTERVIEWER: Have you ever been tempted to write in English?

FUENTES: No, I very soon came to realize that the English language did not need one more writer. That the English language has an unbroken tradition of excellence and when it goes to sleep there is always an Irishman who appears and wakes it up.

INTERVIEWER: Knowing so many languages, which language do you dream in?

FUENTES: I dream in Spanish; I also make love in Spanish—this has created tremendous confusion at times, but I can only do it in Spanish. Insults in other languages don't mean a damn thing to me, but an insult in Spanish really sets me hopping. Let me tell you about a curious experience I had this summer. I was writing a novella about the adventures of Ambrose Bierce in Mexico. Bierce went to Mexico during the Revolution, in 1914, to join up with Pancho Villa's army. I had the problem that the voice had to be Bierce's, and it was extremely difficult to render in Spanish. I had to make Bierce speak with his voice, which is available to me in his stories, so I wrote the novella in English. It was an absolutely terrifying experience. I would be writing along in English when suddenly from under the table Mr. Faulkner would appear and say aah,

aah, can't do that, and from behind the door Mr. Melville would appear and say, can't do it, can't do it. All these ghosts appeared; the narrative tradition in English asserted itself so forcefully that it hamstrung me. I felt very sorry for my North American colleagues who have to write with all these people hanging from the chandeliers and rattling the dishes. You see, in Spanish we have to fill in the great void that exists between the seventeenth and the twentieth centuries. Writing is more of an adventure, more of a challenge. There is only a great desert between Cervantes and ourselves, if you except two nineteenth-century novelists, Clarín and Galdos.

INTERVIEWER: Is this one of the reasons for the epic surge in Latin American novels, this effort to encompass more social and historical perspectives in each work?

FUENTES: Well, I remember ten years ago I was talking to an American writer, Donald Barthelme, and he said, "How do you do it in Latin America? How do you manage to write these immense novels? Come up with all these subjects, these very, very long novels? Is there no paper shortage in Latin America? How do you do these things? We find we have great difficulty in the United States as American writers to find subjects. We write slim books, slimmer and slimmer books." But what I answered on that occasion is that our problem is that we feel we have everything to write about. That we have to fill four centuries of silence. That we have to give voice to all that has been silenced by history.

INTERVIEWER: You do feel that Latin American writers are trying to create a cultural identity for themselves?

FUENTES: Yes, and here I think we have a very strong link with the writers of Central and Eastern Europe. If you had asked me today where the novel is alive and kicking, I would say it's basically in Latin America and in so-called Eastern Europe which the Czechoslovaks insist on calling Central Europe. They think of Eastern Europe as Russia. In any case, there you have two cultural zones where people feel that things have to be said, and if the writer does not say them, nobody will say them. This creates a tremendous responsibility; it puts a tremendous weight on the writer, and also creates a certain confusion, because one could say, Oh, the mission is important, the theme is important, therefore the book has to be good, and that is not always the case. How many novels have you read in Latin America that are full of good intentions— denouncing the plight of the Bolivian miner, of the Ecuadorian banana picker—and turn out to be terrible novels which do nothing for the Bolivian tin miner or the Ecuadorian banana picker, or anything for literature either... failing on all fronts because they have nothing but good intentions.

But still, we had a whole past to talk about. A past that was silent, that was dead, and that you had to bring alive through language. And so for me writing was basically this need to establish an identity, to establish a link to my country and to a language which I— along with many other writers of my generation—felt we in some way had to slap around, and wake up, as if we were playing the game of Sleeping Beauty.

INTERVIEWER: Can it be said, though, that you are speaking for several generations of Spanish and Latin American writers who have a double culture, who have one foot in their local culture and the other in an external, Western culture?

FUENTES: One of the basic cultural factors of Latin America is that it is an eccentric branch of the culture of the West. It is Western and it is not Western. So we feel that we have to know the culture of the West even better than a Frenchman or an Englishman, and at the same time we have to know our own culture. This sometimes means going back to the Indian cultures, whereas the Europeans feel they don't have to know our cultures at all. We have to know Quetzalcoatl *and* Descartes. They think Descartes is enough. So Latin America is a constant reminder to Europe of the duties of its universality. Therefore, a writer like Borges is a typically Latin American writer. The fact that he is so European only indicates that he is Argentine. No European would feel obliged to go to the extremes Borges does to create a reality, not to mirror a reality but to create a new reality to fill in the cultural voids of his own tradition.

INTERVIEWER: Which writers are missing from the evolution of fiction in Spanish? You mentioned Faulkner and Melville, and I could easily imagine Balzac and Dickens.

FUENTES: They are all present because we have appropriated them. Your question is important because it emphasizes the fact that Latin American writers have to appropriate the writers of other traditions in order to fill a void. Sometimes, to our astonishment, we discover an extraordinary sense of coincidence. A lot of fuss has been made about the great influence of Joyce and Faulkner on the Latin American novel. Well, two things have to be said: First, the poets of the Spanish language in the earlier part of this century coincide with the great poets of the English language. Neruda is writing at the same time as Eliot, but Neruda is writing in a rain-drenched town in southern Chile where there are no libraries. Nevertheless, he is on the same wavelength as Eliot. It is the poets who have maintained the language for us novelists: without the poets, without Neruda, Vallejo, Paz, Huidobro, or Gabriela Mistral, there would be no Latin American novel. Second, the great modern novelists of Europe and the United States have revolutionized the sense of time in the Western novel as it had been conceived since the eighteenth century, since Defoe, Richardson, and Smollett. This breaking up of time, this refusal to accept the singular concept of linear time which the West had been imposing economically and politically, coincides profoundly with our sense of circular time, which comes from the Indian religions. Our idea of time as a spiral, our basic historical vision, is derived both from Vico and from our everyday experience of times that coexist. You have the Iron Age in the mountains and the twentieth century in our cities. This recognition that time is not linear is particularly strong in Faulkner because he is a baroque writer and because he shares the Baroque with Latin America. He is probably the only Western novelist in the twentieth century who has the same sense of defeat and loss that we have.

INTERVIEWER: But Faulkner is also re-creating a post-agrarian culture.

FUENTES: The passage from an agrarian culture to a post-agrarian culture is our own situation, but more than anything Faulkner is a writer of defeat. He is the one American writer who says "We are not only a success story; we are also the history of defeats," and this he shares with us. Latin America is made up of historically and politically failed societies, and this failure has created a subterranean language—since the Conquest. The Baroque in Latin America was the response of the New World to the Old World: it took a form of European culture, the Baroque, and transformed it into a hiding place for Indian culture, for Black culture, for the great syncretism which is the culture of Spanish and Portuguese America. We insert ourselves into that tradition when we write today.

INTERVIEWER: This burden of the past we mentioned earlier is extremely important, isn't it? It creates a heavy load that every Latin American writer has to bear. It also deforms language because every word resounds into the past as well as into the future.

FUENTES: I think it was Allen Tate who disparagingly referred to Faulkner as a Dixie Gongorist, which I think is really the highest praise because it links Faulkner to this culture of the incomplete, of the voracious, of the intertextual which is the Baroque. There is a culture of the Caribbean, I would say, that includes Faulkner, Carpentier, García Márquez, Derek Walcott, and Aimé Césaire, a trilingual culture in and around the whirlpool of the Baroque which is the Caribbean, the Gulf of Mexico. Think of Jean Rhys's *Wide Sargasso Sea*.

INTERVIEWER: Did you get this sense of cultural perspective as you were growing up or as you were writing?

FUENTES: As I was growing up. Let me explain: a few years ago, a friend of mine, Tito Gerasi, got permission from Jean-Paul Sartre to write his biography. He said, "I have a great idea; I'm going to ask Sartre to write down the books he read as a child, and from there I'll see what his intellectual formation was." Later Gerasi came back to me and said, "What are these books? I've never heard of them." The books Sartre had read as a child were the books we read in the Latin world, which I read as a child: Emilio Salgari, without whom there would be no Italian, French, Spanish, or Latin American literature. Also Michel Zévaco. These authors are part of our tradition but are not part of the Anglo-Saxon tradition. I was lucky because I had both: I read Salgari and Zévaco as well as Mark Twain and Robert Louis Stevenson. Ed Doctorow told me that he became a writer because he read Sabatini, the author of *Captain Blood*. You're invited into such a marvelous world in those books! You are sailing towards that island on a wonderful Spanish galleon! I never want to get off; I want to spend the rest of my life looking for Treasure Island.

INTERVIEWER: But I was wondering if as you grew up you had a sense of somehow representing your culture to other cultures.

FUENTES: I did. Let me tell you another anecdote. I was a Mexican child growing up in Washington in the thirties. I went to public school, I was popular, as you must be to be happy in an American school, until the Mexican government expropriated foreign-owned oil holdings on March 18, 1938. I became a leper in my school, nobody would talk to me, everyone turned their backs on me because there were screaming headlines every day talking about Mexican communists stealing "our" oil wells. So I became a terrible Mexican chauvinist as a reaction. I remember going to see a Richard Dix film at the Keith Theater in Washington in 1939, a film in which Dix played Sam Houston. When the Alamo came around, I jumped up in my seat shouting "Death to the gringos! *¡Viva México!*" When the war started, Franklin Roosevelt organized a meeting in December of 1939 of children from all over the world to speak for peace. I was chosen to represent Mexico and I was dressed as a little Mexican *charro* with a big sombrero and I went and made my speech for peace in the name of Mexico.

INTERVIEWER: I asked you about it because you have an objective vision of what Mexico is and at the same time you seem to feel that Mexico is within you.

FUENTES: I am grateful for my sense of detachment because I can say things about my country other people don't say. I offer Mexicans a mirror in which they can see how they look, how they talk, how they act, in a country which is a masked country. Of course, I realize that my writings are my masks as well, verbal masks I offer my country as mirrors. Mexico is defined in the legend of Quetzalcoatl, the Plumed Serpent, the god who creates man and is destroyed by a demon who offers him a mirror. The demon shows him he has a face when he thought he had no face. This is the essence of Mexico: to discover you have a face when you thought you only had a mask.

INTERVIEWER: Is Stendhal's image of the novel as a mirror moving along a highway ironic for you?

FUENTES: It poses a problem because I don't think literature can content itself with being either a mask or a mirror of reality. I think literature creates reality or it is not literature at all. You have to write "*La marquise sortit à cinq heures,*" to copy the banal details of life, but this is not enough. The mirror is also a way to augment reality; it augments reality or it does nothing.

INTERVIEWER: We seem to have interpolated Alice's mirror here. There is the mirror in which we see ourselves, the mirror we present to others, and the mirror we pass through. But as you grow up this third mirror is frightening.

FUENTES: It is a neurotic mirror. It's related to desire and to holes. The baroque poet Quevedo is very close to me in my conception of literature as a mirror. For Quevedo the purity of the mirror and the impurity of the asshole are invariably linked. After all, in Spanish, mirror is *espejo*, a *speculum* which contains the word *culo*—asshole. It's the center of the world for Quevedo, the pleasure hole through which you receive and expel desire. So Quevedo can sing of the purity of the reflection in the mirror. I always have him with me in a painting by Cuevas in which he is holding up a mirror saying "look at yourself in this mirror." It's as though the mirror were the mind and the mouth and the eyes which will finally expel reality through the *culo*, the *speculum*. I've always thought this way when thinking about the mirror: the mirror and the latrine are inseparable.

INTERVIEWER: How does the germ of the text take root in your imagination? Where does the subject matter of your work begin?

FUENTES: I think my books are derived from city images, and the city of my dreams or nightmares is Mexico City. Paris or New York just do not stimulate my writing. Many of my stories are based on things I have seen there. The story "The Doll Queen" in *Burnt Water*, for example, is something I saw every afternoon when I was in my teens. There was an apartment house: on the first floor you could see through the windows, and everything was normal. Then at night it was transformed into an extraordinary place full of dolls and flowers, dead flowers and a doll or a girl lying on a bier. I am a city writer and I cannot understand literature outside the city. For me it is Mexico City and its masks and mirrors, the twitchy little images I see when I look at the base of this totem-city, in the mud of the city—the city a space where people move, meet, and change.

INTERVIEWER: I don't mean to ask you a reductive question, but what hooks you, what makes you start writing?

FUENTES: That wonderful thing Hamlet says about "a fiction, a dream of passion." My fiction is a dream of passion, born of a cry that says "I am incomplete. I want to be complete, to be enclosed. I want to add something." So *Artemio Cruz*, for example, is a novel of voices. I think literature is born from a voice: you discover a voice and you want to give it a body of paper, but it is the voice that will be the reality of the novel.

INTERVIEWER: You heard Artemio Cruz's voice?

FUENTES: Yes, it was his voice that said, "I am dying in this present. I am a body and I am losing my existence. It is draining out of me." He had a past and was going to die and his memory was going to die. And another voice, the collective voice said, "We will outlive this individual and we will project a world of words with language and memory which will go on." But it was simply a question of many voices meeting in a literary space and demanding their incarnation.

INTERVIEWER: *Aura*, published in the same year, seems so different from *Artemio Cruz*, so experimental.

FUENTES: *Aura* is written in the second person singular, the voice poets have always used and that novelists also have a right to use. It's a voice that admits it doesn't know everything, and after all you are a novelist because you don't know everything. Unlike the epic poet who does know everything. Homer knows exactly how doors close and, as Auerbach says, closing a door in Homer takes four verses and the death of Hector takes four verses because they are equally important. But this poetic voice says that we are not alone, that something else accompanies us. In writing *Aura*, I was consciously using a particular tradition and without tradition there can be no creation. *Aura* came to me from a great Japanese film, *Ugetsu*. In it, a man goes to war just after he marries a young courtesan, who becomes the purest of wives. When he comes back, he finds she has committed suicide. The town had been taken by some soldiers and in order to avoid rape she killed herself. He goes to her grave and finds her beautiful body perfectly preserved. The only way he can recover her is through an old crone who captures the girl's voice and speaks to him. This is an extraordinary tradition: the old woman with magic powers. Here I insert myself into a tradition that goes back to Faulkner, to Henry James, to Miss Havisham in Dickens, to the countess in Pushkin's *Queen of Spades*, and back to the White Goddess. I'm very much in agreement with Virginia Woolf when she says that when you sit down to write, you must feel the whole of your tradition in your bones, all the way back to Homer.

INTERVIEWER: You also gave voice in *Aura* to a subject not often discussed, Napoleon III's intervention in Mexico, Maximilian and Carlota.

FUENTES: I am obsessed with Carlota: she is one of my ghosts. But my country is a land where the life of death is very important as is the death of life. It is curious that I wrote *Artemio Cruz* and *Aura* at the same time. They complement each other in that *Artemio Cruz* is about the death of life and *Aura* is about the life of death.

INTERVIEWER: The witch in *Aura* is a specific type of woman. What other female images appear in your work?

FUENTES: I've been attacked for depicting very impure women, but this is because of the negative vision my culture has had of women. A culture that combines Arabs, Spaniards, and Aztecs is not very healthy for feminism. Among the Aztecs, for example, the male gods all represent a single thing: wind, water, war, while the goddesses are ambivalent, representing purity and filth, day and night, love and hate. They constantly move from one extreme to another, from one passion to another, and this is their sin in the Aztec world. There is a pattern of female ambiguity in my novels.

INTERVIEWER: In this idea of an image of woman created by men, you automatically conjure up movie actresses, and this reminds me of Claudia Nervo in *Holy Place*.

FUENTES: Oh, of course. She would be the supreme example. But last summer I wrote a play about two women, two great symbols of the face in Mexico, María Félix and Dolores del Río. It is called *Orchids in the Moonlight*, from the camp tango in the old Hollywood musical *Flying Down to Rio*. The two women think they are María Félix and Dolores del Río and behave as such, and you might well assume that they are the actresses in exile in Venice until you discover that it is Venice, California, that the women are two *chicanas*, and that nothing is what it seems. But the real faces of the actresses are there, projected on the stage, those incredible faces never aging, because as Diego Rivera once said to them, "Skulls as beautiful as yours never grow old."

INTERVIEWER: In *Holy Place* you deal with the impact of the female on the male: the protagonist, Mito, seems to lose his identity in the presence of his mother. Like Carlota or the witch, she seems to be an extreme feminine type.

FUENTES: No, because I don't think Claudia Nervo is an extreme. On the contrary, it is Mexican men who make an extreme of her. She is only defending herself. She is a central figure and the men won't allow women to be central figures; they are banished to the extremes because Mexico is a country where women are condemned to be whores or nuns. A woman is either la Malinche, the Indian who helped Cortés and betrayed her race, or Sor Juana Inés de la Cruz, the nun who divests herself of her voice and her personality, under pressure from religious and political authority. Nowadays in Mexico women are saying they are neither whores nor nuns but many things. They are usurping a role that men have reserved for themselves. Things are changing.

INTERVIEWER: You have seen Mexico undergo a tremendous change, from the Mexico that nationalized the oil fields in 1938 to Mexico today. I assume the society has crumbled the way it has here, that the entire value structure has been transformed. I was wondering how that historical reality enters your very mythical vision of the culture.

FUENTES: In Mexico all these changing realities only point up the fact that there is a tradition, that myths are a tradition, that myths breathe, and that they nourish the epics, the tragedies, and even the melodramas of our contemporary life. Because the society is crumbling, we are in a terrible situation of stock-taking. Mexico, all of Latin America in fact, has been fooled by the illusion of progress. If only we could imitate the United States, France, and Great Britain we could become rich, prosperous, and stable. This has not happened. Suddenly we are in 1980 and we know that in your world too, progress has become an illusion, so now we must look back on our tradition, which is all we really have. Our political life is fragmented, our history shot through with failure, but our cultural tradition is rich, and I think the time is coming when we will have to look at our own faces, our own past—look into this mirror we have been talking about.

INTERVIEWER: Has Mexican culture fallen the way it has in New York, where money is the only index of worth? Has materialism leveled Mexican society?

FUENTES: No. Your culture has no past; it lives only in the present. Mexico is a culture with many coexisting times. We have a horrible bourgeoisie in Mexico, much worse than yours, a know-nothing bourgeoisie proud of being ignorant. But we also have the majority of the people who have the spiritual value of religion. Ah yes, now it appears that religion, which we have attacked so much in the past, is a cultural value that exists in the depths of Mexico. I mean the sense of the sacred, not Catholic values, the sense that the rabbit can be sacred, that everything can be sacred. If you go to the land of the Tarahumaras you see they don't care a hoot about material things. They care about reenacting the origins, being present at the origins all over again. They find their health in the past, not in the future.

INTERVIEWER: But as you have already shown in your spy novel *The Hydra Head,* Mexico with its vast oil reserves is going to be thrown into the center of things.

FUENTES: Yes. Oil is going to affect the society. I am writing a novel, *Cristóbal Nonato,* that takes place on October 12, 1992, the five hundredth anniversary of the discovery of the New World. I'm wondering what Mexico City and the country will be like then, when we take stock of having been discovered by Europeans five centuries ago.

INTERVIEWER: What is your projection? Don't tell all your secrets, just give us an idea.

FUENTES: Oh, it's a gloomy projection. This is not a science fiction novel: there are no gadgets. The story is told by an unborn child and it is what he hears that creates his impression of the world into which he is going to be thrown. The life of Mexico City will almost have been destroyed because you can't have a city of thirty million people with all its physical problems—being high up in the sky, cold, surrounded by mountains that keep the smog down, with water having to be brought from far away, and sewage having to be pumped out. The city will drown in shit; that's what will happen to Mexico.

INTERVIEWER: I can't help thinking of *Terra Nostra:* that novel also takes place in the future, between June and December of 1999. Of course, in that novel your primary concern is the past and your scope is vast.

FUENTES: This is a much more comical novel. Its scope is much more concentrated. The very fact that the narrator is inside his mother's womb limits its possibilities drastically. The information he receives is limited—what he hears and what his genes tell him. I am not trying to do anything like *Terra Nostra,* which is an excursion into Mediterranean culture, into all the worlds we come from, and into the creation of power in our society.

INTERVIEWER: Now that you have given us a glimpse of *Cristóbal Nonato* I wonder if you would mind talking about a text I know of only by hearsay, a book you wrote as a boy in Chile after you left Washington in 1941. Do you remember that book?

FUENTES: I remember it very well. I have always been trapped in a way by English because of living in Washington, so when we moved to Chile I found myself recovering Spanish. That was when I was eleven. Chile at that moment was the country of the great poets—Gabriela Mistral and Pablo Neruda in particular. It was also the most politicized country in Latin America. I ended up, of course, in a British school because the British schools in Chile and Argentina were the best. I was promptly dressed up in a blazer, a school tie, and a little grey cap. We did calisthenics at seven A.M. alongside the Andes, got caned, and celebrated allied victories: every time Montgomery won a battle, we had to throw our caps in the air and shout hip, hip, hurrah. There were many budding writers in the school, The Grange it was called: Luis Alberto Heyremans, a playwright now deceased, and both José Donoso and Jorge Edwards, novelists. One of my best friends, who has now become a great Kant scholar, was Roberto Torretti: he and I wrote that novel together. We had many problems because there we were, a Mexican and a Chilean writing a novel that started in Marseilles. Novels had to start in Marseilles because that was where the Count of Monte Cristo made his appearance. Where else could a ship set sail from if not Marseilles with the Château d'If out ahead? The problem, which Dumas did not have, was how to make the people talk: would it be in Mexican or Chilean? We compromised and made them speak like Andalusians. From Marseilles, the novel moved on to Haiti: we had read *Jane Eyre* and were very impressed by mad women in attics. We included a gloomy castle on top of a mountain, Sans Souci—all of this before Alejo Carpentier had written his novel about Haiti, *The Kingdom of This World.* The novel took place there in those gloomy surroundings with mad women chained to their beds and young masters making love to mulatto girls. It went on for about four hundred pages.

INTERVIEWER: Did anyone ever read this Gothic tome?

FUENTES: Not exactly. I read it out loud to David Alfaro Siqueiros the muralist. He was my victim. He had to flee Mexico because he was involved in an assassination attempt on the life of Trotsky. He went to Chile and was painting a bombastic mural in a small town, Chillán, to which Mexico had donated a school after an earthquake had destroyed the local school. My father was chargé d'affaires, and since Siqueiros was not making much money, and depended some-what on the Embassy, we invited him over quite often. He was a charming man, so after dinner I told him to sit down and listen to my novel. He had no way out. He dozed off, of course, and had a good siesta.

INTERVIEWER: So you combined the English Gothic novel, Dumas, and Salgari?

FUENTES: Yes. It was very dramatic, not at all picturesque. We thought it very gloomy and Brontë-like. We were greatly influ-enced by Charlotte and Emily Brontë, as was everyone in our group in Chile. Branwell Brontë was the height of decadence for us. You had to be like the Brontës to be good artists.

INTERVIEWER: Those puritans were the height of decadence?

FUENTES: Well, we thought so—the Moors, the hints of incest. Imagine how the Brontës are seen by thirteen-year-olds in Chile in 1942.

INTERVIEWER: Did you write a great deal before publishing?

FUENTES: Yes. When I moved back to Mexico City I was put into a Catholic school—for the first time in my life. We had left Chile and moved to Buenos Aires, but I couldn't stand the schools there—it was the beginning of the Perón period and the fascist influence on education was intolerable. So I demanded to go to Mexico. Alas, when I got there I was put in a Catholic school. The school made me into a writer because it taught me about sin, that everything you did was sinful. So, many things could be sins and therefore became so pleasurable that they set me to writing. If things were forbidden, one had to write them, and things are pleasurable if they are forbidden.

INTERVIEWER: Has the idea of sin as a stimulus to writing stayed with you?

FUENTES: Yes. I suppose I started to write *Terra Nostra* in that Catholic school in Mexico City. St. John Chrysostom says that purely spiritual love between a man and a woman should be condemned because their appetites grow so much and lust accumulates. This is an essential point in *Terra Nostra*, where people can never meet in the flesh and have others do the actual fornication for them. I learned a lot in Catholic school.

INTERVIEWER: What brand of Catholicism did you have in Mexico City?

FUENTES: It was a very political Catholicism totally allied to the conservative interpretation of Mexican history. There was a teacher there who would arrive with a calla lily at the beginning of each school year. He would say, "This is a pure Catholic youth before he goes to a dance." Then he would throw the lily on the floor and trample it. After, he would pick up the rag of a lily and say, "This is a Catholic after he goes to a dance and kisses a girl." Then he would throw the flower into the waste basket. They rewrote Mexican history in favor of Maximilian, in favor of Porfirio Díaz, the dictator who precipitated the Revolution, and all images of law and order. I was thrown out of school for a month because I dared to celebrate the birthday of Benito Juárez, the Indian who became president of Mexico, an image of liberalism in our country.

INTERVIEWER: We see how you began to write: how did you decide *what* to write at the beginning of your professional career?

FUENTES: I decided I had to write the novel of the Mexico I was living. The Mexican novel was locked into certain genres: there were Indian novels, novels of the Revolution, and proletarian novels. For me those were like medieval walls constraining the possibilities of Mexican fiction. The Mexico City I was living in belied those restraints because it was like a medieval city that had suddenly lost its walls and drawbridges and sprawled outside itself in a kind of carnival. You had European nobility stranded in Mexico because of the war, an up-and-coming bourgeoisie, unbelievable bordellos lit up in neon near the fish markets where the smell of the women and the smell of the fish mingled. The writer Salvador Elizondo would go there and slit the prostitutes' armpits while he made love to them so he could make love in a gush of blood. Then mariachi music all night long. Mexico City found in the late forties and fifties its baroque essence, a breaking down of barriers, an overflow. I remember dancing the mambo in astounding cabarets and that was the origin of *Where the Air Is Clear:* Mexico City as the protagonist of post-Revolutionary life in Mexico. I felt that nothing had been said about that in a novel.

INTERVIEWER: Were there any other writers or artists in your family?

FUENTES: Not particularly: my father was a diplomat, my mother a housewife. My father's brother was an interesting poet, but he died of typhoid at twenty. My great-aunt was a sort of Grandma

Moses for poetry in Vera Cruz. She wrote about the tropics, the lakes, and the sea, and was quite well known.

INTERVIEWER: Were there any myths about either your uncle or your great-aunt that might have created a literary prototype for you?

FUENTES: The only myth was a great-grandmother, Clotilde Vélez de Fuentes. She had her fingers cut off by bandits when she was on the stagecoach between Vera Cruz and Mexico City. She wouldn't take off her rings so they chopped off her fingers. She's the only myth I can remember.

INTERVIEWER: How did your family react to your becoming a writer, to your earning a living by writing?

FUENTES: Well, my parents told me to study law because they said I would die of hunger if I tried to live off my writing in Mexico. I also visited the great poet and humanist Alfonso Reyes and he reminded me that Mexico is a very formalistic country and that if I had no title people wouldn't know how to deal with me. "You'll be like a teacup without a handle," he said. I wasn't unhappy about studying law once I began. First, I went to Geneva, my first trip to Europe, where I learned discipline. Back in Mexico I was able to study with great teachers who had fled Spain during the Spanish Civil War. The former dean of the University of Seville, Manuel Pedroso, told me that if I wanted to understand criminal law I should read *Crime and Punishment* and that if I wanted to understand mercantile law I should read Balzac, and forget the dreary statutes. He was right, so I immediately found a conjuncture between the social and narrative dimensions of my life. I might have become a corporate lawyer, but I wrote *Where the Air Is Clear* instead. What energy I had then: I wrote that novel in four years while finishing law school, working at the University of Mexico, getting drunk every night, and dancing the mambo. Fantastic. No more. You lose energy and you gain technique.

INTERVIEWER: Your second novel quickly followed the first.

FUENTES: My second was actually my first. I was already writing *The Good Conscience,* a more traditional book, when it was washed away in the flood of *Where the Air Is Clear.* That novel was more than a book for me: it was my life. It made a big splash: it was praised to heaven and damned to hell. One critic said it was only fit to be flushed down the toilet. Now I find to my chagrin that it is required reading for fifteen-year-old girls in the Convent of the Sacred Heart in Mexico City.

INTERVIEWER: So we have the creation of a world which takes on its own shape, a kind of Faulknerian or Balzacian world. Is it still alive?

FUENTES: I've never left it. In the preface I wrote for *Burnt Water,* I mention an imaginary apartment house in Mexico City: Artemio Cruz lives in splendor in the penthouse and Aura the witch lives in the basement. Somewhere in between I have all my other characters. I think I have always been caught in the tension of illusory realism because the realism of these novels is illusory. I hope I am a decent reader of Cervantes, and he, after all, inaugurated realism by casting doubt on reality. This illusory realism is one pole of my writing and the other pole is the fantastic dimension which is extremely real because it takes place in the mind. People think of Balzac merely as a realistic social writer, they forget his fantastic novels. So the lesson of Balzac is deeper for me than appearances would suggest.

INTERVIEWER: You are very much aware of the continuity of your writing.

FUENTES: In a sense my novels are one book with many chapters: *Where the Air Is Clear* is the biography of Mexico City; *The Death of Artemio Cruz* deals with an individual in that city; *A Change of Skin* is that city, that society, facing the world, coming to grips with the fact that it is part of civilization and that there is a world outside that intrudes into Mexico. There is a collective psyche in these books which is negated and individualized. But no character speaks alone because there is the sense, I hope, that there is a ghost on every page, with every character. All of this culminates in *Distant Relations,* a ghost story about the ghost of literature, about this world as a creation of fiction, a dangerous fiction you are afraid to hand over to the reader. *Distant Relations* is the novel I care most for. It says the most about me as a writer and my interests in literature. It is about writing, the only novel I have ever written about writing.

INTERVIEWER: It hasn't come out in English yet; could you tell us about it?

FUENTES: It is a story told by one character to another who in turn tells it to me, Fuentes. I will not be satisfied until the story is completely told. I must know the whole story, but once I have it I must pass it on to you readers like a gift from the devil. As the title suggests, it is a story about distant relations, about a family in the New World and the Old World whose whole story cannot be told because no text could contain the whole story. It also deals with the influence of France on the Caribbean nations, the ghosts of French writers who came from Latin America, like Lautréamont or Heredia. The novel deals with the origins of fiction, how no story can ever be fully told, how no text can ever be fully exhausted.

INTERVIEWER: Both *Terra Nostra* and *Distant Relations* deal with origins: the first maps out the Mediterranean and Spanish sources of Spanish-American culture and the second describes the origin of the literary text, your vain attempt to absorb and express a total history. This desire we see in both novels for a totality of one kind or another reflects one of the common concerns of the novelists of the so-called boom of the Latin American novel during the sixties. How do you understand this "boom"?

FUENTES: I would say with García Márquez that we are writing one novel in Latin America, with a Colombian chapter written by García Márquez, a Cuban chapter written by Carpentier, an Argentine chapter by Julio Cortázar and so on. We live in a continent where the novel is a recent development, where many things have been left unsaid. It is difficult to speak of individuals because a fusion has taken place: characters from *Artemio Cruz* appear in *One Hundred Years of Solitude*, while in *Terra Nostra* there are characters from *One Hundred Years of Solitude*, from Carpentier's *Explosion in a Cathedral*, Cabrera Infante's *Three Trapped Tigers*, and Cortázar's *Hopscotch*. There is a constant intertextuality which is indicative of the nature of writing in Latin America.

INTERVIEWER: So you never felt isolated as a Mexican writer, or that your work was for Mexicans only?

FUENTES: I think I was conscious from the very beginning of my career that it was ridiculous to speak of Mexican literature or Peruvian literature, or Chilean literature, that if we were to have any meaning, any universality, it would have to be within the wider range of this tattered, mendicant language we call Spanish.

INTERVIEWER: Some Spanish-American writers have suggested that it was only during the sixties that they could imagine a readership that extended from Mexico City to Buenos Aires.

FUENTES: This was not the case for me. I founded and directed a lively magazine in the fifties called *Revista mexicana de literatura*, and in 1955, we were publishing Julio Cortázar's early short stories, Cuban poets like Cintio Vitier and José Lezama Lima, even a short story coauthored by Jorge Luis Borges and Adolfo Bioy Casares. By the mid-fifties I felt the traditional barriers had been broken down. The readership was developing at the same time so that there was an intellectual and even a material underpinning for the boom when it appeared. There were publishing houses, distributors, and the authors' knowledge that we belonged to the same linguistic community.

INTERVIEWER: Why were the sixties so favorable to a communal spirit among the writers?

FUENTES: The Cuban Revolution certainly provided a meeting place. Such fervor and hope were raised by the Cuban Revolution! Havana became a focal point until the Cubans developed their tropical socialist realism and began to excommunicate people. Ultimately they destroyed the possibility of a community, but the Cuban Revolution played a fundamental role in creating a sense of unity. I was there when Castro came into Havana. That was a galvanizing moment in our lives, and retrospectively it still is. An extraordinary thing happened then in the history of Spanish-American literature: everybody prominent in the Boom was a friend of everybody else. Now this has sadly ended. Now that we enter middle age the friendship has broken, and people have become enemies for personal or political reasons. We look back with nostalgia.

INTERVIEWER: Your personal vision of the boom reminds me of the paucity of biographical and autobiographical materials in the Hispanic world. Only now are we beginning to see writers describing their relation to historical events in Latin America. There are texts like José Donoso's *Personal History of the Boom,* but there is no tradition of memoirs or autobiographies.

FUENTES: I'll tell you why: there is a fear of what is written because it compromises you. I remember arriving at the Mexican embassy in Paris and asking for some information left, I thought, by one of my predecessors. I was interested in his ideas about French politics: it turned out that he never wrote anything because some day it might be used against him.

INTERVIEWER: You have mentioned the influence of *Citizen Kane* on *Artemio Cruz*. Have films been important to your writing?

FUENTES: I'm a great moviegoer. The greatest day in my life as a child was when my father took me to New York City to see the World's Fair and *Citizen Kane*, when I was ten years old. And that struck me in the middle of my imagination and never left me. Since that moment, I've always lived with the ghost of *Citizen Kane*. There are a few other great movies which I am conscious of when I write. Buñuel's work would be another. Von Stroheim would be another one, especially the great version of *The Merry Widow* he did as a silent film, without the waltzes. Great scenes of love between John Gilbert and Mae Murray, in beds of black sheets, and beautiful women playing the flute and tambourine around them with their eyes blindfolded. And finally when the love comes to a climax, they pull the curtains of the little bed, so they are totally isolated from sight; we are there seeing the absence of sight—a series of reflections unseen and imagined, which I found very powerful. But beyond that I don't view it as an influence.

I think the comedians have influenced everybody, the Marx Brothers are among the greatest artists of the twentieth century. The greatest anarchists and revolutionaries, and destroyers of property. The people who make the world shriek and explode with laughter and absurdity. I think they have influenced practically everybody. Keaton and Chaplin. But then literature is another thing. It's a verbal process which is very different from the film, very, very different.

INTERVIEWER: Then you don't feel that film will usurp the novel?

FUENTES: I was talking a few months ago in Mexico with one of the great filmmakers of our time, Luis Buñuel. He was eighty years old, and I was asking how he looked back on his career and on the destiny of the film. He said, "I think films are perishable, because they depend too much on technology, which advances too quickly and the films become old-fashioned, antiques. What I hope for is that technology advances to the point that films in the future will depend on a little pill which you take; then you sit in the dark, and from your eyes you project the film you want to see on a blank wall."

INTERVIEWER: Somebody would come along and close your eyes.

FUENTES: Yes, there will be censors. But the film would be projected inside your head, then. They'd have to kill you. It would be the final proof of artistic freedom.

INTERVIEWER: What do you do to promote your own work? Do you submit to talk shows?

FUENTES: Perhaps each nation has the Siberia it deserves. In the Soviet Union a writer who is critical, as we know, is taken to a lunatic asylum. In the United States, he's taken to a talk show. There they have to deal with the KGB; here they have to deal with Johnny Carson, which is much more withering, I suspect. Philip Roth has said, in comparing his situation to that of Milan Kundera, the Czech writer, that in the United States, everything goes and nothing is important. In Czechoslovakia, nothing goes and everything is important. So this gives the writer an added dimension he doesn't have here.

I was in Paris last year. A book of mine was being launched and they said that I had to go on television. I didn't want to. They said no, no, it sells a lot of books—the program, called *Apostrophes,* is very popular; it's seen by about thirty million people in France. I said, "Okay, let's go and see what happens." It was a terrifying experience because there was a petulant Frenchman who kept cutting me off, so I couldn't express my ideas. He wanted things to go very quickly, and I couldn't say anything. I was very unhappy at what had happened and with what I had said. I went back with Sylvia, my wife, to the apartment. The concierge was waiting up for us and she said, "Ah, I just turned off the television. How wonderful. It was magnificent, marvelous." I said, "No, it was terrible. It was awful. I didn't like the things I said." And she said, "But Mr. Fuentes, I didn't hear anything you said. I saw you. *I saw you.*" People who are glued to the television are really in the deepest recess of their soul, hoping to see themselves, because this will be the apotheosis of their identity. Walter Benjamin says a very good thing about the real revolution of the nineteenth century being the invention of photography. All throughout history, people had been faceless, and suddenly people had a face. The first photographs were kept in jewel boxes lined with velvet because they were precious. They were your identity. Now suddenly you have this possibility of being seen by thirty, forty, fifty million people. You have an identity. You exist. You are someone. No matter how fleetingly, no matter how briefly. Talk about the end of feudalism. There it is. The end of feudalism happens in front of your TV.

INTERVIEWER: Have you ever contemplated writing your memoirs?

FUENTES: Oh yes. I want to do that very much when the time comes and I keep lots of interesting notes. I think that in Mexico and Latin America it is a good idea to start thinking of the genre of the memoir, of leaving something, of creating in that genre. My generation has done a great deal to create a narrative tradition and we probably have time to create a memoir tradition. After all, it has existed in the past, in Cortés's letters and in Bernal Díaz del Castillo's personal history of the conquest of Mexico. And now I see this promise in Guillermo Cabrera Infante's book of boyhood in Havana.

INTERVIEWER: Do you think you will continue to write at the same rate you have been?

FUENTES: Well, it has become physically easier for me to write. Time passes and the past becomes the present. What you were living and thought you had lost forever is ancillary to your work. Then suddenly it acquires a shape, it exists in an order of time all its own and this order of time demands a literary form. So then these presences of the past are there in the center of your life today. You thought they were unimportant or that they had died, but they have just been looking for their chance. If you try to force a theme when you are twenty-five and have lived less, you find you can't do a thing with it. Suddenly it offers itself gratuitously. At fifty I find there is a long line of characters and shapes demanding words just outside my window. I wish I could capture all of them, but I won't have enough time. The process of selection is terrifying because in selecting you necessarily kill something.

INTERVIEWER: This is a fantastic image, a double apprenticeship: an initial phase of writing being itself a gestation period followed now by a period of painful plenitude.

FUENTES: When your life is half over, I think you have to see the face of death in order to start writing seriously. There are people who see the end quickly, like Rimbaud. When you start seeing it, you feel you have to rescue these things. Death is the great Maecenas, Death is the great angel of writing. You must write because you are not going to live any more.

—*Alfred MacAdam*
*Charles Ruas*

# Guillermo Cabrera Infante

© Jerry Bauer

Guillermo Cabrera Infante was born on April 22, 1929, in Gibara, a small town along the northern coast of Cuba—also the birthplace of Fulgencio Batista and Fidel Castro. From a young age he was exposed to radical politics; his parents founded the local chapter of the Communist party and his family was persecuted throughout the 1930s. In 1941, Cabrera Infante attended the University of Havana, and he was thrown in jail briefly for using obscenities in the literary journal *Bohemia;* thereafter he adopted the pseudonym G. Cain. He began his career writing film reviews, and went on to develop a collection of short stories in 1960 titled *Así en la paz como en la guerra* [As in Peace, So in War].

After working briefly for the Bureau of Cultural Affairs under Castro's new regime and serving as director of the literary journal

*Lunes de Revolución,* Cabrera Infante's revolutionary fervor waned. He left Cuba for Belgium in 1965, never to return. During the sixties and seventies, his work spanned genres from prose to nonfiction, including *Un oficio del siglo XX* [A Twentieth-Century Job] (1963), *Vista del amanecer en el trópico* [A View of Dawn in the Tropics] (1974), and *Arcadio todas las noches* (1978). He was awarded Spain's Biblioteca Breva Prize for an unfinished novel that would later become *Tres tigres tristes* [Three Trapped Tigers].

*Tres tigres tristes,* Cabrera Infante's tour de force, appeared in final form in 1967 and established him as both a master of wordplay and an incisive commentator in Cuban politics. The novel follows a group of friends as they experience Havana nightlife, and incorporates multiple perspectives and humorous linguistic gymnastics. Gregory Rabassa, translator and writer, dubbed Cabrera Infante "the punmaster of Spanish-American literature."

His experience growing up in Havana served as fodder for his next and most autobiographical novel, *La Habana para un infante difunto* [Infante's Inferno] (1979), which demonstrates, above all, ruthless self-investigation in search of a fixed identity. That same year Cabrera Infante became a British citizen, and in 1986 he published his first book in English, *Holy Smoke: Anatomy of a Vice.* He published several works in the nineties, the most notable being *Mea Cuba* (1993), a collection of essays, criticism and letters.

—

*This interview took place in 1982, during the spring semester at the University of Virginia where Cabrera Infante and his wife of twenty-one years, the actress Miriam Gómez, had rented for the semester a charming, yellow, mock-Georgian home that belonged to an English professor. It is decorated in a loosely eighteenth-century style, and contains a large collection of books, mostly by eighteenth-century British authors.*

*Cabrera Infante, a devotee of small work spaces, himself a smallish person, works upstairs in a tiny, untidy study adjacent to the master bedroom. When he is not writing or talking on the telephone, he birdwatches, joining Miriam Gómez, binoculars and Peterson guide in hand, among the trees surrounding the house, or peruses* TV Guide *in pursuit of old movies.*

*The high-ceilinged living room where we talk is decorated with prints of*

También tenemos el honor de tener entre nuestra selectísima con-
currencia al coronel Cipriano Suárez Dámera, M.M.,M.M. y P., pun-
donoroso militar y correcto caballero, acompañado, como siempre,
por su bella y gentil y elegante esposa Arabella Longoria de
Suárez Dámera. Una buena noche feliz para usted coronel, en com-
pañía de su bella esposa!

Tropicana! Del mundo de la cultura viene a engalanar nuestras noches de Tropicana la bella, elegante y culta poetisa Minerva
Cruz, recitadora de altos quilates dramáticos y tremendada y fina
voz: los versos se hacen rimas de terciopelo en su voz suave
acariciadora. Luz, ¡luz¡ LUZ (coño) Minerva, Minerva
Cruz para ustedes público gentil. Un aplauso. Eso es. Quiero anun-
ciarles que desde el próximo día primero, Minerva engalanará con
sus ademanes clásicos y su figura escultura y su voz
que es la voz de la cultura, el último show en cada noche de
Tropicana. Gracias Minerva. ¡Y éxitos. No, Minerva gracias a
ti que eres la musa de mesas.
Y ahora... and now... señoras y señoras... ladies and gentlemen...
público que sabe lo que es bueno... Discriminatory public... Sin
traducción... without translation...Sin más palabras que nuestras
exclamaciones y sin más ruido que vuestros calurosos aplausos...
Without word but your and your applause... Sin palabras
pero con música y sana alegría y esparcimiento... without words
but with music and happiness and joy... Para ustedes!...To you all!
Nuestro primer gran show de la noche....Our first great show of the
evening... Arriba el telón!..Curtains up!

*A manuscript page from the prelude to* Three Trapped Tigers.

*Hogarth's* Rake's Progress. *Outside, a subject of great interest to Naso, the family cat, are large numbers of cardinals, robins, and starlings gathered to eat the seeds Miriam Gómez has scattered for them—her desire to feed and watch birds in conflict with her love for cats. Above the sofa where Cabrera Infante sits, Hogarth's women crowd around the drunken Rake and provide a curious counterpoint to the interview: their silent brawling mocks our supposedly genteel conversation.*

INTERVIEWER: How do you write?

CABRERA INFANTE: Do you mean the position I assume at the desk?

INTERVIEWER: No, no. I mean your writing habits.

GUILLERMO CABRERA INFANTE: In fact I don't really write all that much. I type. Nowadays I type on my brand-new Praxis 35, an Olivetti made in Japan—the old Rome-Tokyo Axis having now become a merger. The problem is that this typewriter, instead of becoming unruly like all my old typewriters and old girlfriends, started out imitating my wife, Miriam Gómez, by trying to do my thinking for me. It's like living in a totalitarian state. No wonder they named it Praxis. That's what Marxists call "thought in action." Praxis may make perfect for them, but not for me.

INTERVIEWER: Do you jot down notes on the typewriter too?

CABRERA INFANTE: I used to, but the notes became pages and sometimes short stories. I write down notes in my acromegalic handwriting, with letters as big as fingers on a small pocket notebook or on steno pads, which I keep everywhere—on my desk, my night table, in the kitchen. Steno pads should have a better name...

INTERVIEWER: What better name could they have?

CABRERA INFANTE: Sterno pads. In honor of Laurence Sterne, digressor.

INTERVIEWER: Sterne? Lots of critics—to say nothing of students forced to read him—attack him because of his digressions.

CABRERA INFANTE: I don't have to defend Sterne; he is his own defense, the Sterne line. And I certainly agree when he says that "digressions are the sunshine, the life, the soul of reading."

INTERVIEWER: Swift was no less devoted to digression than Sterne. What do you think of him?

CABRERA INFANTE: The digressor as aggressor. The difference is that Swift was all *saeva indignatio* and that savage indignation was the motor of all his writings. You couldn't find a less playful writer among his contemporaries. Compared to Swift, Pope was a stand-up comedian.

INTERVIEWER: You seem to have an affinity for English eighteenth-century satire—something people might not expect from a Cuban writer. How do you understand satire, as a literary genre?

CABRERA INFANTE: Look, my friend, who knows what to expect from a Cuban writer, or any writer anywhere? Why not Sterne and Swift? Or Armour and Swift? At best, satire is didactic. At worst, political. This means that satires are not ludic or playful but just the opposite. They are the play wherein the satirist catches the conscience of the audience, which is why they are so closely related to sermons, religious tracts, and political pamphlets. Personally, I feel closer to Swift's motto, "*Vive la bagatelle*," than to his epitaph. Long live trivia! Where he and I part company is the grave, where his satire is most serious, and where I would rather turn that bagatelle into "bag-a-Stella." Swift wanted to use satire, literature, "to mend the World." To me this makes writing, which should be an end in itself—literature—into something political. Any literary work that aspires to the condition of art must forget politics, religion, and, ultimately, morals. Otherwise it will be a pamphlet, a sermon, or a morality play. Even the greatest moralist of our century, Joseph Conrad, was first and foremost an entertainer.

INTERVIEWER: What would you say about Solzhenitsyn?

CABRERA INFANTE: Solzhenitsyn is a failed artist but a very successful moralist. His novels are pretentious junk, but his political writings, *The Gulag Archipelago* books, for example, are precious masterpieces of indictment.

INTERVIEWER: Is George Orwell, then, also a failure?

CABRERA INFANTE: Yes, a failure as an artist, but a superb pamphleteer. His political essays, together with Camus's, are the best written in Europe since World War II. These men are heroes because they fight swords with words—but that doesn't make them artists.

INTERVIEWER: You raise the difficult problem of reading. How do we read a satirist such as Swift?

CABRERA INFANTE: A critic or, let's say an attentive reader, reads *Gulliver's Travels* and decides that Swift must either be right as an artist and wrong as a moralist or the other way around. But Swift had no such problem: he was concerned with moral issues and with deploying his arguments with the best rhetorical devices he could muster. He succeeds as an artist, but to appreciate that aspect of his work we have to set aside his moral issues. Mind you, deep down he was right about something we are not ready to admit, namely, that man is a beast, a predator, evil without redemption.

INTERVIEWER: What about the fact that Swift was Dean Swift, a cleric?

CABRERA INFANTE: That's a big problem for Swiftians: Swift believed man to be rotten through-and-through. For him the only hope for humanity lay in beasts. The whole structure of eigh-teenth-century faith in the goodness of man collapses at the first whinny of the Houyhnhnm. That's where the slogan "Four legs good, two legs bad" really originated. But Swift was serious where Orwell was mischievous.

INTERVIEWER: Do you agree with this misanthropic theory?

CABRERA INFANTE: Totally. I think Creation, Evolution, or, what it is probably—Chance—made a mistake. Man is the most danger-ous mistake in the universe, a glorious but miserable mistake. He is about to destroy the entire planet, and it's the rest of Nature that will pay for it. Man, to put it in Swiftian terms Swift could never utter, is the cancer of the planet!

INTERVIEWER: Is that exclamatory tone the one you use in the pulpit?

CABRERA INFANTE: All right, you're right. The tone is too high, but the tune is true. Besides, I share Swift's love for horses and women. The difference is that I like to play with women and he lacked any erotic vocation. He was sexually active, but I think he spurned in-tercourse finally because while he liked the foreplay he hated what Sade loved and Yeats lamented—that sex takes place in the site of the excreta. Add to that the idea that sex meant entering a body in the places where foul things were trying to exit. Remember that in the eighteenth century sex was a prelude to venereal disease, or, even worse, the procreation of evil. You know, I think "A Modest Proposal" is meant as much as a form of belated birth control as a comic remedy for poverty and hunger in Ireland. He knew that if horses (the perfect animal) were to survive, man had to cease to exist. The notion that a beast could be more perfect than man was, of course, perfectly un-Christian, so he has to be read as a comic writer or as a madman. We defuse his message by turning him into a humorist, the author of a children's book.

INTERVIEWER: Perhaps we might return to Swift on the matter of digression.

CABRERA INFANTE: We never left it: this was a digression on aggression.

INTERVIEWER: Let me be specific: could you have written Swift's "Digression in Praise of Digressions"?

CABRERA INFANTE: I'll answer if you use the Johnsonian "Sir" to ask me.

INTERVIEWER: Just this once then: "Sir."

CABRERA INFANTE: Thank you. Yes, I could have written most of it, especially the part about having heard of many attempts to write the *Iliad* in a nutshell and having seen a nutshell in an *Iliad*. And that quip that people use books as men use lords: they only know their titles but claim their acquaintance. I also like the way he sets up a polemic so he can attack both sides. One fault: Swift begs the reader's pardon for "digressing from himself" and claims it's a necessity. This for Sterne would be an *excusatio non petita*.

INTERVIEWER: What literary device does Swift's writing hinge on?

CABRERA INFANTE: Parody, sheer parody. If he weren't a parodist he couldn't have written "A Modest Proposal." And *Gulliver's Travels* is a parody of travel literature and, of course, *Robinson Crusoe*. There is an important parodic strain that runs through most of my favorite English writers: Swift, Sterne, even Lewis Carroll. In fact, the three could be said to have written a single book, with chapters called *A Tale of a Tub*, *Sentimental Journey*, and *Sylvie and Bruno*. Their remote ancestor is the *Satyricon*, with which they share a will to fragmentation and black humor.

INTERVIEWER: None seems terribly concerned with plot, or, for that matter, character.

CABRERA INFANTE: I don't know what plot and character are. Dickens created all possible (and impossible) characters, so that takes care of character. And plot, for me, belongs in mystery stories and movies. I am concerned with literary space, which is language, and not literary time. When we talk about character, we inevitably drift toward psychology: Choderlos de Laclos was the first and the last to use it properly.

INTERVIEWER: You know, you manage to make Swift, Sterne, and even Carroll sound rather melancholy.

CABRERA INFANTE: *Mea culpa!* Don't forget we live a heritage of humorless thinkers like Kierkegaard, Heidegger, or Sartre. When you have a sense of humor, you can laugh off your philosophic melancholy even when you know the joke is on you. I'll bet none of those English writers we've mentioned really believed in God.

INTERVIEWER: Even Reverend Dodgson?

CABRERA INFANTE: He was too good a logician to believe in so absurd a Maker. I think he believed man was made by the daughter of Chance and Fate, Miss Fortune.

INTERVIEWER: How does all this British misanthropy, parody, satire, and humor relate to your first major book, *Three Trapped Tigers*?

CABRERA INFANTE: *TTT* is an English book written elsewhere. It's not British and it's not short, but at least it's nasty and therefore true to life.

INTERVIEWER: The word "sad" is in the Spanish title: why did you excise that hint to the reader in the translation?

CABRERA INFANTE: In *Tres tristes tigres,* sadness is just a word, part of a tongue-twister that means nothing. *Three Sad Tigers,* at best, sounds like the title of a children's book. It's not a happy book, but I tried to make it one because, with Jefferson, I feel man has a right to the pursuit of happiness.

INTERVIEWER: I'm not sure, but I think Jefferson first put the word "property" where "happiness" is today.

CABRERA INFANTE: Then like an American Proudhon, I can say that happiness is theft. I should write a sequel to *TTT,* in which the writer Silvestre would find the actor Arsenio Cué a fugitive from a soap opera, unkempt and unshaved. Before disappearing, Cué would parody Paul Muni's memorable last words in *I Was a Fugitive from a Chain Gang* to answer Silvestre's question about how he was doing and say, "I steal."

INTERVIEWER: Since you mention *TTT,* I would like to ask you some questions about your other books. Why have you disowned your first book, the story-cycle *Así en la paz como en la guerra* (1960)?

CABRERA INFANTE: There's juvenilia in that book but also some senilia. It was mostly written when I started writing movie criticism in the mid-fifties. I have nothing against the stories. In fact, half a dozen or so may be salvageable. But it's the book itself I object to.

INTERVIEWER: But why?

CABRERA INFANTE: Because it's a book not written but collected under the perverse influence of Sartre and his idea that a writer must not only write about a moment in History (like Marx he always capitalized the word), but also comment on his writing as well. Sartre also demands that the writer include *all* of society. It's aesthetically hideous, a kind of social realism with a human face or a species of naturalism with a socialist conscience. Believe me, that book was collated with evil glue.

INTERVIEWER: I've heard it said that you actually began writing because after you read Miguel Angel Asturias's *El señor presidente* (1941) you said that you could certainly do no worse than Asturias. Is that true, and, if so, where is the story?

CABRERA INFANTE: It's true; the year was 1947, the yarn was published in the magazine *Bohemia*, but if you think I'm going to talk about it you're crazy.

INTERVIEWER: I see, you're not only modest but discreet. Perhaps instead you'd tell me about the publication history of *TTT*, how it began life as a book called *View of Dawn in the Tropics*?

CABRERA INFANTE: It's a simple story. The book that won the Spanish Biblioteca Breve Prize in Barcelona in 1964 was vetoed by Franco's censors. That happened while I was forcibly detained in Cuba in 1965. Then I had second thoughts about the book. I began toying with the idea of changing it and wrote what is now the final fragment, "Bachata." When I finally managed to get out of Cuba, I found out what had happened to the old manuscript. I rewrote it all then and there under the new title, which was its title before it won the prize. There was still some censoring, but there was lots of genuine rewriting.

INTERVIEWER: The way you link the two, it would seem the censor was also a kind of editor.

CABRERA INFANTE: As a matter of fact, that Spanish censor was more creative than my publisher or any of his editors. He made twenty-two cuts, mostly concerning the female bosom, his fondest obsession. Wherever I wrote "tits," he substituted "breasts." He eliminated oral indelicacies of any kind—even though such things do not abound in *TTT*, which is rather a chaste book about friendship rather than sex. But the censor had more than sex on his mind, especially if men were involved, so if a character went to a military academy and turned into a homosexual later on, the censor simply crossed out "military" making the academy more Platonic than Prussian. At the end of the book, the censor got really creative. The ending is a long speech by a madwoman I had copied down years before and was now using as an Epilogue. The old woman talked endlessly, always repeating herself. She was a religious fanatic, damning Catholicism, the Pope, and priests. The censor cut all that and with it all that was repetitious and neorealist in the speech. The last sentence in his version, all in lower case and without punctuation was *cant go no further.* Who could ask for a better ending?

INTERVIEWER: Your readers in English have *TTT* and the collection of vignettes from Cuban history called *View of Dawn in the Tropics* (1974) available to them, but they have had little opportunity to read your nonfiction. Would you comment on that other side of your writing?

CABRERA INFANTE: Gladly. I'll begin with a book called, depending on the reader, *Oh* or *Zero—O* (1975) in Spanish. It's a combination of previously published pieces and some essays I wrote for the book. The one I like best is "An Innocent Pornographer." It's about Corin Tellado, a writer of cheap, romantic novels—the kind called *novela rosa* or rosy romance in Spanish. She is the most widely read author writing in Spanish today and has been manufacturing a novelette a week for the past twenty-five or thirty years. I'm proud to say that I was the first person to write about her seriously and that since the time of my essay (mid-1967), she has been the subject of countless articles, interviews, even television programs. Nobody saw that the essay was written with a tongue in my rosy cheek.

INTERVIEWER: Your other book of essays seems closer to your literary writing. Why is that?

CABRERA INFANTE: *Exorcismos de esti(l)o* (1976) is definitely another kettle of fish. The title is obviously an homage to Raymond Queneau and, at the same time, an advertisement for itself because of its complicated asymmetry. It means many things: the exorcizing of style, exercises in summertime, even the lure of the pen—all in a send-up of *Exercises de Style*. This is one of my favorites among my own books and it closes the cycle begun in my collected movie reviews, *Un oficio del siglo xx* (1962). In *Exorcismos*, I expanded my experience (not experiment, a word I loathe when I see it applied to art instead of science) with Havanese, the idiom of *habaneros*, who might perhaps be called *hablaneros* or total talkers. Most of it was written while I was a cultural attaché at the Cuban embassy in Brussels (1962)—and it shows. It contains many messages from an Edmond Dantés, who read his own name as Inmundo Dantesco, the prisoner of Ifs, waiting for some Abbé Faria and passing time scratching graffiti on the filthy walls of his cell. One of the writings on the wall is a piece on Brillat-Savarin (1765–1826), the gourmet and amateur musician trapped by the French Revolution. I also like a short (one page) biography of Stalin's embalmer, a man the tyrant exiled to Siberia. I can still feel the embalmer's ghoulish glee as he ripped open the belly of the beast. For a moment I was the embalmer and Stalin had a Spanish name.

INTERVIEWER: *Un oficio del siglo xx* (1962) is more than a collection of film reviews. After all, you write there about your own pseudonym, G. Cain, as if he were deceased. How do you understand the book?

CABRERA INFANTE: As a novel. The Prologue, the Intermission, and the Epilogue are biographical comments on G. Cain, the critic. The reviews, his criticism, are the corpus—that is, his body. The whole book is a rite of passage conducted over his dead body. That's what a novel is, don't you think?

INTERVIEWER: If you say so. What about the title though, how would you like it translated?

CABRERA INFANTE: I'm finicky about titles. I'd like it as ambiguous as possible. Not *A Trade of the Twentieth Century* but *A Twentieth Century Job*. This gives readers an embarrassing choice: is it a job lot or Job or just a job? A better title might be *Job's Lot,* so everything would go to Cain's heirs.

INTERVIEWER: I want you to talk about your literary-political writings, particularly "Bites from the Bearded Crocodile," which appeared in the *London Review of Books* (June 1981).

CABRERA INFANTE: That article *had* to be written. Its original title was "Culture in Castro's Cuba: The Renaissance That Never Was." Let's go back in history a bit: the first time I ever attempted to write anything of a literary-political nature was in July of 1968, to answer an interview for an Argentine magazine, *Primera plana,* that was a combination of *L'Express* and *Time.* It caused a scandal. Just imagine: a person (me) whose parents were founders of the Cuban Communist Party, who wrote in his youth for *Hoy,* the Party newspaper, who was brought up in grinding poverty, who struggled to become a writer, who became Cuba's first real film critic, the youngest editor of a high-circulation magazine, then founding editor of the most influential literary supplement in the Spanish-speaking world, who then becomes a diplomat in the Castro government, who leaves Cuba silently—and all of a sudden shouts from a London rooftop that the mighty king is a naked tyrant.

INTERVIEWER: Why did you feel the time had come to speak out?

CABRERA INFANTE: There are too many people who go around saying that despite shortcomings the Revolution has at least done a great job on education and public health. This is like praising Hitler for pulling Germany out of the economic quagmire of the Weimar Republic and exactly like those damned Italian trains that always arrived on time under Mussolini. Those fellow train travelers were saying this time that culture was now a big thing in Cuba because Fidel Castro had taught everybody to read and write. What's the use of being literate if you lack the freedom to write, publish, and read what you want? The Sforzas, the Gonzagas, and of course the Medicis were upstarts and boors compared to this Cuban *condottiere,* this self-made patron of the arts and sciences. These were, of course, the lies of the land. The article, by the way, has been widely translated—even into Norwegian and Japanese!

INTERVIEWER: The article on Cuba was a spontaneous response to a political situation, but your essay on the fate of the writers José Lezama Lima and Virgilio Piñera under the Castro regime—a masterpiece in my opinion—is of a different nature. How does it fit in with your other writings?

CABRERA INFANTE: With me you always have to begin with the title. "*Vidas para leerlas*" may be roughly translated as "Lives to be Read," but that way you lose the Plutarchian pun, because "Parallel Lives" and "Lives to be Read" sound very similar in Spanish. Understanding this play on words is essential for understanding the whole piece. Here I must refer to another Cuban writer (living in France), Severo Sarduy, a disciple of Piñera and a follower of Lezama, who wrote a book of essays on writing called *Written on a Body*. The notions of writing on human skin and living lives to be read are complementary and apposite for writers like Piñera and Lezama, who were very different writers, the one writing stark, naked prose and the other composing heavily ornate poems and preciously robed prose. At the same time, they were both very sensual writers, both homosexuals who suffered because of it. I wrote the lives of the poets after the poets' deaths, which I think is not different from writing fiction.

INTERVIEWER: The pun is your trademark, but why use it when you are being serious?

CABRERA INFANTE: That's just the point. Writing for me, even what you call serious writing, is play. Puns, you see, are words whose meaning depends on play; it's the player who calls the shots. A great player, Lewis Carroll, saw that, but being a reverend he put the words in Humpty Dumpty's mouth. The question about language is not who is right or wrong but, in the old Hegelian scheme, who is the master and who the slave? Puns are my freedom and my control.

INTERVIEWER: Since you pun in so many of your titles, I suppose we'd better go back to them: please explain why you say your titles are the essence of your work.

CABRERA INFANTE: The title always comes first, to me and to the reader. I've written many stories and articles just by doggedly following the title. Sometimes I use a working title, sometimes I find a title suitable for a given subject. Take my most recent novel, *La Habana para un infante difunto* (1979). It had a different title when I began: *Las confesiones de agosto*, a clever allusion to confession and to Saint Augustine's *Confessions*. I had begun writing the book in August, so that was included as well. Then one day I heard a title, *La Habana para un infante difunto*, just like that, the same way Saint Augustine heard the voice in the garden. With the new title in mind, I rewrote the whole book.

INTERVIEWER: So you believe in inspiration?

CABRERA INFANTE: Let's call it *embullo*, a Cuban word that means easy eagerness, a particularly gracious way of climbing on the bandwagons of the mind. I write every time the Holy Ghost whispers some sweet something in my ear. Of course I also write to meet deadlines, but that's not really writing. Sometimes it comes just because I sit down at the typewriter.

INTERVIEWER: Speaking of inspiration, and a prolonged one at that, *La Habana para un infante difunto* is almost eight hundred pages long and yet it has outsold all your other books. Why?

CABRERA INFANTE: Filth, my dear MacAdam, filth. It is the first truly erotic book written in Spanish—a language and a literature that recoils in horror at living filth. That's what made it a bestseller. My first big book, *TTT*, is about friendship, and *La Habana* is about love, the biography of a single-minded character's search for the tamed screw. But in both books disillusion outlasts love. In *TTT,* friendship breeds betrayal, and in *La Habana,* before the flowers of sex fade, sex fades.

INTERVIEWER: The link between the two books seems to be a very Spanish, very baroque idea, *desengaño,* the moment when the scales of earthly illusion—friendship, the joys of the flesh—fall away and the protagonist sees both the abyss and salvation before him. Would you say you are part of the neobaroque movement that is so important in Spanish-American and particularly Cuban writing in our times?

CABRERA INFANTE: Certain writers, Borges and José Lezama Lima, have used a complex style it was convenient to call baroque. Other Cuban writers, Severo Sarduy and Alejo Carpentier, have both written about baroque and neobaroque and written in a baroque style. My themes may coincide with the baroque, but they are much more universal than you make them out to be. After all, the main theme of *La Habana* is not simply love but the pursuit of happiness across the empty space of loneliness. One of the more outrageous scenes is one a critic has called an "Ode to Masturbation." It isn't merely the sight of a human worm mating with his other end, but love in solitary confinement. This paean to onanism, with all due respect to Genet and Proust, takes place in a bathroom that is bare, small, and putrid. A cell or dungeon where the loving self conquers reclusion in the Devil's Island of the body and the mind that we call poverty.

INTERVIEWER: That last word might give the unsuspecting reader the impression that you write in a realist or naturalist style.

CABRERA INFANTE: That's a coy decoy. But after all, betrayal is the name of the game in *TTT:* betrayal of life through language and literature. The ultimate betrayal is in translation, of literature and of language, of life. So why not betray the reader's expectations as well?

INTERVIEWER: I just can't seem to dissociate these ideas from a baroque vision of the world.

CABRERA INFANTE: I'll go this far with you: *La Habana* is my own version of the Don Juan myth, beginning with the protagonist's complete innocence and ending in his complete guilt, which comes from his knowledge of the antagonist. Like my characters in *TTT,* these in *La Habana* are look-alikes, mirror images, ego and alter-ego. I've given the narrator many of my own traits. For example (remember, my mother brought me to a movie when I was twenty-nine *days* old), the narrator ends up in a movie, inside a big woman. Not in her womb, but down her vagina. The final phrase of the book—"Here's where we came in"—could mean that this is just one more movie or just one more woman. But only a few pages earlier, the now amniotic memoirist remembers that Virgilio Piñera told him a similar story as a dirty joke. It's curious that Virgilio, the Cuban poet, was a pederast, frightened by women, with a horror of the vagina. Curiouser and curiouser! I had published this ending years earlier (it was the first section of the book I wrote) with the title *Facilis Descensus Averni,* a line I stole from Virgil, also a pederast, who dreaded chasms and considered them to be the moral faults of Mother Earth. May we leave, on that note, the baroque barouche?

INTERVIEWER: Yessir. Perhaps you'd talk about your work-in-progress.

CABRERA INFANTE: It looks more like a work in re-gress to me. I confess with chagrin that I've been working on the same project since 1968 and even earlier. It's a long, long book called *Cuerpos divinos,* which for once you can translate into English without playing hide-and-seek with the reader, as *Divine Bodies.* This project, which by now seems too vast ever to be completed, has changed form many times, but it has not changed subject. Once more, as in *TTT* and in *La Habana,* it is Havana, this time the city and what happened to it between March 13, 1957, and a week in October 1962.

INTERVIEWER: Why such precise dates?

CABRERA INFANTE: March 13, 1957, was the day the Presidential Palace, in the heart of Old Havana, was attacked by anti-Communist terrorists. It was a suicide mission carried out at three o'clock in the afternoon, doomed, as the terrorists knew, to failure. And yet, they almost killed Batista, they almost seized power in the capital, while Fidel Castro and his small band of guerrillas were a thousand miles away in Oriente Province. Had they won, Cuban history would have been totally different. And by implication, the present and future history of the Caribbean.

INTERVIEWER: And the second date?

CABRERA INFANTE: That's the time of the so-called Missile Crisis. Kennedy confirmed Castro's regime—for a second time: the first was in the Bay of Pigs fiasco, when he unwittingly made Castro legitimate. During the Missile Crisis he seemed to know what he was doing. After that, Castro became a totalitarian tyrant and that was the end of Cuba as a free country. That was also the end of Havana as a carefree city. And that's where my book ends.

INTERVIEWER: It sounds like the literary reconstruction of a historical period some critics denounced *TTT* for not being.

CABRERA INFANTE: It's just the opposite. The book evokes only Havana, specifically La Rampa, a street, not really a street, three blocks where El Vedado, which I call the Forbidden City, meets Havana. It's a street that goes down to the sea in a ramp-like incline. I write almost exclusively about that street that never sleeps—in my books, that is.

INTERVIEWER: Is it like Damon Runyon's Broadway?

CABRERA INFANTE: It is, but where Damon Runyon had only parody and repartee, I have parody and paronomasia. The main character in my books, especially this one, is language. The prime task, the objective of my writing is to make the word an object. Not to convey thought, but to eliminate thought with words. Not sound, but words loose upon the world. In any case, *Cuerpos divinos* is not only anti-Runyon but anti-Thomas as well.

INTERVIEWER: Thomas who?

CABRERA INFANTE: Lord Thomas, Hugh Thomas—the British historian who has written the best history of Cuba to date. It's a pity he begins with the British seizure of Havana in 1762. But fortunately he ends his book in 1962, just as I do. *Cuerpos divinos* and Hugh Thomas's history show how the novel and history-writing converge and diverge. History is to politicians what posterity is to artists, and all politicians, Fidel Castro included, aspire to the condition of history. The difference is that the writer's posterity can be instant posterity, also known as success—a book that is read. But no politician would ever accept the idea that his posterity is a mere book called History.

INTERVIEWER: Surely you believe in immortality, a niche in that book called Literary History?

CABRERA INFANTE: I don't believe in immortality, either of the body or of the written word, my corpus. Remember, when we talk about those immortal writers, like Homer, we are not talking about the writers but their writing. Dead men don't write. Dead writers don't last. Homer exists as a continuous process of rewriting called reading and translation.

INTERVIEWER: And *Cuerpos divinos* is about the difference between history for writers and politicians?

CABRERA INFANTE: It simply points out the difference between speech and speeches. By the way, *Cuerpos divinos* has become three books plus a settlement of accounts called *Separata,* in which three characters, one of them a mulatto midget, talk and talk and talk. Most of the writing is done by the midget, a peculiar sort of writer who has never written a line and who cannot because he cannot really speak.

INTERVIEWER: That's one paradox too many for me.

CABRERA INFANTE: The midget is very verbal and loquacious, even garrulous. But he, as one of my characters in *TTT* remarks, tries to turn Spanish into a dead language. He speaks in English, and because his English is not very good, he keeps on making puns and jokes. He is condemned, not to silence but to speaking gibberish. That is the language of Babel, which is what Havana once was, Babelonia, where we spoke in tongues.

INTERVIEWER: Why haven't you finished it?

CABRERA INFANTE: My life keeps getting in the way. I started it in 1968, as I said, but in 1969, I had to stop to write a screenplay, entitled *Vanishing Point.* So I went to Hollywood in 1970. In Hollywood, under orders from Richard Zanuck (the man who was *Jaws*), I wrote a screenplay based on a dime spy novel called *The Salzburg Connection* that was never made into a film. (The title was, though, under another name, with another plot.) But I earned more money than I had ever seen in my life. In 1971, I went back to the book, but because *Vanishing Point* was such a success Joseph Losey engaged me to write a screenplay of Malcolm Lowry's *Under the Volcano.* I ended up in the loony bin, a.k.a. a *bedlam* in London. From there, under the power of eighteen electroshocks that practically eradicated what I use most to write (except for my typewriter)—I mean my memory—I went into clinical depression, an insidious illness that has lasted for years. It still lasts—so I must take life with a pinch of lithium salt. In the meantime, subsidized by my points (i.e., shares) in *Vanishing Point,* I managed to complete, rewrite, or compose a few books. And then I went back to *Cuerpos divinos,* which I again interrupted to write *La Habana para un infante difunto.* I thought it would take only a few months, but it took me three years and two different versions.

INTERVIEWER: Do you really mean that writing the screenplay for *Under the Volcano* drove you mad?

CABRERA INFANTE: Let's say it was the final stage of a process. I was writing (this was 1971) *Cuerpos divinos* when my agent at the time (he must remain anonymous because he's a powerful Hollywood producer now) casually asked me if I knew of a book called *Volcano.* I said I had heard of it when it was still called *Under the Volcano.* "So you know the book?" "Sure." I lied because at the time I still hadn't read the book. He then advised me to get on a plane and go to Rome to talk to Joe Losey. "He needs a fresh script." I was about to leave for Rome when my agent gave me one last piece of advice: "Take the book with you, willya?" I took his advice and the book and read it on the plane. I was so enthralled, so taken by it, so much into the character of Consul Firmin, that we went mad together. This didn't happen in the plane but back in London, while I wrote the script—a word I have tended to pronounce ever since as this "creep." If I feel suicidal, I call it simply this "crypt."

INTERVIEWER: Douglas Day, Lowry's biographer, says your script is superior to the novel.

CABRERA INFANTE: Douglas Day is kind to me and unkind to Malcolm Lowry. *Under the Volcano* is one of the truly tragic novels of this century and at moments it may be compared to the best tragic writing of Tolstoy or Dickens. For my money, Lowry's novel belongs in the same class with a few of Faulkner's books and with *The Death of Virgil.* Lowry has an advantage over both Faulkner and

Broch in that he is easier to read. It's a pity Losey couldn't make the picture because he is that rare bird, a film director who is cultured and, more important, intelligent.

INTERVIEWER: We've talked a good deal now about your writing and your fascination with spoken language, especially that of Havana, and with the act of writing, the continuous flow you spin into books. Embedded in your talk about talking there are two other kinds of discourse: images (including pictures and movies) and sound (especially popular music). Could we talk about your life now in terms of those other aspects?

CABRERA INFANTE: The three are inseparable, but let's try to emphasize images and music this time. As I said earlier, my mother brought me to the movies when I was twenty-nine days old. As a child I watched anything and everything that moved. And even things that didn't move—the funnies. Incidentally, it was the comic strips that bridged the gap between pictures and words for me because I learned to read by deciphering the words in the little balloons.

INTERVIEWER: What could you have seen in your Cuban home-town?

CABRERA INFANTE: I saw serials with Ken Maynard, Johnny Mack Brown, and my favorite cowboy star, Buck Jones. I wept when he died in the Coconut Grove fire in 1941. According to legend, he died trying to save a chorine. According to the press he burned because he was too drunk to move. Like John Ford in the movie *The Man Who Shot Liberty Valance,* my memory printed only the legend. I even remember Kermit Maynard, Ken's brother. You name me any 1930s movie, serial, short, or cartoon and I'll tell you all about it. In Gibara, my hometown, my uncle was the projectionist, so I got in free. In Havana, where we moved in 1941, there were other possibilities. All of that is in *TTT* and *La Habana.*

INTERVIEWER: Were the close-up kisses the source of your erotic impulses?

CABRERA INFANTE: The only kind of movie I wasn't keen on were love movies. Kissing time was yawning time for me. I still don't care much for romantic movies. Give me a *motion* picture and you give me emotion.

INTERVIEWER: Did you listen to radio serials?

CABRERA INFANTE: We were too poor to own a radio until well into the forties, but I would listen to the neighbors', both in Gibara and Havana. With the exception of "Tarzan," all my favorite programs were Cuban, even "The Spirit," and "Raffles," which borrowed freely from the comic strips and the novel of the same title. But those were in the forties. In the late thirties, my favorite programs were "The Red Serpent," with a Chinese detective, and "The Mad Monk," a take-off on "The Shadow," not on Monk Lewis.

INTERVIEWER: So the radio provided another link, words: spoken words, sound effects, and, of course, music.

CABRERA INFANTE: I was a real radio ham. Some of my parodies of radio programs reappear in *TTT*. And it was radio that led me to love classical music, because Cuban programs could use commercial recordings as background music without paying for them. My early passions were both visual and aural, in the form of movies and comic strips or radio serials and popular music.

INTERVIEWER: That popular music is simultaneously a kind of background to your novels and a code to which your characters allude.

CABRERA INFANTE: Especially the narrative music, the *son* (beat) and the *bolero*, which is a Cuban song with a faint rhythm base. I still remember those old songs that talked about the marimba, the musical instrument, as wood blocks that could sing with the voice of a woman. Or even better, a *bolero* in praise of some dark lady's eyes in whose shadows you could see palm trees drunk with the wine of sunshine. Good grief! The only reason I didn't become a composer is that I can't carry a tune.

INTERVIEWER: Did you ever do any drawing?

CABRERA INFANTE: When I was about ten, I would draw all the planes that appeared in the "Smilin' Jack" strip and I still remember a particularly elaborate hydroplane that earned me praise from my granduncle. I was fairly good at drawing and as an adolescent in Havana I thought I might become some kind of Cuban painter. That illusion turned to disillusion (*engaño* vs. *desengaño*) when my younger brother, who was only twelve at the time, showed me who was going to be the painter in the family.

INTERVIEWER: Was it then, when you were a teenager, that you began to write?

CABRERA INFANTE: I did write a radio play at that time and even taped it on a very cheap, primitive wire recorder. It was modeled on "The Spirit," the American comic strip, not the radio serial. A homage to Will Eisner, it wasn't all that bad. As a matter of fact, I became an amateur radio actor for a while, playing on a Sunday radio program sponsored by a Catholic association. I wrote some of the plays myself: they were all saints' lives. I took the parts of Arabs, Orientals, and heretics and took my acting style not from Peter Lorre, as you might have thought, but from Jesús Alvariño, a great Cuban radio personality who played Tamakún, a prince who was an Oriental adventurer and an amateur detective. Alvariño became chief of programming for Cuba's biggest radio station, and it was to him I delivered my first "professional" writing, a pilot for a radio program based on the Sherlock Holmes story "The Speckled Band." He rejected it flat and saved me from becoming a radio scriptwriter.

INTERVIEWER: Did you only write screenplays later, as an adult?

CABRERA INFANTE: When I was about twenty, around 1949, I wrote a story in the form of a screenplay. It was based on the folklore of my Oriental hometown, Gibara, and it was even published. The title, oddly enough, was "The Howling." A horror piece, naturally.

INTERVIEWER: What was your first real screenplay?

CABRERA INFANTE: The one I wrote in London in the summer of 1966. It was never shot. I wrote it in English, but the title was *El Máximo*. Over the past few years there has been a vogue for novels on South American tyrants among my Spanish-American colleagues, but most of those books turn out to be trite versions of the Spaniard Ramón del Valle Inclán's brilliant *Tirano Banderas* (1926). I wrote this script about a Caribbean dictator who flees to Ibiza (as Batista fled to Madeira) and there reproduces his presidential palace, complete with bodyguards, honor guards, and receptions attended only by scruffy islanders. I based the story on the life of the late Trujillo, the bloody ridiculous dictator of the Dominican Republic, but my title contained an oblique reference to a still active Cuban bleeding tyrant. The producer got cold feet, of course. I would like to rewrite that script someday because it was funny, but perhaps not funny enough. It had too many paper gags— jokes that work well on paper but fall flat on the screen. When I started writing screenplays, I had to learn that no matter how good your dialogue *looks* on the page, it sounds different when spoken by actors. It seems unreal because of course it is. Dialogue in fiction is always written to be read in silence. The page is the limit. Dialogue on stage and on the screen is meant to be spoken. The voice is the limit. Dickens discovered this when he started reading his books in front of audiences.

INTERVIEWER: Could you tell some more about that 1970 trip to Hollywood?

CABRERA INFANTE: In Hollywood I felt like a visitor from outer space. When I checked into the Chateau Marmont Hotel, I called my agent. Before I could recite my full name, his secretary asked me if I were Hungarian. First I said no, but when I thought about how many Hungarians had triumphed in Hollywood—Michael Curtiz, Peter Lorre, Bela Lugosi—I said I was from Buda but no pest. The secretary just giggled. That was my welcome to Hollywood. What I did mostly was to explore Raymond Chandler's territory. You know, I hope, that one of the models for *TTT* is *The Long Goodbye*.

INTERVIEWER: Did you have any experiences there like those we associate with Fitzgerald or Faulkner, those high-pressure story conferences?

CABRERA INFANTE: I never attended a story conference. The Chandler, Fitzgerald, and Faulkner days were long gone when I arrived. Mine was truly a pleasant stay—all expenses paid. The only thing like a story conference that happened to me took place when I met Richard Zanuck. He asked me what the title *Vanishing Point* meant, and I told him all about linear perspective and the end of a man as a convergence of life lines. He thanked me and that was that. The only suggestion came from Big Boss Darryl Zanuck himself. I was flattered and surprised that the eighty-year-old man would even bother to read the script. I wrote in what he suggested, a small, connective scene, but my director never shot it. At the end of that year, the old man kicked his son out of the studio and came back. In Hollywood, old pros die with their kicking boots on.

INTERVIEWER: Was your director axed by Zanuck the elder?

CABRERA INFANTE: He succumbed to his own lack of talent.

INTERVIEWER: Is the translation of your script into visual images in *Vanishing Point* the same sort of displacement you describe in noting the difference between written and spoken dialogue?

CABRERA INFANTE: What the spectator sees on the screen is the mirror image of my screenplay. *Vanishing Point* is my script as seen on the white mirror of the screen, in De Luxe color, at an aspect ratio of 1:85, running at twenty-four frames per second, in Stereo Sound—much more than I ever wrote or could write. That's a movie. I just wrote the screenplay. Thanks to John Alonzo, a cine- matographer of genius, my screenplay is now a piece of Americana, a cult film, and a very successful movie. I *wrote* a motion picture about a man with a problem in a car. My director made a movie about a man in a car with problems. Cars in the film are actors and the movie may be taken as a paean to cars or to death by car. By the way, I don't drive.

INTERVIEWER: Would you ever do another screenplay?

CABRERA INFANTE: Sure. Not for the glory but certainly for the money. I'd like to do Conrad's *Nostromo* because it's the best of Conrad's novels and because I'm in the perfect position to make a good script of it. I even talk English with a Polish accent.

INTERVIEWER: What about film reviews? After your brilliant reviews in *Un oficio del siglo xx* and the equally stunning essays on Welles, Huston, Hitchcock, Minnelli, Ford, and Hawks in *Arcadia todas las noches* (1978), it seems a shame that you would give up film criticism.

CABRERA INFANTE: Flattery will lead this interview nowhere, you know. Early in 1960, I realized I couldn't go on reviewing films in Havana because the Eastern-bloc films they were showing were beyond criticism. In fact they were beneath contempt even. So when *Carteles,* the magazine where I had started writing film reviews, was closed down (in June of that year), I decided my time was up. Besides, I was beginning to burn out as a reviewer. I was no longer capable of going to the movies just for fun because I had to be a critic all the time.

INTERVIEWER: You felt you were intellectualizing too much?

CABRERA INFANTE: Are you kidding? I just got tired of being a critic. But I understand what you mean because I have always been a staunch defender of Hollywood against charges of commercialism and vulgarity. Hollywood is commercial and vulgar—and a purveyor of popular entertainment. And I refuse to make distinctions between high and low culture, between art and pop art. Movies are for people to enjoy. Films, to make a distinction, are for snobs and pretentious critics. I don't like films: you can have Godard, Antonioni, Bergman, Bertolucci, and all the German *auteurs*. Give me the directors I wrote about in *Arcadia todas las noches*, and if you can't, give me Spielberg, De Palma, Romero, or Scorsese—even Blake Edwards now.

INTERVIEWER: What? Do you actually like Julie Andrews as a sex symbol?

CABRERA INFANTE: She's as appetizing as a eunuch in drag, but I like the comedies her husband has been turning out. Well, perhaps not *Victor/Victoria* so much, but *S.O.B.* is such a ruthless comedy about Hollywood that if Blake Edwards were to make one about Washington, Bob Hope would be playing the White House—and not as a stand-up comedian.

INTERVIEWER: I'd like to return to literature if I may. Ever since Borges shared the Formentor Prize with Beckett in 1961, Latin American literature has been the dominant force in the Spanish-speaking world. Do you feel you owe anything to your Latin American elders?

CABRERA INFANTE: First let me say that I despise the term "Latin America." Better call us Mongrelia. We are mongrels, a messy mix of white, black, and Indian. Second, aside from the elements I absorbed from the culture I grew up in I owe nothing to those "elders" you mention, especially if they wrote in Spanish.

INTERVIEWER: What are you talking about?

CABRERA INFANTE: Well, Borges, an elder I admire, writes in Borgese, a private dialect composed of quaint and formal English that condescends to employ Spanish words with Anglo-Saxon syntax. I owe him a lot, but I owe nothing to his Spanish.

INTERVIEWER: Do you owe your—I hate to say it—Latin American contemporaries anything?

CABRERA INFANTE: Not even money. For me there's Borges and the rest. They are the rest, a silent majority for me because I can't hear a word they're writing.

INTERVIEWER: But you are a part of the boom of the Latin American novel of the sixties!

CABRERA INFANTE: Like hell! They were only a sonic boom, a wake. But since you press me, I confess I have a debt with Carlos Fuentes.

INTERVIEWER: What is it? A theme—Fuentes's interest in film?

CABRERA INFANTE: I met Carlos in Mexico City in 1959. He entered my field of vision waving a hand and smiling as he crossed a screening room. It happened at Producciones Barbachano Ponce. I was there with Manuel Barbachano and Luis Buñuel, whose only claim to fame then was *Los olvidados* (an utterly forgettable film). We were watching rushes of Buñuel's latest picture, *Nazarín,* which he made for Barbachano. Watching your rushes in private can be very boring so we were keeping Buñuel company. Suddenly the door opened and in came Carlos with a small metallic object in his hand. I thought it was a derringer, but he rubbed his face with it! His smile turned into a grimace as he stretched the skin on his jowl and rolled up his eyes. Carlos was much more entertaining than *Nazarín.* Actually, he was shaving. I had never seen a cordless razor before and I couldn't wait to buy one. Back in Cuba, I used it thinking, "If Carlos could only see me now." That's my debt to Carlos Fuentes.

INTERVIEWER: That's your debt?

CABRERA INFANTE: That's it. But it's a lot more than my debt to Cortázar, who didn't have to shave at all when I met him. Vargas Llosa wore sideburns in those days and shaved with a cut-throat razor. And García Márquez had a mustache when I met him in Havana back in 1961. I met Donoso, the only true gentleman of the bunch, in London in 1970. Too late for the two of us. You see, he had the longest beard I ever saw, and I wore a goatee. Barababoom!

INTERVIEWER: Don't you think you're being a little bitchy?

CABRERA INFANTE: Yes, because I don't want to get lost in the crowd. We all write on our own, and I want to be read on my own. Feeling better now?

INTERVIEWER: I think we've exhausted that topic. Perhaps exile might be our last subject. Here in the United States we've seen a tidal wave of Cuban exiles pour onto our shores in recent years. How did you leave Cuba?

CABRERA INFANTE: By plane. I was a lucky exile, unlike those who left on the Freedom Flotilla. I left on a *Cubana* flight with my two daughters (by my first marriage), a Raymond Chandler novel, and little else. The tickets came compliments of the Cuban government. The man who is now number three in the regime, who had known me since I was a boy and who fancies himself a literary critic, figured it would be better all around if I left in good standing. He probably thought the rigors of capitalism or the cold climate would drive me home.

INTERVIEWER: Were you sad to leave Cuba and Havana for good?

CABRERA INFANTE: I left that pitiful place feeling pity. Actually I was grinning like Paul Muni when he escaped from the chain gang.

INTERVIEWER: Your writing is full of nostalgia. *TTT* even has an epigraph, taken from *Alice in Wonderland,* about imagining the light of a candle after the candle is blown out. Don't you ever feel homesick?

CABRERA INFANTE: Show me a man who longs for jail and I'll show you a warden on his day off, spent at the zoo, of course. I had become, to use the regime's metaphor, a *gusano,* a worm. That was Fidel Castro's invention, although Goebbels really had the copyright when he referred, in 1933, to Jews as *Ungeziefer* (vermin). I was no Gregor Samsa; I was leaving Kafkaland behind, so I took my metamorphosis in stride.

INTERVIEWER: Thinking now about the total phenomenon of Cuban exile, how do you understand the Mariel phenomenon?

CABRERA INFANTE: An event without precedent in the history of diplomacy. In less than seventy-two hours eleven thousand people took refuge in the Peruvian embassy in Havana. Mariel took place so that Fidel Castro could cover up his own blunder, his having removed the Cuban guards from around the Peruvian embassy.

INTERVIEWER: So it was a *coup de théâtre*?

CABRERA INFANTE: Yes, with the greatest producer making everyone play his part. Some, like the novelist Reinaldo Arenas, were expelled because they were known homosexuals—there are no gays allowed in clean-cut Communist Cuba—but others had to swear they were pederasts, prostitutes, or parasites to be let out.

INTERVIEWER: Are you friendly with these recent exiles, like Arenas?

CABRERA INFANTE: I have the most cordial relationship with several. Carlos Franqui, the former editor of *Revolución,* is an old friend. He showed me I could be a writer. Reinaldo Arenas is a new friend who shares my passion for writing. Heberto Padilla I've known for many years and is another good friend.

INTERVIEWER: Padilla is a rather special case in the history of Latin American and Cuban literature.

CABRERA INFANTE: Around 1970, Padilla said a lot of ugly things about me and others in print, so I retorted. He had written them under pressure from the Cuban police, who viewed him with distrust. Later he was jailed, tortured, and forced to make a public confession, now famous, in which he denounced a few friends in Cuba and abroad, me included. He also confessed some minor literary crimes—like writing a couple of mildly critical poems the Security Police deemed subversive—and abominated himself and his wife, Belkis, also a poet. Fascist states like Cuba just don't like dissidents, real and potential. Padilla was about to become a historical enemy. Homosexuals, it seems, are natural dissidents, strangers in a Communist paradise.

INTERVIEWER: Would you say that you all constitute a Cuban "Lost Generation"?

CABRERA INFANTE: I don't think even the Lost Generation was a real generation. They were never lost, only drunk. All I can talk about is the writers, painters, and musicians who gathered around *Lunes,* the Monday literary supplement to the newspaper *Revolución,* a cultural wonder created by Carlos Franqui that became the most popular and powerful paper in Cuban history.

INTERVIEWER: Was *Lunes* as successful?

CABRERA INFANTE: We were a knockout, in more senses than one. Imagine a literary weekly that prints a quarter of a million copies, in a country in revolution, distributed along with the official newspaper. There were some really talented people working on *Lunes:* Virgilio Piñera, then almost sixty, was the oldest and Severo Sarduy, at twenty, was the youngest. In between there were Oscar Hurtado (his last name means "stolen" and he was a bit of a plagiarist), Walterio Carbonell, a Paris-educated, black Marxist ideologue, José Baragano, a surrealist poet (deceased), Padilla, Pablo Armando Fernández, who returned from New York to take part in *Lunes,* as had Padilla. There was Raúl Martínez, an abstract painter who did our covers and layout, Natalio Galán, a composer and music critic who now lives in New Orleans. Calvert Casey, who learned his art of literary economy from Virgilio Piñera. Antón Arrufat, today back in precarious favor after being persecuted with Padilla. José Triana, the dramatist, who now lives in Paris. What a cast! But we chose the wrong production, of course. Mind you, *Revolución* gave me my only chance to be a war correspondent.

INTERVIEWER: When was that?

CABRERA INFANTE: At what you call the Bay of Pigs and what the Cubans call Playa Girón.

INTERVIEWER: Would you care to talk about it?

CABRERA INFANTE: Why not? On the night of April 18, 1961, I went down to the editorial offices of *Revolución* to volunteer to be a war correspondent and pick up my ID card. I didn't have to go, but I was curious and held the mistaken belief that war is good for writers. It was an adventure. Anyway, Carlos Franqui had a problem: too many war correspondents and only one war. He even had foreign correspondents. While I was there, I also found out about the international situation. One of the Prensa Latina people was down there and we asked him how things were going on the international front. He said everything was shipshape except for a spot of trouble in New York. It seemed the fellow in charge of the agency in Manhattan had left town in such a hurry that he hadn't even bothered to lock the office door. We asked him who that was. "Oh nobody, just a Colombian journalist, of no importance, named García Márquez."

INTERVIEWER: You're joking.

CABRERA INFANTE: No. Anyway, I left and headed for the front at about three o'clock in the morning, driving my Austin-Metropolitan convertible. The Bahía de Cochinos goes inland (as bays will) to form the Ciénaga de Zapata—Zapata Swamps (not named for Marlon Brando's look-alike)—and you reach it by driving east along the Central Highway across Havana and through Matanzas Province, looking for the Jaguey Grande road that you hit at the end of the province, where Matanzas meets Las Villas Province and the swamps. President Kennedy chose the landing spot, apparently for humanitarian reasons. The original site on Eisenhower's landing plans was near Trinidad, a small colonial city decaying in isolation at the foot of the Escambray Mountains, where there had been peasant uprisings against Castro since 1960. The landing place was a strip of sand between the swamp and the Caribbean.

INTERVIEWER: You drove out there alone?

CABRERA INFANTE: No. Walterio Carbonell, the brilliant Cuban Marxist who was a lawyer and once the leader of the Young Communist League, was with me. Carbonell was expelled from the Party in 1953 after he sent a telegram to Fidel Castro, a friend from university days, but then in Batista's prison. The telegram simply congratulated Castro for surviving the Moncada Barracks attack, but Carbonell sent it right to the jail and signed it. The Party was terrified Batista might link them to the plot, so out he went. Fausto

Canel, a young film director and *Revolución's* movie critic, and a very young writer and TV critic (also my former brother-in-law) named Luis Aguero were also in the car.

INTERVIEWER: The Austin sounds more like a Greyhound.

CABRERA INFANTE: Well, we were all underdeveloped. At dawn, still on Central Highway, we were detained for more than an hour by traffic—not all of it war correspondents. There were hundreds of trucks, tanks, jeeps, even motorcycles jamming the narrow highway. I remember thinking that a single enemy plane could have blown the convoy sky high—and us along with it! Fortunately the inefficiency of our army was matched by an absolute lack of contingency-planning by the enemy: Cubans at war. We skirted around Treasure Pond and headed for Jaguey, which looked like a border town in the Old West, with people peering through half-closed windows at war as if it were a showdown. At the end of the town the road was blocked by two jeeps and four soldiers. Only when I waved my ID card—which Franqui had concocted the night before with the printers—did they let us pass. There was no more traffic, only a solitary, very forbidding road to war. We all looked back. To go on might mean death, but to go back would mean a loss of face. We chose war. Near the coast we met a group of very young soldiers, mere children, jumping up and down and shouting "Dia-lang! Dia-lang!" They weren't Cuban Viet Cong, but uncouth youths trying to say "Díaz Lanz." They thought they had caught Díaz Lanz, the former head of Castro's air force, who was (and is) a defector in the U.S. But Díaz Lanz never came. They had found a U.S. Army camouflage parachute, whose former owner was probably drowned in the swamp or devoured by the infamous alligators of Zapata. We went on to the beach, Playa Larga, where the first landing took place. It looked like a Bacardi commercial: there was nothing on the beach except what God created and the tracks where the enemy had placed their heavy artillery. There was not a single weapon to be seen.

INTERVIEWER: You mean they took everything back off?

CABRERA INFANTE: There were no bodies, no blood, no empty shells, no weapons of any kind. Maybe they practiced retreating too much and advancing too little. The only enemy we could see was about four miles offshore—several American warships. They looked like big gray rocks made of solid lead. Reversing the shot, I tried to imagine what they might see through their binoculars: four tiny civilians (the tallest only five feet seven) standing around a tiny British sportscar painted white, parked on the very spot where their invading surrogates had been such a short time before. We must have been a bizarre or sorry sight! I was the only one dressed in something vaguely military: my *milicia* uniform—olive-green trousers, blue *mesclilla* shirt and black beret and boots. Fausto had on a short-sleeved shirt and slacks, as did Aguero. Walterio Carbonell was wearing a pinstriped black double-breasted 100% wool suit he bought at Aquascutum in London. He did take off his vest and dress shirt and replaced them with a yellow Lacoste—a concession to the climate. Then, problems John Wayne never had—my car wouldn't start. But an army jeep came by and in it was an old friend of mine from journalism school, Angel Guerra, a good name (Angel of War) for a very martial-looking lieutenant. He offered us a lift to war, just like that.

INTERVIEWER: Was there really a front? Were you far from it?

CABRERA INFANTE: Not very far, but what mattered was fear: fear of not getting to the war and fear of getting too much into it. On the side of the road there were two cows grazing peaceably, as we sped by on a two-lane blacktop highway recently built for tourists. Then we stopped near a house and a dark, heavy man in fatigues, sweating and dirty, came up to us gesturing and shouting like mad: "Are you in command here?" He was talking to me. All I could reply was, "Come on, man, I come from Havana." Then Angel jumped out of the jeep and calmed the hysterical sergeant down. The sergeant went back into the din and confusion and I got scared.

Bombs started falling and I ran for cover in the shack by the road. All hell broke loose and I found I was blasted *down* (I know it sounds illogical) to the floor. There I was "biting the dust"—the house had a dirt floor. Punishment came from above, a clap of thunder and a pair of boots.

INTERVIEWER: What boots?

CABRERA INFANTE: A pair of boots with feet in them, all connected to legs and the whole thing pressing against my head and shoulders. I looked up and saw who it was: a young black soldier trying to dig a foxhole with his bare hands and fear for a spade. I decided it was better to be killed by a bullet than let this young Othello make me into an urbane Turk and smite me thus, strangling me like an uncircumcised dog of war. I went out and found Angel calmly smoking. He told me never to go into a house during a bombing raid because pilots always attack what they can see— houses for example. I headed for a sheltering tree where I found César Leante, another minute man from *Revolución*. I asked him how far we were from the front and he told me we were at the front. I was suddenly Fabrizio del Dongo at Waterloo without knowing it. Fausto joined us and I woke up Luis Aguero, who was having a rather improbable nap, to tell him we were pulling out. Suddenly they were shelling our rear! We found out that the shelling was the product of Núñez Jiménez: he was a geographer Castro had made head of the Agrarian Reform Office. He was a nature lover now turned into an artillery officer. He wasn't so hot with a howitzer, because the shells were landing *away* from the beach—and *on* our way out. We were confused—so was everyone else—but we jumped on a truck leaving the war zone. We reached the newspaper late that night and found that the war was over.

INTERVIEWER: What about the others?

CABRERA INFANTE: There was a major crackdown after the Bay of Pigs. A documentary, *P.M.,* shot by my brother Sabá, was seized and banned by the Censorship Board. *Lunes* protested and was suppressed. Then Franqui was made to take a trip to Europe and was later fired as editor of *Revolución*. I was sent as cultural attaché to Belgium. Carbonell was named ambassador to Tunisia and got in trouble when he accidentally ran down a Tunisian Jew. He happened to be with a buxom blond French girl at the time and the Cuban Communists turned the event into a scandal. He was recalled and came home to write a brilliant, truly Marxist essay that demonstrated that Cuban literature had a slave culture for background. For this he ran afoul of the Stalinist literary commissars. Then he got into even more trouble by explaining to a delegation of French writers invited by the Cuban government that there was no freedom of speech in Cuba and telling all about *P.M.* and *Lunes*. He was called to the Writers' Union to recant, but delivered a scathing speech instead. He was expelled from the union, of course, lost his job and made destitute. Then he tried to form a Black Power movement in Cuba: that got him four years at hard labor.

INTERVIEWER: And the others?

CABRERA INFANTE: Fausto married a French girl, left Cuba, and is now a (divorced) Frenchman, working in Spain as a film director. Luis Aguero tried to leave through the Writers' Union, but ended up in the slammer for two years. César Leante became a socialist success. He was Cuba's cultural attaché in Paris, then a successful novelist in Havana, and later a high official in the Ministry of Culture. In 1981, he was sent to East Berlin. The plane stopped in Madrid and César asked the security man aboard permission to stretch his legs. Permission granted. He stretched them all the way to immigration to ask for asylum!

INTERVIEWER: No other happy endings?

CABRERA INFANTE: Well, when I got back home that night, I expected a hero's welcome from my consort Miriam Gómez. All she did was banish me to the bath to remove all the soot that had turned me into a kind of Cuban Al Jolson. Then we went to bed.

INTERVIEWER: Now, after you left Cuba, when you lived in Spain and later in London, how did you live?

CABRERA INFANTE: As I've always lived: by my wits, which is the lowest form of wit and not, as Addison says, the pun. I was not permitted to work—either for pay or for free—at all when I first got to England. But a clever lawyer told me that writing was not working. I agreed then and I still do. He meant that I could concoct stories, articles, screenplays—whatever—and that these would constitute a product I would manufacture and sell.

INTERVIEWER: Surely you were shocked at the idea of not being allowed to earn a living.

CABRERA INFANTE: Not really. You see, I've always had friends. I merely lived on the charity of my closest ones. Two Cuban writers in exile, Juan Arcocha and Calvert Casey (who later killed himself in Rome), lent me money through my French publisher at that time, Gallimard, to create for the Home Office the illusion I was receiving income from abroad. Later I wrote for *Mundo Nuevo*, the most important Spanish-language literary magazine of the late sixties, which was then edited by Emir Rodríguez Monegal (who now teaches at Yale) in Paris. He is a dear friend. I entered the jungle of exile when I was barely thirty-six and officially left it at fifty, when I became a subject of Her Majesty Queen Elizabeth II. Now, I'm the only English writer who writes in Spanish.

—*Alfred MacAdam*

# MANUEL PUIG

Manuel Puig was born in Argentina on December 28, 1932, the son of a businessman and a chemist. Puig described his hometown of General Villegas as "a place that had nothing, far away, very far away from the sea and the mountains and from Buenos Aires." He sought escape through film, going to the cinema five times a week as a boy. In 1950 he attended the University of Buenos Aires, studying philosophy and architecture, and in 1953 he got a job as a translator in the Argentine Air Force.

In 1955, Puig received a scholarship to study film in Rome. He subsequently taught Spanish and Italian in London, worked as an assistant film director in Rome and Paris, a dishwasher in Stockholm, a film director in Buenos Aires, a film subtitler in Rome, and ended up as a clerk for Air France in New York in the mid-1960s.

Puig's first novel, *La traición de Rita Hayworth* [Betrayed by Rita Hayworth], first appeared in Buenos Aires in 1968 but was initially received warily due to the homosexual undertones in the protagonist, Toto. In 1969 it was translated into French and hailed by *Le Monde* as one of the best novels of the year. Puig's next two novels, *Boquitas pintadas: Folletín* [Heartbreak Tango: A Serial] (1969) and *The Buenos Aires Affair: Novela policial* [The Buenos Aires Affair: A Detective Novel] (1973), were incisive parodies of pulp romance and detective novels, while at the same time appealing to grander themes of social exclusion and alienation.

Although his international success gained him recognition in his home country, Puig's books could no longer be published there due to political repression. In 1976, Seix Barral, a Barcelona publisher, published Puig's most famous novel, *El beso de la mujer araña* [Kiss of the Spider Woman]. It tells the story of the relationship between Molina and Valentín, a gay man and a Marxist revolutionary, trapped together in a prison cell. The novel's inclusion of an overtly homosexual protagonist was groundbreaking both as a stand for gay rights and as a critique of political, social, and sexual repression. In 1985, Hector Babenco turned the novel into a movie that won William Hurt an Academy Award for the role of Molina. Eight years later, Terrence McNally adapted the book into a musical that earned a Tony Award in 1993. During the late seventies and early eighties, Puig published four books: *Pubis Angelical* (1979), which draws on the stereotypical romance and science fiction novels to detail the exploitation of three women in different eras, *Maldición eterna a quien lea estas páginas* [Eternal Curse on the Reader of These Pages] (1980), *Sangre de amor* [Blood of Requited Love] (1982), and his last novella, *Cae la noche tropical* [Tropical Night Falling] (1988).

Puig spent his final months in Cuernavaca, Mexico, where he died from complications of AIDS on July 22, 1990.

———

*Puig has lived little of his adult life in Argentina, but all of his novels, with the exception of* Blood of Requited Love, *are about Argentina or Argentines coping with exile. When we met in Puig's home in Rio de Janeiro, I was struck by his very Argentine manner: a grave courtesy and reserve which*

CARLOS - O sobrenome nunca soube.

YAN - Não me faz entrar?

CARLOS - Desculpe. Entre. É que a surpresa foi muito grande.

YAN. - Há vinte anos que você não me vê. Mas eu já te vi. Cantando
    em Nova York, Paris, em Buenos Aires mesmo.

CARLOS - E nunca veio me dar um alô.

YAN - Eu não tinha coragem... Mas nesta noite de fim de ano... com
    todo mundo fazendo loucuras, até você. Não foi?

CARLOS - (interrompendo) Você está linda. *Je l'étêl como esse quadros de nuestra* C:... NADIA: Nunca vi uma quad
YAN - Obrigada. *na parede Dufy, Braque, Matisse... C: São da minha coleçã particular. N: Sempre os teve com você? C: Fora me fazerem comp Mas muitas veze esses parede pra mim parecem estar cobertas, com eu pas Prata*

CARLOS /Senta aqui. Me conta, onde está morando?

YAN - Viajo muito. Mas minha casa é aqui mesmo, em Montecarlo.
    Não me casei com um milionário, como alguns dizem. Só tive
    foi sorte nos negócios.

CARLOS - Valparaíso.

YAN - Mas é uma história chata. Só de cifras, bons investimentos,
    só. ~~De~~ *Mas* você, ~~porém,~~ eu sei tudo. ~~Tenho seguido sua carreira
    desde que começou a gravar discos.~~ A tua glória não me sur-
    preendeu. Eu sempre soube disso.

CARLOS - É mesmo?

YAN - Sim. Você tinha o sucesso ~~escrito~~ *gravado* na testa.

CARLOS - ~~Pala seriamente?~~ *Ata nada* *Agora eu vejo outras coisas gravadas aí.*

YAN - Você ~~era~~, e continua sendo, alguém que dá certo em tudo. Por
    que tem talento... *não somente acreditava ~~nas pessoas~~ na sua musica, acreditava* ~~e a outra coisa.~~ *nas pessoas, amava as pessoas.*

CARLOS - ~~Que outra coisa?~~

YAN - ~~É difícil explicar. Você não somente acreditava na sua mú-
    sica... e a amava. Você acreditava nas pessoas, amava elas.~~

CARLOS - ~~É isso que achava de mim?~~

YAN - ~~E pelas suas últimas músicas, eu sinto que você sempre ficou
    assim, no fundo... apesar do sucesso... além de toda a
    vaidade.~~

CARLOS - ~~Yankele~~ *Nadia*... Posso chamá-la assim?

YAN - Por favor...

CARLOS - ~~Yankele~~ *Nadia*... ~~você falou que eu acreditava nas pessoas. O
    que quer dizer com isso? porque eu... não acredito em ninguém.
    Pelo menos agora.~~

*A manuscript page from Manuel Puig's* Gardel, *a play
about tango singer Carlos Gardel.*

*set him apart from the more free-wheeling Brazilians. He is slender, with a handsome, tanned face and expressive dark eyes. He doesn't care much for interviews, but he did agree to three meetings at six-month intervals. The first he agreed to on the condition that we confine it to a morning's conversation. The morning in question was a cool, rainy Saturday in May 1988. We sat on comfortable sofas at one end of a pleasant living room with a polished tile floor, many plants, and a poster of Argentine tango idol Carlos Gardel on one whitewashed wall. The interview began somewhat formally in Spanish, and loosened up a bit when we switched to English. As we talked, I saw why it was that interviews exhausted him: he is attentive, thoroughly engaged, and careful about choosing precisely what word he wants, even in a foreign language. When he hits upon it his face lights up.*

INTERVIEWER: What is the difference between movie and book material?

MANUEL PUIG: In my experience, an epic story translates very well into film. Realistic novels—the kind made up of small details and constructed using a certain analytical approach—don't make good films. Films are syntheses. Everyday grayness, everyday realism is especially tough to translate to the screen. I remember discussing this once with a filmmaker, who said, "Yes, but look at the realistic films the Italians made, such as De Sica's *Umberto D.*" I disagreed. There's nothing of everyday grayness in *Umberto D*—it's about suicide, about deciding whether to kill yourself or not. It's an epic film *disguised* as an everyday realistic one. What I like to do in my novels is to show the complexity of everyday life; the subtexture of social tensions and the pressures behind each little act of ours. That's very difficult to put into film. I feel much more comfortable with films dealing with allegorical, larger-than-life characters and stylized situations.

INTERVIEWER: Is that why you liked American films of the 1940s?

PUIG: Sure. They were dreams, totally stylized—the perfect stuff of films because dreams allow you the possibility of a synthetic approach.

INTERVIEWER: Have you ever found that the dialogue of those 1940s films helped with fictional dialogue?

PUIG: I learned certain rules of story-telling from the films of that time. Mainly how to distribute the intrigue. But what interests me more about those films is examining the effect they had on people.

INTERVIEWER: On the people you grew up with?

PUIG: Well, yes—on my characters. My characters have all been affected by those cinematic dreams. In those days, movies were very important to people. They were their Mount Olympus. The stars were deities.

INTERVIEWER: Obviously you were intrigued by movies as a child. What about books?

PUIG: One of the very first books I read was André Gide's *Pastoral Symphony.* In 1947 he won the Nobel Prize. At the same time a film had been made of the novel, so he had come into the territory of my immediate interest, which was, of course, film. I read the novel and was immensely impressed. Soon after, I remember being impressed by Faulkner's *The Wild Palms.* Such contrasting authors— Gide all measure and economy, and Faulkner sprawling all over the place.

INTERVIEWER: Did you read *The Wild Palms* in English?

PUIG: No, I read Borges's Spanish translation, which is a beautiful work. I read Faulkner's other books in English. I never went back to *The Wild Palms,* but for me it's always an example of intuitive writing.

INTERVIEWER: So a writer's imagination is either calculated or intuitive?

PUIG: It goes from one extreme to the other. In between you have all these shadings. I have trouble reading fiction these days. So I've lost that immense realm of pleasure. Thank God I still enjoy movies and plays.

INTERVIEWER: You mean you don't read *any* fiction now?

PUIG: Writing has spoiled the pleasure of reading for me, because I can't read innocently. If you are an innocent reader, you accept the fantasy of others; you accept their style. These days another writer's problems of style immediately recall my own stylistic problems. If I read fiction, I'm working; I'm not relaxing. My only sector of interest now is biographies. Those I read with great relish, because the facts are real and there is no pretense of style.

INTERVIEWER: Even your later novels are concerned with 1940s films. Do you ever go to contemporary movies?

PUIG: Rarely. I simply got tired of walking out in the middle. It's a pity, because I know I may be missing some good things, but the price of viewing hours and hours of trash is too high. Of course, I receive films from all over the world—very strange films from Barcelona, Rome, Los Angeles, London. I barely have time to see *them.*

INTERVIEWER: People send them to you because they know you like old movies?

PUIG: Yes, I've established a network. There are many like me who are interested in certain periods and nationalities. For instance, I'm extremely interested in Mexican films from the forties and fifties. The world doesn't know what it's missing. There is a very silly prejudice against certain movie nationalities, so many films are simply discarded, though they're gems. In fact, I think the best Latin American films come from Mexico, at least from that very particular period. From a sociological point of view, the Argentine films are also of interest to me.

INTERVIEWER: There isn't much news from Argentina in the Brazilian papers. I wonder if you feel as remote here, in a neighboring country, as you might in Mexico or New York.

PUIG: New York is totally removed. Mexico feels closer.

INTERVIEWER: Do you find it easy to adapt yourself to different cultures?

PUIG: I learn languages easily, except German. My experience in Rome, New York, and Mexico was that you have to either integrate yourself or leave. For me there's always this desire to belong and become part of the country. Here in Brazil I had a very bad experience with the literary establishment and at the same time a very positive one on the human side.

INTERVIEWER: What was the bad experience?

PUIG: I published a book with a Brazilian setting called *Blood of Requited Love;* the literary establishment here decided to ignore it, as if it hadn't even been published.

INTERVIEWER: Wasn't the Josemar character in the novel a carpenter who worked on your house?

PUIG: There are very few words in the book that are not his. I simply edited our conversations. Mainly my job was to bring all the material out of him, put him in a mood to talk and express himself.

INTERVIEWER: Did he ever read the book?

PUIG: He barely reads. It was odd because he received a huge amount of money. He made more money on that book than I did. I thought it was going to be a big success—here, especially—so we made a fifty-fifty arrangement. But then he preferred to get a fixed amount and with that he bought himself a new house. It was ironic, because his tale was about the loss of a house; by telling it he got a new and better house. I felt very good about all this. Not only had I written a new novel, but I had helped someone. I expected gratitude, at least to inspire a warm feeling. But it wasn't the case.

INTERVIEWER: He felt burdened by your help?

PUIG: He tried to blackmail me. After the book was published, he said he'd had threats against his life and had had to give people money. I reminded him of the contract, which said that he was responsible for any references made to living persons. I had changed the names of the people and places, there was no publicity about his identity. That was enough to dissuade him. What he'd said was all lies. If it had been true, he would have come to me in despair. Thank God I had a very good contract. I was really appalled. The fact of telling me the story, of unburdening himself, was already positive for him. What's more, I paid him per hour while he was talking.

INTERVIEWER: The reverse of psychoanalysis.

PUIG: Yes. And on top of it all he got a house, which was so symbolic of all he had lost. The book is really about the loss of a father, so similar to my own *Betrayed by Rita Hayworth*. I felt terribly identified with him. I always write about people who somehow reflect my problems. In general they are similar to me, though I make many changes. In this case, the guy was Brazilian, not Argentine. He was thirty, not fifty. He was extremely strong and handsome; I am not. He has fantastic health, which I don't have. He was illiterate; I was supposed to be a writer. He doesn't question machismo, while machismo for me is the basic question of my existence. What we shared was this father problem—a ghost of a father. By the end there was such a brotherhood between us. It came to nothing as far as human relations go, but I'm very glad it happened because the novel has a certain interest; and I'm glad because I helped him.

INTERVIEWER: Was the process of writing that novel different from that of your other books?

PUIG: Very much so. I'd never worked with a tape recorder. With *Eternal Curse on the Reader of These Pages* there was also a real character present, but the writing process was different. I created a character myself—the old man Ramírez—so I could establish a dialogue with him. I didn't have much trouble feeling and imagining myself as Ramírez, because in 1978 and 1979, when I was working on the book, I was going through a very dark period.

INTERVIEWER: So you wrote the novel from the dialogue that was going on between the two of you as one between Ramírez and this other person.

PUIG: We practically wrote it together. He was beside me the whole time; it was a sort of psychodrama typed as it happened.

INTERVIEWER: Using this extraordinary method, how do you control your material?

PUIG: If you know a character—as much as it's possible to know another—and you put that person into a certain circumstance, you should be able to predict the reaction, especially the verbal reaction.

INTERVIEWER: Doesn't the book take all sorts of unexpected turns?

PUIG: It should be the opposite. It should be a situation where, well, I know all about them and I can probably guess what their reactions would be in a given situation. So it's just a matter of watching. But of course, they are delicate relationships. You cannot impose anything on characters. They help you, they give you all, but you have to respect them.

INTERVIEWER: So you get to know your characters and then turn them loose.

PUIG: You should be able to put a character in a situation that never happened in real life and predict what that character would have done or said.

INTERVIEWER: What if a person you're interviewing says or does something different from what you had in mind?

PUIG: Both in *Blood of Requited Love* and *Eternal Curse on the Reader of These Pages* I didn't have anything that the characters hadn't said. Of course, I did my own weaving. The yarn is presented by the characters and I work with that.

INTERVIEWER: What most writers like about fiction is the idea of making up characters and having them do whatever they want.

PUIG: Oh, no, no, no, no. I try to respect my characters. If you know them well, you won't make them do any nonsense.

INTERVIEWER: If you're reproducing real conversation verbatim, what is the difference between this kind of fiction and ... well, documenting?

PUIG: My characters' ways of thinking and talking have their musical and pictorial qualities. I take these qualities and I do my own embroidery. In aesthetic terms, a writer can use any method he wants. What counts, and what makes it fiction, is how it's done. The writer who uses the third person in his fiction is using an orthodox, established method or code. I am interested in the individual kinds of speech, however flawed and limited, of real people. That may limit me, but the use the writer makes of whatever method is limited only by his talent.

INTERVIEWER: What kind of characters do you pick as these "collaborators"?

PUIG: I can only tell a story about a character who reflects my most burning problems. I believe in characters as vehicles of exposition. Their voices are full of hidden clues, and I like to listen to them. That's why I work so much with dialogue. What they *don't* say sometimes expresses more than what they *do* say. Mine is not the classic third-person voice.

INTERVIEWER: Obviously you have to edit them.

PUIG: In my novels I try to reproduce everyday language. Of course, there's a certain concern about length. You can't have people expounding on themselves forever in novels the way they do in real life.

INTERVIEWER: Is it easier to write in the first person?

PUIG: Yes. When I deal with first-person dialogue and I know the character well, it's just a matter of lending an ear.

INTERVIEWER: You prefer not to have the novelist in the novel?

PUIG: I'm not interested in listening to my voice that much. I have no ego.

INTERVIEWER: But the voice of Manuel Puig is always there.

PUIG: My view of things comes out in the long run, let's hope. I remember at the beginning of my career a very nasty established writer said, "Oh, I know how Manuel Puig's characters talk but how does *he* talk? He doesn't have a persona." I thought the world of movies and acting provided the pure height of vanity, but I was mistaken.

INTERVIEWER: There's a lot of jealousy among writers.

PUIG: They're supposed to be people with more insight and distance, but it's not always the case.

INTERVIEWER: In some of your novels, particularly *The Buenos Aires Affair,* it seems as though people live in an artistic world because they can't live in the day-to-day world. Do you ever yearn for a life that has nothing to do with art?

PUIG: It's not a solution. With that book I meant to suggest there are other sources of energy and strength. But a life totally devoid of the imagination would be very boring.

INTERVIEWER: Do you think fiction can show people how to live?

PUIG: Direct experience is best, but then you'd need a thousand lifetimes. Books have that wonderful quality of showing you other lives. They can be a great nourishment.

INTERVIEWER: What are the easiest and hardest parts of writing for you?

PUIG: The beginning is exciting because I get an idea. Then I start looking for the shape to use to present it. The content always comes from the form, in my case. I think it should be like that, but I know other writers work differently. Then comes the critical moment, when I look for the voices of the narrators. Sometimes it's easy; sometimes not. If I find the narrator quickly, that's great, but it doesn't always happen that way. I have to find a voice that convinces me, and that's very difficult. Only when I believe in the narrator does it fall into place. Actually, the hardest part of writing for me is the typing and tidying things up. I don't dare try a word processor. I find it useful to type the different drafts—going from the rough draft to the second. As you're typing a clean copy you make decisions. I have been writing novels for almost thirty years, and I'm used to a certain technique of polishing. I've been told, "Try that machine, that processor, you'll love it." But not yet. Maybe next time. I like to keep track of the first draft. I like to see the scratching in ink. I do a lot of scratching.

INTERVIEWER: Are your revisions very radical?

PUIG: It depends. *Kiss of the Spider Woman* had almost no corrections. I wrote that novel with the greatest ease. *The Buenos Aires Affair* and *Pubis Angelical* were the toughest, because there were many changes in narrators. The last one, *Cae la noche tropical,* came out quite easily.

INTERVIEWER: How much of the book do you have in mind before you start?

PUIG: Most of it. But with this last novel, something very peculiar happened. I was shaping it, working on a real character—Ferreira in the book—but then he just disappeared. I couldn't get all the information I needed from him. So somehow another interesting person—actually someone I was considering for another story— came into the picture. I thought perhaps I could shift him into this novel. Absolutely accidental. But then *he* disappeared. It was very, very strange. Both were people in the neighborhood whom I could talk to and both of them disappeared. But that gave the final shape to the novel. The fact that they would disappear was essential. It was their nature. At a certain point they couldn't take the responsibility and they would leave. So it was reality, absolutely dictating the course of the novel. Nothing like that had ever happened to me before. But it wasn't a problem; it turned out to be an advantage.

INTERVIEWER: Do you think that people are determined by their circumstances?

PUIG: This is the awful thing: we are all *so* determined by our culture. Mainly because we learn to play roles. For me it starts with the very unnatural and hideous sexual roles. I think that sex is totally banal, devoid of any moral meaning or weight. It's just fun and games, innocence itself. But at a certain point somebody decided that sex has a moral weight. A patriarch invented the concept of sexual sin to distinguish between the saintly woman at home and the prostitute on the street.

INTERVIEWER: And men have a very different morality applied to them?

PUIG: Men are subject to no morality! A man full of sexual energy is a stallion, a model of health. A woman with strong sexual needs, up to a certain time ago, was considered a victim of her glands. She was not trusted, because it was thought that if she had sex so easily there must be something wrong with her, physically and mentally. The minute sex becomes of moral importance, horrible problems are created needlessly. The principle of sex is pleasure, that's all. I consider sex to be an act of the vegetative life, vegetative in the sense of eating and sleeping. Sex is as important as eating or sleeping but as devoid of moral meaning.

INTERVIEWER: At the end of *Pubis Angelical,* when Ana realizes she's sexless, like an angel, she begins thinking about the people whom she loves. It seems like you're saying that once people get over sex they can begin to love each other.

PUIG: Yes, once that problem is settled—or you don't imagine it as a problem. Once you've eliminated sex as a means of superiority or inferiority, sex is of no meaning.

INTERVIEWER: Do you think eliminating sex roles is possible in this world?

PUIG: At this moment, it's only a utopian ideal. But I see it as the only answer. The changes since 1968 point to that. You're very young; you don't know what this world was like in the forties. I remember very intelligent women saying strange things such as, "I cannot enjoy sex unless I fear a little the man who embraces me." There was all this myth of the macho superiority.

INTERVIEWER: Both sexes accepted it.

PUIG: Since you learned to enjoy sex that way, as an act of possession, it was something you wouldn't argue with. The general belief is that it was an unfair situation for women, but a natural one. If you went against it, you were unnatural. A woman had to be soft and surrender, and that way she would achieve pleasure. Afterwards, with experience, she would begin to find something phony in all this. So then she'd try to get even in some other way. We are so immersed in sexual repression, it's impossible to think of a world without it—but it will come.

INTERVIEWER: In *The Kiss of the Spider Woman*, there is a little utopia created under dire circumstances in the prison cell. Did you feel that Molina and Valentín transcended their traditional roles?

PUIG: It happens. I'm not just fantasizing; what I know comes from experience.

INTERVIEWER: If you weren't a writer, could you imagine yourself in another occupation?

PUIG: Something I'd enjoy? I'd like to sing, but I have no voice. Or maybe play an instrument. I'd enjoy anything creative. I wasn't bad at drawing, but I never developed it.

INTERVIEWER: Why did you become a writer? Do you feel it's something you need to do?

PUIG: For me it was a blessing. At first, I thought films were my thing, but I didn't like the work on the set and collaborating with lots of people. So I decided to write film scripts. I never sold them; they were training, pre-literary practice. Later when I finally started writing novels I found them to be the great solution— because what I'd wanted to do all along was to tell stories. With images, or with words, it didn't matter; I like to re-create reality in order to understand it better. But writing was something I could do on my own. I could do all the revisions I wanted and without the pressures of budgets. I could make a living out of it, and also it was an enjoyable activity. Of course, there are the secondary aspects, which are a little bothersome.

INTERVIEWER: Like being interviewed?

PUIG: Well, more or less. Even worse is the accounting, dealing with the publishers, all that. But what's really a bore and downright unpleasant is the relationship with the critics. They can be very irresponsible people. There are exceptions, but few. I've been rescued in a way by the colleges. There you find a different attitude. But it comes much later; when you've just published a book, what you feel immediately is the contact with the press.

INTERVIEWER: Universities don't pick up books for several years.

PUIG: No, and their reaction doesn't have much impact. But it's wonderful to know that somebody accepts your work. The reviewers from newspapers and magazines just want to amuse the person who buys the paper. They do it at the expense of the authors. Many, many times it's dishonest as well, because the critics belong to groups that don't like you—it's a horror. I'm published in twenty-four different languages, so I know critics. In Spanish I have to deal with the attitudes of the Mexicans, of the Argentines, of the Chileans. Each Spanish-speaking country has a special syndrome. I don't find it stimulating at all.

INTERVIEWER: Do you worry much about this?

PUIG: Well, critics have power, unfortunately. With time the book will outlive anything. But they have the power to retard it a lot. I've had a very bad relationship with the critics. I don't have to say thank you to them.

INTERVIEWER: Do you think that writing is something that can be taught?

PUIG: No, but you can discuss it. What I did when I taught at City College and at Columbia University was to discuss my own experiences and then suggest exercises. I don't like to go into a classroom and sit and listen to somebody reading.

INTERVIEWER: Did teaching help your writing at all?

PUIG: It always does, because you're always discussing the questions that plague you.

INTERVIEWER: What was it like for you to teach Americans?

PUIG: I found it interesting because I could see what their phobias, fears and problems were. I've found that in both America and Latin America, the young writer usually doesn't like the system, with a capital "S," in his country. But in Latin America the possibility exists of actually shaking that system, because Latin American systems are shaky. Young writers who don't like the American way of life feel impotent, because it's really tough to shake Wall Street. You may not like Wall Street, but it works somehow. That's also the case in countries like Germany. Ironically, Latin American countries, in their instability, give writers and intellectuals the hope that they are needed. In Latin America there's the illusion that a writer can change something; of course, it's not that simple.

INTERVIEWER: Do you have a reader in mind when you write?

PUIG: I could say that each novel has been written for somebody, to convince somebody in particular. It's almost an act of seduction.

If not seduction, at least an attempt at explaining something to somebody.

INTERVIEWER: Tell me about your schedule as a writer. Do you write every day?

PUIG: I adore routine. I cannot work away from it. It has to be the same thing every day. It takes a long time for me to wake up, so in the morning I write letters, revise translations—things that don't demand too much. At noon, I go to the beach and swim for twenty minutes. I come back, eat, and take a nap. Without that nap there is no possibility of creation. From four to eight I really work. Then I have dinner and that's it. I cannot work after eating. I stop and see something on the video machine. I hate to interrupt this for weekends. Then it's very hard to go back to work.

INTERVIEWER: You can't pretend that the weekends are weekdays?

PUIG: Friends take me out of my routine.

INTERVIEWER: Which of your novels do you like best?

PUIG: It's difficult to say. There isn't one I dislike more than the others. They all have their problems, but I must admit if I published them it's because I believe that there's something worthwhile in them. That I cannot hide from you.

—*Kathleen Wheaton*

# MARIO VARGAS LLOSA

© Jerry Bauer

Mario Vargas Llosa was born on March 28, 1936, in Peru. His family life was marked by turmoil: his parents separated at the time of his birth, and he was raised in his maternal grandfather's home. Vargas Llosa attended schools in Bolivia and Peru, ending up at the infamous Leoncio Prado Military Academy, whose unethical practices he later exposed in his novels. In 1953 he attended San Marcos University in Lima, where he became involved in university politics and held various part-time jobs as newscaster, journalist, and librarian; later on he moved to Paris and joined the literary community burgeoning there.

Vargas Llosa's first novel, *La ciudad y los perros* [The Time of the Hero], published in 1963, is a thinly veiled account of the corruption Vargas Llosa himself experienced at the Leoncio Prado Military Academy. In response, the school burned hundreds of copies in the courtyard, while the novel quickly garnered international acclaim. His reputation was confirmed with the publication of his second novel, *La casa verde* [The Green House], which won the Rómulo Gallegos Prize of Venezuela in 1967. From there, Vargas Llosa wrote the novella *Los cachorros* [The Cubs] (1967), which explores the brutal rite of passage from adolescence to adulthood by telling a story of a boy emasculated by a dog.

As Vargas Llosa continued to write, his works became increasingly political in tone, as exemplified by *Conversación en la catedral* [Conversation in the Cathedral] (1975), in which Vargas Llosa paints the backdrop of his college experience under General Manuel Odría's oppressive dictatorship, and *Pantaleón y las visitadoras* [Captain Pantoja and the Special Service] (1973), a scathing satire of the Peruvian army. His fifth novel, *La tía Julia y el escribidor* [Aunt Julia and the Scriptwriter], walks the line between fact and fiction, recounting the story of a young writer's love affair with his aunt.

Vargas Llosa's masterpiece, *La guerra del fin del mundo* [The War of the End of the World] (1981), presents a detailed representation of Latin American history and epic storytelling. During the eighties Vargas Llosa became both a prolific writer, expanding his canon with three plays—*La Señorita de Tacna* [The Young Lady from Tacna] (1981), *Kathie y el hipopótamo* [Kathie and the Hippopotamus] (1983) and *La Chunga* (1986)—and a prominent political figure in Peru. In 1990 he campaigned for the presidency of Peru and lost to Alberto Fujimori, whom he heavily criticized in lectures and essays.

His most recent works combine scathing political commentary with complex literary style, and include novels such as *El hablador* [The Storyteller] (1987) and *Lituma en los Andes* [Lituma in the Andes] (1993), and nonfiction works such as *El pez en el agua* [A Fish in the Water] (1994).

———

*In this interview Mario Vargas Llosa speaks of the inviolable mornings he spends in his office writing, seven days a week. In the fall of 1988, however, he decided to interrupt this otherwise strictly kept schedule to run as the Libertad party candidate for the presidency of Peru. Vargas Llosa had long*

Pero, aunque nunca admitiría en voz alta semejante cosa,
cuando ~~estaba~~ a solas, como àhora, Doña Lucrecia se preguntaba
si el niño no estaba efectivamente ~~descubriendo su vida~~ el
despuntar del deseo, la poesía del cuerpo, aliéndose de ella
como maestra. La actitud de Alfonsito la intrigaba. ?Era con=
ciente de que, al echarle los brazos ~~al cuerpo~~ como lo hacía,
al besarla en el cuello de esa manera ~~remolona~~ y ~~⬛~~ buscarle
los labios, infringía los límites de lo tolerado? Imposible
saberlo. Tenía una mirada tan franca, tan directa, que a Do=
ña Lucrecia le párecía imposible que aquella cabecita rubicun=
da pudiera albergar pensamientos sucios, escabrosos.

"Pens aientos sucios, susurró, la boca contra la almohada,
escabrosos ¡Jajajá!" Se sentía de buen humor y un calorcito
~~delicioso~~ corría por sus venas, como si ~~la~~ sangre se hubiera
transubstanciado en vino tibio. No, ~~seguramente~~ el niño no podía ~~serse~~
~~sospechaba~~ que aquello era jugar con fuego, seguramente que
esas efusiones las dictaba un oscuro instinto, un tropismo
inconsciente. Pero, aun así, no dejaban de ser juegos peli=
grosos ¿verdad, Lucrecia? Porque cuando lo veía, pequeñín,
arrodillado en el suelo, contemplándola ~~arrobado~~ como si fue=
ra una aparición, o cuando sus bracitos y su cuerpo frágil
se soldaban a ella y sus labios delgados, casi invisibles, se

*A manuscript page from Vargas Llosa's novel* In Praise of the Stepmother.

*been outspoken on the subject of Peruvian politics and has made Peruvian political issues the subject of several of his novels. Yet until the most recent elections he had always resisted suggestions that he run for political office. During the campaign he mentioned his difficulty with the empty emotionalism and rhetoric that are the language of electoral politics. Following the multiparty election, he lost a runoff to Albert Fujimori on June 10, 1990.*

INTERVIEWER: You are a well-known writer and your readers are familiar with what you've written. Will you tell us what you read?

MARIO VARGAS LLOSA: In the last few years, something curious has happened. I've noticed that I'm reading less and less by my contemporaries and more and more by writers of the past. I read much more from the nineteenth century than from the twentieth. These days, I lean perhaps less toward literary works than toward essays and history. I haven't given much thought to why I read what I read.... Sometimes it's for professional reasons. My literary projects are related to the nineteenth century: an essay about Victor Hugo's *Les Misérables,* or a novel inspired by the life of Flora Tristan, a Franco-Peruvian social reformer and "feminist" *avant-la-lettre.* But then I also think it's because at fifteen or eighteen, you feel as if you have all the time in the world ahead of you. When you turn fifty, you become aware that your days are numbered and that you have to be selective. That's probably why I don't read my contemporaries as much.

INTERVIEWER: But among your contemporaries that you do read, whom do you particularly admire?

VARGAS LLOSA: When I was young, I was a passionate reader of Sartre. I've read the American novelists, in particular the lost generation—Faulkner, Hemingway, Fitzgerald, Dos Passos—especially Faulkner. Of the authors I read when I was young, he is one of the few who still means a lot to me. I have never been disappointed when I reread him, the way I have been occasionally with, say, Hemingway. I wouldn't reread Sartre today. Compared to everything I've read since, his fiction seems dated and has lost much of its value. As for his essays, I find most of them to be less important, with one exception perhaps: "Saint Genet: Comedian or Martyr," which I still like. They are full of contradictions, ambiguities, inaccuracies and ramblings, something that never happened with Faulkner. Faulkner was the first novelist I read with pen and paper in hand, because his technique stunned me. He was the first novelist whose work I consciously tried to reconstruct by attempting to trace, for example, the organization of time, the intersection of time and place, the breaks in the narrative, and that ability he has of telling a story from different points of view in order to create a certain ambiguity, to give it added depth. As a Latin American, I think it was very useful for me to read his books when I did because they are a precious source of descriptive techniques that are applicable to a world which, in a sense, is not so unlike the one Faulkner described. Later, of course, I read the nineteenth-century novelists with a consuming passion: Flaubert, Balzac, Dostoyevsky, Tolstoy, Stendhal, Hawthorne, Dickens, Melville. I'm still an avid reader of nineteenth-century writers.

As for Latin American literature, strangely enough, it wasn't until I lived in Europe that I really discovered it and began to read it with great enthusiasm. I had to teach it at the university in London, which was a very enriching experience because it forced me to think about Latin American literature as a whole. From then on I read Borges, whom I was somewhat familiar with, Carpentier, Cortázar, Guimaraes Rosa, Lezama Lima—that whole generation except for García Márquez. I discovered him later and even wrote a book about him: *García Márquez: Historia de un Deicidio*. I also began reading nineteenth-century Latin American literature because I had to teach it. I realized then that we have extremely interesting writers—the novelists perhaps less so than the essayists or poets. Sarmiento, for example, who never wrote a novel, is in my opinion one of the greatest storytellers Latin America has produced; his *Facundo* is a masterwork. But if I were forced to choose one name, I would have to say Borges, because the world he creates seems to me to be absolutely original. Aside from his enormous originality, he is also endowed with a tremendous imagination and culture that are expressly his own. And then of course there is the language of Borges, which in a sense broke with our tradition and opened a new one. Spanish is a language that tends toward exuberance, proliferation, profusion. Our great writers have all been prolix, from Cervantes to Ortega y Gasset, Valle-Inclán or Alfonso Reyes. Borges is the opposite—all concision, economy and precision. He is the only writer in the Spanish language who has almost as many ideas as he has words. He's one of the great writers of our time.

INTERVIEWER: What was your relationship to Borges?

VARGAS LLOSA: I saw him for the first time in Paris, where I lived in the early sixties. He was there giving seminars on the literature of the fantastic and *gauchesca* literature. Later I interviewed him for the Office de Radio Television Française, where I was working at the time. I still remember it with emotion. After that, we saw each other several times in different parts of the world, even in Lima, where I gave a dinner for him. At the end he asked me to take him to the toilet. When he was peeing he suddenly said, "The Catholics, do you think they are serious? Probably not."

The last time I saw him was at his house in Buenos Aires; I interviewed him for a television show I had in Peru and I got the impression he resented some of the questions I asked him. Strangely, he got mad because, after the interview—during which, of course, I was extremely attentive, not only because of the admiration I felt for him but also because of the great affection I had for the charming and fragile man that he was—I said I was surprised by the modesty of his house, which had peeling walls and leaks in the roof. This apparently deeply offended him. I saw him once more after that and he was extremely distant. Octavio Paz told me that he really resented that particular remark about his house. The only thing that might have hurt him is what I have just related, because otherwise I have never done anything but praise him. I don't think he read my books. According to him, he never read a single living writer after he turned forty, just read and reread the same books....

But he's a writer I very much admire. He's not the only one, of course. Pablo Neruda is an extraordinary poet. And Octavio Paz—not only a great poet, but a great essayist, a man who is articulate about politics, art and literature. His curiosity is universal. I still read him with great pleasure. Also, his political ideas are quite similar to mine.

INTERVIEWER: You mention Neruda among the writers you admire. You were his friend. What was he like?

VARGAS LLOSA: Neruda adored life. He was wild about everything—painting, art in general, books, rare editions, food, drink. Eating and drinking were almost a mystical experience for him. A wonderfully likable man, full of vitality—if you forget his poems in praise of Stalin, of course. He lived in a near-feudal world, where everything led to his rejoicing, his sweet-toothed exuberance for life. I had the good fortune to spend a weekend on Isla Negra. It was wonderful! A kind of social machinery worked around him: hordes of people who cooked and worked—and always quantities of guests. It was a very funny society, extraordinarily alive, without the slightest trace of intellectualism. Neruda was exactly the opposite of Borges, the man who appeared never to drink, smoke or eat, who one would have said had never made love, for whom all these things seemed completely secondary, and if he had done them it was out of politeness and nothing more. That's because ideas, reading, reflection, and creation were his life, the purely cerebral life. Neruda comes out of the Jorge Amado and Rafael Alberti tradition that says literature is generated by a sensual experience of life.

I remember the day we celebrated Neruda's birthday in London. He wanted to have the party on a boat on the Thames. Fortunately, one of his admirers, the English poet Alastair Reid, happened to live on a boat on the Thames, so we were able to organize a party for him. The moment came and he announced that he was going to make a cocktail. It was the most expensive drink in the world with I don't know how many bottles of Dom Perignon, fruit juices and

God knows what else. The result, of course, was wonderful, but one glass of it was enough to make you drunk. So there we were, drunk every one of us, without exception. Even so, I still remember what he told me then; something that has proven to be a great truth over the years. An article at the time—I can't remember what it was about—had upset and irritated me because it insulted me and told lies about me. I showed it to Neruda. In the middle of the party, he prophesied: "You are becoming famous. I want you to know what awaits you: the more famous you are, the more you will be attacked like this. For every praise, there will be two or three insults. I myself have a chest full of all the insults, villainies, and infamies a man is capable of withstanding. I wasn't spared a single one: thief, pervert, traitor, thug, cuckold…everything! If you become famous, you will have to go through that."

Neruda told the truth; his prognosis came absolutely true. I not only have a chest, but several suitcases full of articles that contain every insult known to man.

INTERVIEWER: What about García Márquez?

VARGAS LLOSA: We were friends; we were neighbors for two years in Barcelona, we lived on the same street. Later, we drifted apart for personal as well as political reasons. But the original cause for the separation was a personal problem that had no relation whatsoever to his ideological beliefs—which I don't approve of either. In my opinion, his writing and his politics are not of the same quality. Let's just say that I greatly admire his work as a writer. As I've already said, I wrote a six-hundred-page book on his work. But I don't have much respect for him personally, nor for his political beliefs, which don't seem serious to me. I think they're opportunistic and publicity-oriented.

INTERVIEWER: Is the personal problem you mentioned related to an incident at a movie theater in Mexico where you allegedly fought?

VARGAS LLOSA: There was an incident in Mexico. But this is a subject that I don't care to discuss; it has given rise to so much speculation that I don't want to supply more material for commentators. If I write my memoirs, maybe I'll tell the true story.

INTERVIEWER: Do you choose the subjects of your books or do they choose you?

VARGAS LLOSA: As far as I'm concerned, I believe the subject chooses the writer. I've always had the feeling that certain stories imposed themselves on me; I couldn't ignore them, because in some obscure way, they related to some kind of fundamental experience—I can't really say how. For example, the time I spent at the Leoncio Prado Military School in Lima when I was still a young boy gave me a real need, an obsessive desire to write. It was an extremely traumatic experience which in many ways marked the end of my childhood—the rediscovery of my country as a violent society, filled with bitterness, made up of social, cultural and racial factions in complete opposition and caught up in sometimes ferocious battle. I suppose the experience had an influence on me; one thing I'm sure of is that it gave rise to the great need in me to create, to invent.

Up until now, it's been pretty much the same for all my books. I never get the feeling that I've decided rationally, cold-bloodedly to write a story. On the contrary, certain events or people, sometimes dreams or readings, impose themselves suddenly and demand attention. That's why I talk so much about the importance of the purely irrational elements of literary creation. This irrationality must also, I believe, come through to the reader. I would like my novels to be read the way I read the novels I love. The novels that have fascinated me most are the ones that have reached me less through the channels of the intellect or reason than bewitched me. These are stories capable of completely annihilating all my critical faculties so that I'm left there, in suspense. That's the kind of novel I like to read and the kind of novel I'd like to write. I think it's very important that the intellectual element, whose presence is inevitable in a novel, dissolves into the action, into the stories that must seduce the reader not by their ideas but by their color, by the emotions they inspire, by their element of surprise, and by all the suspense and mystery they're capable of generating. In my opinion, a novel's technique exists essentially to produce that effect: to diminish and if possible abolish the distance between the story and the reader. In that sense, I am a writer of the nineteenth century. The novel for me is still the novel of adventures, which is read in the particular way I have described.

INTERVIEWER: What's become of the humor in your novels? Your most recent novels seem far from the humor of *Aunt Julia and the Scriptwriter*. Is it hard to practice humor today?

VARGAS LLOSA: It's never occurred to me to ask myself whether today I will write a funny book or a serious one. The subjects of the books I've written in the last few years just didn't lend themselves to humor. I don't think *War of the End of the World* and *The Real Life of Alejandro Mayta* or the plays I've written are based on themes that can be treated humorously. And what about *In Praise of the Stepmother?* There's plenty of humor there, isn't there?

I used to be "allergic" to humor because I thought, very naively, that serious literature never smiled; that humor could be very dangerous if I wanted to broach serious social, political, or cultural problems in my novels. I thought it would make my stories seem superficial and give my reader the impression that they were nothing more than light entertainment. That's why I had renounced humor, probably under the influence of Sartre, who was always very hostile to humor, at least in his writing. But one day, I discovered that in order to effect a certain experience of life in literature, humor could be a very precious tool. That happened with *Captain Pantoja and the Special Service*. From then on, I was very conscious of humor as a great treasure, a basic element of life and therefore of literature. And I don't exclude the possibility that it will play a prominent role again in my novels. As a matter of fact it has. This is also true of my plays, particularly *Kathie and the Hippopotamus*.

INTERVIEWER: Can you tell us about your work habits? How do you work? How does a novel originate?

VARGAS LLOSA: First of all, it's a daydream, a kind of rumination about a person, a situation, something that occurs only in the mind. Then I start to take notes, summaries of narrative sequences: somebody enters the scene here, leaves there, does this or that. When I start working on the novel itself, I draw up a general outline of the plot—which I never hold to, changing it completely as I go along, but which allows me to get started. Then I start putting it together, without the slightest preoccupation with style, writing and rewriting the same scenes, making up completely contradictory situations....

The raw material helps me, reassures me. But it's the part of writing I have the hardest time with. When I'm at that stage, I proceed very warily, always unsure of the result. The first version is written in a real state of anxiety. Then once I've finished that draft—which can sometimes take a long time: for *The War of the End of the World*, the first stage lasted almost two years—everything changes. I know then that the story is there, buried in what I call my "magma." It's absolute chaos but the novel is in there, lost in a mass of dead elements, superfluous scenes that will disappear or scenes that are repeated several times from different perspectives, with different characters. It's very chaotic and makes sense only to me. But the story is born under there. You have to separate it from the rest, clean it up, and that's the most pleasant part of the work. From then on I am able to work much longer hours without the anxiety and tension that accompanies the writing of that first draft. I think what I love is not the writing itself, but the rewriting, the editing, the correcting.... I think it's the most creative part of writing. I never know when I'm going to finish a story. A piece I thought would only take a few months has sometimes taken me several years to finish. A novel seems finished to me when I start feeling that if I don't end it soon, it will get the better of me. When I've reached saturation, when I've had enough, when I just can't take it anymore, then the story is finished.

INTERVIEWER: Do you write by hand, on the typewriter, or do you alternate?

VARGAS LLOSA: First, I write by hand. I always work in the morning, and in the early hours of the day, I always write by hand. Those are the most creative hours. I never work more than two hours like this—my hand gets cramped. Then I start typing what I've written, making changes as I go along; this is perhaps the first stage of rewriting. But I always leave a few lines untyped so that the next day, I can start by typing the end of what I'd written the day before. Starting up the typewriter creates a certain dynamic—it's like a warm-up exercise.

INTERVIEWER: Hemingway used that same technique of always leaving a sentence half-written so he could pick up the thread the next day....

VARGAS LLOSA: Yes, he thought he should never write out all he had in mind so that he could start up more easily the next day. The hardest part, it always seems to me, is starting. In the morning, making contact again, the anxiety of it... But if you have something mechanical to do, the work has already begun. The machine starts to work. Anyway, I have a very rigorous work schedule. Every morning until two in the afternoon, I stay in my office. These hours are sacred to me. That doesn't mean I'm always writing; sometimes I'm revising or taking notes. But I remain systematically at work. There are, of course, the good days for creation and the bad ones. But I work every day because even if I don't have any new ideas, I can spend the time making corrections, revising, taking notes, et cetera.... Sometimes I decide to rewrite a finished piece, if only to change the punctuation.

Monday through Saturday, I work on the novel in progress, and I devote Sunday mornings to journalistic work—articles and essays. I try to keep this kind of work within the allotted time of Sunday so that it doesn't infringe on the creative work of the rest of the week. Sometimes I listen to classical music when I take notes, as long as there's no singing. It's something I started doing when I lived in a very noisy house. In the mornings, I work alone, nobody comes up to my office. I don't even take phone calls. If I did, my life would be a living hell. You cannot imagine how many phone calls and visitors I get. Everyone knows this house. My address unfortunately fell into the public domain.

INTERVIEWER: You never let go of this spartan routine?

VARGAS LLOSA: I can't seem to, I don't know how to work otherwise. If I started to wait for moments of inspiration, I would never finish a book. Inspiration for me comes from a regular effort. This routine allows me to work, with great exultation or without, depending on the days.

INTERVIEWER: Victor Hugo, among other writers, believed in the magical force of inspiration. Gabriel García Márquez said that after years of struggling with *One Hundred Years of Solitude*, the novel wrote itself in his head during a trip to Acapulco in a car. You have just stated that inspiration is for you a product of discipline, but have you never known the famous "illumination"?

VARGAS LLOSA: It's never happened to me. It's a much slower process. In the beginning there's something very nebulous, a state of alert, a wariness, a curiosity. Something I perceive in the fog and vagueness which arouses my interest, curiosity, and excitement and then translates itself into work, note cards, the summary of the plot. Then when I have the outline and start to put things in order, something very diffuse, very nebulous still persists. The "illumination" only occurs during the work. It's the hard work that, at any given time, can unleash that…heightened perception, that excitement capable of bringing about revelation, solution, and light. When I reach the heart of a story I've been working on for some time, then, yes, something does happen. The story ceases to be cold, unrelated to me. On the contrary, it becomes so alive, so important that everything I experience exists only in relation to what I'm writing.

Everything I hear, see, read seems in one way or another to help my work. I become a kind of cannibal of reality. But to reach this state, I have to go through the catharsis of work. I live a kind of permanent double life. I do a thousand different things but I always have my mind on my work. Obviously, sometimes it becomes obsessive, neurotic. During those times, seeing a movie relaxes me. At the end of a day of intense work, when I find myself in a state of great inner turmoil, a movie does me a great deal of good.

INTERVIEWER: Pedro Nava, the memorialist, went as far as to draw some of his characters—their face, their hair, their clothes. Do you ever do that?

VARGAS LLOSA: No, but in certain cases, I do make up biographical sheets. It depends on the way I sense the character. Although the characters do sometimes appear to me visually, I also identify them by the way they express themselves or in relation to the facts surrounding them. But it does happen that a character is defined by physical characteristics that I have to get down on paper. But despite all the notes you can take for a novel, I think that in the end what counts is what the memory selects. What remains is the most important. That's why I have never taken a camera with me on my research expeditions.

INTERVIEWER: So, for a certain time, your characters are not related to each other? Each has his or her own personal history?

VARGAS LLOSA: In the beginning, everything is so cold, so artificial and dead! Little by little, it all begins to come alive, as each character takes on associations and relationships. That's what is wonderful and fascinating: when you begin to discover that lines of force already exist naturally in the story. But before getting to that point, it's nothing but work, work, and more work. In everyday life, there are certain people, certain events, that seem to fill a void or fulfill a need. Suddenly you become aware of exactly what you need to know for the piece you're working on. The representation is never true to the real person, it becomes altered, falsified. But that kind of encounter only occurs when the story has reached an advanced stage, when everything seems to nourish it further. Sometimes, it's a kind of recognition: "Oh, that's the face I was looking for, that intonation, that way of speaking...." On the other hand, you can lose control of your characters, which happens to me constantly because mine are never born out of purely rational considerations. They're expressions of more instinctual forces at work. That's why some of them immediately take on more importance or seem to develop by themselves, as it were. Others are relegated to the background, even if they weren't meant to be, to begin with. That's the most interesting part of the work, when you realize that certain characters are asking to be given more prominence, when you begin to see that the story is governed by its own laws which you cannot violate. It becomes apparent that the author cannot mold characters as he pleases, that they have a certain autonomy. It's the most exciting moment when you discover life in what you've created, a life you have to respect.

INTERVIEWER: Much of your work was written outside of Peru, in what one might call a voluntary exile. You stated once that the fact Victor Hugo wrote out of his own country contributed to the greatness of a novel like *Les Misérables*. To find oneself far from "the vertigo of reality" is somehow an advantage for the reconstruction of that same reality. Do you find reality to be a source of vertigo?

VARGAS LLOSA: Yes, in the sense that I've never been able to write about what's close to me. Proximity is inhibiting in the sense that it doesn't allow me to work freely. It's very important to be able to work with enough freedom to allow you to transform reality, to change people, to make them act differently, or to introduce a personal element into the narrative, some perfectly arbitrary thing. It's absolutely essential. That's what creation is. If you have the reality before you, it seems to me it becomes a constraint. I always need a certain distance, time-wise, or better still, in time and place. In that sense, exile has been very beneficial. Because of it, I discovered discipline. I discovered that writing was work, and for the most part, an obligation. Distance has also been useful because I believe in the great importance of nostalgia for the writer. Generally speaking, the absence of the subject fertilizes the memory. For example, Peru in *The Green House* is not just a depiction of reality, but the subject of nostalgia for a man who is deprived of it and feels a painful desire for it. At the same time, I think distance creates a useful perspective. It distills reality, that complicated thing which makes us dizzy. It's very hard to select or distinguish between what's important and what is secondary. Distance makes that distinction possible. It establishes the necessary hierarchies between the essential and the transient.

INTERVIEWER: In an essay you published a few years ago, you wrote that literature is a passion, and that passion is exclusive and requires all sacrifices to be made and makes none of its own. "The primary duty is not to live but to write," which reminds me of something Fernando Pessoa, the Portuguese poet, wrote: "To navigate is necessary, to live is unnecessary."

VARGAS LLOSA: You could say that to write is necessary and to live is unnecessary.... I should probably tell you something about me, so that people will understand me better. Literature has been very important to me ever since I was a child. But even though I read and wrote a lot during my school years, I never imagined that I would one day devote myself exclusively to literature, because at the time it seemed too much of a luxury for a Latin American, especially a Peruvian. I pursued other things: I planned to go into law, to be a professor or a journalist. I had accepted that what was essential to me would be relegated to the background. But when I arrived in Europe with a scholarship after finishing university, I realized that if I continued to think that way, I would never become a writer, that the only way would be to decide officially that literature would be not only my main preoccupation, but my occupation. That's when I decided to devote myself entirely to literature. And since I couldn't support myself on it, I decided I would look for jobs that would leave me time to write and never become priorities. In other words, I would choose jobs in terms of my work as a writer. I think that decision marked a turning point in my life because from then on I had the power to write. There was a psychological change. That's why literature seems more like a passion to me than a profession. Obviously, it is a profession because I make my living off it. But even if I couldn't support myself on it, I would still continue to write. Literature is more than a *modus vivendi*. I believe the choice a writer makes to give himself entirely to his work, to put everything at the service of literature instead of subsuming it to other considerations, is absolutely crucial. Some people think of it as a kind of complementary or decorative activity in a life devoted to other things or even as a way of acquiring prestige and power. In those cases, there's a block, it's literature avenging itself, not allowing you to write with any freedom, audacity, or originality. That's why I think it's so important to make an absolutely total commitment to literature. What's strange is that in my case, when I made that decision, I thought it meant I chose a hard life, because I never imagined that literature could make me enough to live on, not to mention to live well. It seems like a kind of miracle. I still can't get over it. I didn't have to deprive myself of anything essential in order to write. I remember feeling much more frustrated and unhappy with myself when I couldn't write, when I was living in Peru before I left for Europe. I married when I was very young and I had to take any job I could get. I had as many as seven at a time! It was of course practically impossible for me to write. I wrote on Sundays, on holidays, but most of my time was spent on dreary work that had nothing to do with literature and I felt terribly frustrated by it. Today, when I wake up in the morning, I'm often amazed at the thought that I can spend my life doing what gives me the greatest pleasure, and further more, live off it, and well.

INTERVIEWER: Has literature made you rich?

VARGAS LLOSA: No, I'm not a rich man. If you compare a writer's income to a company president's, or to a man who has made a name for himself in one of the professions, or in Peru, to a toreador's or a top athlete's, you'll find that literature has remained an ill-paid profession.

INTERVIEWER: You once recalled that Hemingway felt empty, sad and happy at the same time after he finished a book. What do you feel in those circumstances?

VARGAS LLOSA: Exactly the same thing. When I finish a book, I feel an emptiness, a malaise, because the novel has become a part of me. From one day to the next, I see myself deprived of it—like an alcoholic who quits drinking. It's something that isn't simply accessory; life itself is suddenly torn from me. The only cure is to throw myself immediately into some other work, which isn't hard to do since I have a thousand projects to attend to. But I always have to get back to work immediately, without the slightest transition, so that I don't allow the void to dig itself deeper between the previous book and the next one.

INTERVIEWER: We've mentioned some of the writers whose work you admire. Now let's talk about your own work. You've said several times that *The War of the End of the World* is your best book. Do you still think that?

VARGAS LLOSA: It's the novel I put the most work into, the one I gave the most of myself for. It took me four years to write it. I had to do enormous research for it, read enormous amounts, and overcome great difficulties because it was the first time I was writing about a different country from my own, in an era that wasn't mine, and working with characters who spoke in a language which wasn't the book's. But never has a story excited me as much as that one did. Everything about the work fascinated me, from the things I read to my trip across the Northeast. That's why I feel a singular tenderness for that book. The subject also allowed me to write the kind of novel I've always wanted to write, an adventure novel, where the adventure is essential—not a purely imaginary adventure but one profoundly linked to historical and social problematics. That's probably why I consider *The War of the End of the World* my most important book. Of course, these kinds of judgments are always so subjective. An author isn't capable of seeing his work objectively enough to establish these kinds of hierarchies. The novel became a terrifying challenge that I wanted to overcome. In the beginning, I was very apprehensive. The colossal amount of research material made me feel dizzy. My first draft was enormous, certainly twice the size of the novel. I asked myself how I was going to coordinate the whole mass of scenes, the thousands of little stories. For two years, I was filled with anxiety. But then, I made the trip through the Northeast, throughout the Sertao, and that was the turning point. I had already done an outline. I had wanted to imagine the story first, on the basis of the research material, and then do the trip. The trip confirmed a number of things and offered new insights on others. A lot of people also helped me. Originally, the subject was not meant for a book but for a film directed by Ruy Guerra. At the time, Paramount in Paris was run by someone I knew who called me one day and asked me if I wanted to write the screenplay for a movie they were producing for Guerra. I had seen one of his movies, *Ternos Caçadores* [Sweet Hunters], that I had liked very much; so I went to Paris and met him. He explained to me what he wanted to do. He told me what he had in mind was a story having to do in one way or another with the war at Canudos.* We couldn't make a movie about Canudos, the subject was too broad, but about something that was in some way related to it. I didn't know anything about the war at Canudos, I'd never even heard of it. I started to research it, to read about it, and one of the first things I read in Portuguese was *Os Sertões* by Euclides da Cunha. It was one of the great revelations in my life as a reader, similar to reading *The Three Musketeers* as a child, or *War and Peace, Madame Bovary,* and

---

*In 1897, a large group of disaffected villagers led by the messianic preacher Antonio Maciel occupied the town of Canudos in the Brazilian Sertao of Bahia. Under the control of Maciel, who was also known as "the Councilor," they declared the village an independent state. The uprising was finally put down by an expedition commanded by the Brazilian minister of war, after several other police and military efforts to suppress it had failed.

*Moby Dick* as an adult. Truly a great book, a fundamental experience. I was absolutely stunned by it; it is one of the greatest works Latin America has produced. It's a great book for many reasons but most of all because it's a manual for "Latin Americanism"—you discover for the first time what Latin America isn't. It isn't the sum of its imports. It's not Europe, Africa, pre-Hispanic America, or indigenous societies—but at the same time, it's a mixture of all these elements which coexist in a harsh and sometimes violent way. All this has produced a world that few works have captured with as much intelligence and literary marvel as *Os Sertões*. In other words, the man I truly owe for the existence of *The War of the End of the World* is Euclides da Cunha.

I think I read practically everything ever published about the war at Canudos up until that time. First, I wrote a screenplay for the movie which was never produced because of various problems it ran into, inherent to the film industry. The project reached a very advanced stage, production had already started, but one day Paramount decided the movie wouldn't be made and it wasn't. It was a disappointment for Ruy Guerra, but I was able to continue working on a subject that had kept me fascinated for so long for a measly result—a screenplay isn't much, after all. So I started to read again, to do research, and I reached a peak of enthusiasm that few books have inspired in me. I used to work ten to twelve hours a day on it. Still, I was afraid of Brazil's response to it. I worried it would be considered meddling in a private affair . . . especially since a classic Brazilian writer had already covered the subject. There were some unfavorable reviews of the book, but on the whole, it was received with a generosity and an enthusiasm—by the public as well—that touched me. I felt rewarded for my efforts.

INTERVIEWER: What do you think of the succession of misunderstandings that characterize Canudos: the republican partisans seeing in the rebels the upheaval of the monarchy and British imperialism, while the rebels themselves believed they were fighting the devil? Could one call this a metaphor of sorts for ideology?

VARGAS LLOSA: Perhaps that's where the value of Canudos lies for a Latin American, because the reciprocal blindness produced by a fanatical vision of reality is also the one that prevents us from seeing the contradictions between reality and theoretical visions. The tragedy of Latin America is that, at various points in history, our countries have found themselves divided and in the midst of civil wars, massive repressions, massacres like the one at Canudos because of that same reciprocal blindness. Perhaps one of the reasons I was fascinated by Canudos is that the phenomenon could be observed in miniature, in the laboratory, as it were. But obviously, it's a general phenomenon: fanaticism and intolerance weigh heavily on our history. Whether it's messianic rebellions, socialist or utopian rebellions, or struggles between the conservatives and the liberals. And if it isn't the English at work, it's the Yankee imperialists, or the Freemasons, or the devil. Our history has been marked by our inability to accept differences of opinion.

INTERVIEWER: You wrote once that none of your other works had lent themselves as well to the chimeric ideal of the novel as this book. What did you mean by that?

VARGAS LLOSA: I think the novel as a genre tends toward excess. It tends toward proliferation, the plot develops like a cancer. If the writer follows a novel's every lead, it becomes a jungle. The ambition to tell the whole story is inherent in the genre. Although I've always felt there comes a moment when you have to kill the story so it won't go on indefinitely, I also believe that storytelling is an attempt to reach that ideal of the "total" novel. The novel I went the farthest with in that respect is *The War of the End of the World*, without a doubt.

INTERVIEWER: In *Mayta* and *The War of the End of the World*, you said you wanted to lie in full knowledge of the truth. Can you explain?

VARGAS LLOSA: In order to fabricate, I always have to start from a concrete reality. I don't know whether that's true for all novelists, but I always need the trampoline of reality. That's why I do research and visit the places where the action takes place; not that I aim simply to reproduce reality. I know that's impossible. Even if I wanted to, the result wouldn't be any good, it would be something entirely different.

INTERVIEWER: At the end of *Mayta,* the narrator tells us that the main character, now owner of a bar, has trouble remembering the events that are so important to the narrator. Did that really happen? Did the man really exist?

VARGAS LLOSA: Yes, he exists, though he isn't exactly what the book made of him. I changed and added a lot. But for the most part, the character corresponds to someone who was once a militant Trotskyite and was imprisoned several times. I got the idea for the last chapter when I spoke to him and was surprised to find that what I considered a crucial time in his life had become secondary to him—an adventure among others in a checkered life. It really struck me when I realized during our conversation that I knew more about the affair than he did. He had already forgotten certain facts and there were things he never even knew about. I think the last chapter is crucial because it changes the whole sense of the book.

INTERVIEWER: Tell us about Pedro Camacho in *Aunt Julia and the Scriptwriter,* who writes serials for the radio and starts mixing up his own plots.

VARGAS LLOSA: Pedro Camacho never existed. When I started to work for the radio in the early fifties, I knew a man who wrote radio serials for Radio Central in Lima. he was a real character who functioned as a kind of script machine: he wrote countless episodes with incredible ease, hardly taking the time to reread what he'd written. I was absolutely fascinated by him, maybe because he was the first professional writer I'd ever known. But what really amazed me was the vast world that seemed to escape from him like an exhalation;

and I became absolutely captivated by him when he began to do what Pedro Camacho does in the book. One day, the stories he wrote started overlapping and getting mixed up and the radio station received letters from the audience alerting them to certain irregularities like characters traveling from one story to the next. That's what gave me the idea for *Aunt Julia and the Scriptwriter*. But obviously, the character in the novel goes through many transformations, he has little to do with his model, who never went crazy. I think he left the station, took a vacation.... The ending was much less dramatic than the novel's.

INTERVIEWER: Isn't there also a kind of meta-language in the novel in the sense that Varguitas, who is modeled after you, lives a life as farcical as the lives of Camacho's serial characters?

VARGAS LLOSA: That's about right. When I wrote *Aunt Julia,* I thought I was only going to tell Pedro Camacho's story. I was already well into the novel when I realized it was turning into a kind of mind game and wouldn't be very believable. And, as I've said before, I have a kind of realism mania. So, as a counterpoint to the absurdity of the Pedro Camacho story, I decided to create another, more realistic plot that would anchor the novel in reality. And since I was living a kind of soap opera myself at the time—my first marriage—I included that more personal story and combined it with the other, hoping to establish an opposition between a world of fantasy and one that is almost documentary. In the process of trying to achieve this, I realized that it was impossible to do when you write a piece of fiction, a hint of unreality always seeps into it, against the author's will. The personal story became as delirious as the other. Language itself is capable of transforming reality. So Varguitas's story has autobiographical elements in it that were profoundly altered, as it were, by contagion.

INTERVIEWER: In several articles from recent years, you have made certain assertions that seem very pessimistic. In 1982, for example, you wrote: "Literature is more important than politics. Writers should become involved in politics only in the sense of opposing its dangerous schemes and putting them in their place." Isn't that a pessimistic vision of what politics can do to bring about progress?

VARGAS LLOSA: No. I meant that literature has more to do with what is lasting than politics do, that a writer cannot put literature and politics on an equal footing without failing as a writer and perhaps also as a politician. We must remember that political action is rather ephemeral whereas literature is in for the duration. You don't write a book for the present day; in order for a work to exert influence over the future, time must play its role, which is never or rarely the case for political actions. However, even as I say this, I never stop passing judgments on the political climate or implicating myself by what I write and what I do. I believe that a writer cannot avoid political involvement, especially in countries like mine where the problems are difficult and the economic and social situation often has dramatic aspects. It's very important that writers act in one way or another, by offering criticism, ideas, by using their imagination in order to contribute to the solution of the problems. I think it's crucial that writers show—because like all artists, they sense this more strongly than anyone—the importance of freedom for the society as well as for the individual. Justice, which we all wish to rule, should never become disassociated from freedom; and we must never accept the notion that freedom should at certain times be sacrificed in the name of social justice or national security, as totalitarians from the extreme left and reactionaries from the extreme right would have us do. Writers know this because every day they sense the degree to which freedom is necessary for creation, for life itself. Writers should defend their freedom as a necessity like a fair salary or the right to work.

INTERVIEWER: But I was quoting your statement for its pessimistic view of what politics can do. Should or can writers limit themselves to voicing their opposition?

VARGAS LLOSA: I think it's important that writers participate, make judgments and intervene, but also that they not let politics invade and destroy the literary sphere, the writer's creative domain. When that happens, it kills the writer, making him nothing more than a propagandist. It is therefore crucial that he put limits on his political activities without renouncing or stripping himself of his duty to voice his opinion.

INTERVIEWER: How is it that a writer who has always shown a great distrust of politics became a candidate for the presidency of Peru in the 1990 elections?

VARGAS LLOSA: A country can sometimes find itself in a state of emergency, in a war for example, in which case there is no alternative. The situation in Peru today is catastrophic. The economy is foundering. Inflation has reached record highs. Over the first ten months of 1989, the population lost half its buying power. Political violence has become extreme. Paradoxically, in the midst of this enormous crisis, there appears to be the possibility of making great changes toward democracy and economic freedom. We can rethink the collectivist, socialist model for the state which has been used in Peru since 1968. We shouldn't miss this chance to restore what we've been fighting for these last years: liberal reform and the creation of a real market economy. Not to mention the renewal of the political culture in Peru responsible for the crisis that is sweeping the country. All these reasons made me overcome any reservations I had and led to my involvement in the political struggle—a very naive illusion, after all.

INTERVIEWER: As a writer, what do you think is your greatest quality and your biggest fault?

VARGAS LLOSA: I think my greatest quality is my perseverance: I'm capable of working extremely hard and getting more out of myself than I thought was possible. My greatest fault, I think, is my lack of confidence, which torments me enormously. It takes me three or four years to write a novel—and I spend a good part of that time doubting myself. It doesn't get any better with time, on the contrary, I think I'm getting more self-critical and less confident. Maybe that's why I'm not vain: my conscience is too strong. But I know that I'll write until the day I die. Writing is in my nature. I live my life according to my work. If I didn't write, I would blow my brains out, without a shadow of a doubt. I want to write many more books and better ones. I want to have more interesting and wonderful adventures than I've already had. I refuse to admit the possibility that my best years are behind me, and would not admit it even if faced with the evidence.

INTERVIEWER: Why do you write?

VARGAS LLOSA: I write because I'm unhappy. I write because it's a way of fighting unhappiness.

—*Ricardo A. Setti*
*Translated by Susannah Hunnewell*

# LUISA VALENZUELA

Luisa Valenzuela was born in Buenos Aires in 1938, where she attended the Belgrano Girls' School and went on to Colegio Nacional Vicente López. She began her journalistic career at a young age by contributing to various local papers and magazines, but her first short story, "*Ese canto*," did not appear until 1958, published in the Argentine literary journal *Ficción*. That same year, Valenzuela moved to Paris with her husband and had a daughter, Anna Lisa Marjak. In 1961 she returned to Buenos Aires.

Valenzuela's first novel, *Hay que sonreir*, appeared in 1966, followed almost immediately by a collection of stories, *Los heréticos*, in 1967, both of which were later combined and translated into English under the title *Clara: Thirteen Stories and a Novel*. In 1969 she was awarded a Fulbright grant to participate in the International Writers Program at the University of Iowa, where she wrote her third novel, *El gato eficaz*.

From 1972 to 1974, Valenzuela split her time between Mexico, Paris, and Barcelona, where she wrote the novel *Como en la guerra*, maintaining a permanent residence in New York working under the auspices of a National Foundation of the Arts grant. From there she traveled extensively, attending various international writers' conferences and working for *Crisis* and *La Nación* in South America before she settled in New York once again as a writer-in-residence at Columbia University, teaching and translating, and then as Distinguished Visiting Writer at New York University. Her most well known books, *Cola de lagartija* [The Lizard's Tail] and *Cambio de armas* [Change of Arms], were published during her stay in the United States, and were immediately met with fervent praise.

Valenzuela, perhaps the most prominent female Latin American novelist to date, has published over a dozen books, all of which have been translated across the globe. Aside from having received such prizes as the Guggenheim Fellowship (1983), and twice winning the Plaza y Janés novel prize, she has held prominent titles at universities worldwide. She currently lives in Buenos Aires, where she is working on a novel and a book of essays.

———

*Valenzuela settled in Argentina again in 1989, and currently lives in the Belgrano neighborhood where she grew up. Her living room is open and warm, its ochre walls adorned with numerous paintings by Puppo, Raul Alonso, Batteplanos and Lea Lubins. In the background, the patio—overgrown with tangles of vines, roses and ficus—looks out onto looming skyscrapers. Off the living room is Valenzuela's study, where she does all her writing when in Buenos Aires. Two walls of the study are lined with books—written in Spanish, English, and French. Another wall is covered with masks, which Valenzuela has collected over her years of travel. Her desk occupies the heart of the room, and seems almost alive with the words and images encased under the glass cover. A computer, as well as piles of open books and letters, sits on top of the desk.*

*This interview took place over several meetings during the past year.*

*Esto galeones de sueño no suelen resultar ser embarcación de placer, con los borques fantasmas etc*

## El río - Lecho

He aquí lo inmencionable en este río, río que sin embargo
por momentos logra lo que muchos ansiamos y se sale de madre.
Todos aspiramos a salirnos de madre, a cortar el cordón o las
amarras y bogar a la deriva. A veces este río lo logra y es cuando él y ella más lo aprecian porque ya no corre por su lecho y
no hay que mencionar el lecho.

Ni el uno ni la otra son de aquellos a quienes se les es-
capan las metáforas, por eso se hacen miedo. Se dan miedo, se lo
brindan uno a otra y a veces viceversa a manos llenas. El miedo
como río, el cauce como lecho, el lecho como fondo, inconfesable.
Sobre el lecho el río, sobre el río el galeón como con colchón
de aire, sobre el galeón los mástiles y ellos dos negándose a
bajar del palo de mesana, escapándole al palo mayor como a la
peste. Y eso que muchas veces han estado navegando en otras aguas
y conocen a fondo la terminología. Saben de la arboladura y del
velamen, reconocen la gavia, el trinquete, la vela mayor y hasta
la vela de fortuna. Saben colocar brazas y acolladores. Entien-
den de perchas y de jarcias. Ella sabe
pujamen, él más de una vez ha cargado la vela en lo alto de la
verga

El puño de escota de la vela es pan comido para ellos.
Ella sabe todo lo referente a la relinga del pujamen

esas cosas.

Pero este galeón de sueños navega por cuenta propia, impul-
sado a veces por suspiros secretos. Es un buque fantasma sobre
un río fantasma con lecho la profundidad

*A manuscript page from* "El río," *an unpublished story.*

*Valenzuela has a beautiful, expressive face, which is framed by dark, unruly hair; she speaks slowly and deliberately, with an unmistakable Argentine accent marked with both sophistication and grit. The first conversation was conducted last September in Wisconsin, when Valenzuela was the guest lecturer at the Midamerican Conference. (A multimedia performance based on her story "Other Weapons" premiered there.) Additional conversations took place during Valenzuela's frequent visits to New York City: at a Chinese restaurant in midtown; and over a brief breakfast in the East Village in September 2001 when she came to the city to write about the World Trade Center attacks for* La Nación. *In between the meetings, occasional e-mails were exchanged, some in English and some in Spanish, all of them signed* Abrazos—*hugs.*

—*Sarah Lee*

INTERVIEWER: When did you start writing?

LUISA VALENZUELA: I dictated my first poem to my mother at age six. It was about death. Funny I would connect so early with the one unavoidable subject. The poem describes a beautiful woman with all the obvious metaphors of the time; then a bird comes to her window and says, *Hacia ti viene la muerte* (death comes toward you). It came to me just like that—influenced by Poe, no doubt—and my mother wrote it down. My older sister used to read scary stories aloud to make me eat, so maybe that's where I got the inspiration. In my early years I never thought I would become a writer. Maybe those tales of terror made me decide to write—after all, it's always better to be on this side of the production line.

I published my first story at age twenty—which was also about death. Death is the ultimate mystery, which, alas! love isn't, so it's more enticing as subject matter. We are always trying to have the last word over what will finally have the last word over us.

INTERVIEWER: Your mother was a well-known Argentine writer. What was it like to grow up surrounded by literary figures?

VALENZUELA: One time my mother and Borges composed a story together. I remember the laughter coming from the room they were

*Valenzuela, with her mother (on the left) and her daughter, at her mother's house in the early 1970s.*

working in. The story, "*La hermana de Eloisa*," was published in 1955, but neither one of them liked that story much after a certain time, and it was never reprinted in a book. My mother said that the experience taught her how to edit. Borges would come out of the dining room where they were writing and laughing, and say, "Today we made significant progress—we wrote one full line." Now I am grateful for that experience—they were so happy writing the story that it impressed upon me that writing is a joyous activity. And it is, for the most part.

INTERVIEWER: What was Borges like?

VALENZUELA: He was a walking system of thought. You could see the way his mind worked, since he was offering it so generously—also in a self-centered way, because he didn't care to listen much. He monologued in the most splendid and humorous fashion—he seemed so serious, but was full of wit and naughty humor.

I remember the last days we spent in New York with him. Daniel Halpern would be driving us back and forth from NYU to Columbia, and Borges would be posing impossible questions: In what version of what year of this poem did Auden change such-and-such word for another? Things like that. We took care of the frail old man, protecting him from the students, and then in the evenings his future wife, María Kodama, would call and say, Borges wants to go listen to some jazz, or, Borges wants to take a ride in the park. By the end of the stay we were exhausted.

INTERVIEWER: As a child, were you aware of his greatness?

VALENZUELA: Not then. The people who surrounded him—the group that visited our home during those years—were all great. Borges didn't stand out among the rest; he was so shy. What I do remember are his lectures. I went to every one of them. At times, there would be sudden and long silences; the public suffered, think-

*Valenzuela and Borges, at the opening of La Libreria bookstore in New York City, 1989.*

ing he had lost the thread, but he was simply searching. The minute he opened his mouth again, the exact term emerged like a gem.

INTERVIEWER: His talks were on literature?

VALENZUELA: Yes. Those were Peronist times, and Perón felt threatened by intellectuals. Borges was transferred from his obscure job at a municipal library to inspector of poultry in municipal markets. And since intellectuals do need to earn a living—in spite of the common belief—an organization called Pro Arte organized lectures and courses in private homes such as my mother's. The feeling was great in spite of the fear: everybody felt like conspirators, keeping all the windows closed, the meetings secret.

INTERVIEWER: Could you say a little more about the Pro Arte movement?

VALENZUELA: Things here get lost so easily. There is virtually no trace now of Pro Arte, an association born—honoring the name—to help the artist. Pro Arte started by organizing exhibits, concerts and lectures in public spaces in the forties. During Perón's regime, they had to go underground, or at least into the private domain. Many of the great writers were involved: Borges, Ernesto Sábato, Eduardo Mallea, Manuel Peyrou, Conrado Nalé Roxlo, the poets Amelia Biaggioni, María Emilia Lahitte and Eduardo González Lanuza. Also the émigrés from the Spanish Civil War: Arturo Cuadrado—the publisher of *Botella al mar*—Clemente Cimorra, Amparo Arbajal. I was very young at the time, but remember them vividly. It was a movable, motley crowd. They were an impressive lot.

At least once a week they would get together, sometimes until the wee hours of the morning. Empanadas, sandwiches, and red wine were the usual fare. I remember the ongoing arguments between Borges and Sábato—around politics, around the value of the short story versus the novel. I remember at some point (because of politics and, perhaps, a secret literary rivalry) the situation got out of hand. Pipina Diehl offered a splendid peacemaking dinner, at the end of which she urged Georgie (Borges was called by his nickname while his mother was alive) to apologize. "I wasn't aware that we had quarreled," he answered for everyone to hear, and went on sipping his soup.

INTERVIEWER: How would you compare contemporary literary life in Argentina to literary life back then?

VALENZUELA: Literary life then was passionate. Literature was really alive; it was something to be taken into account, both in the media and the public sphere. Now we run with the times. Individualism is rampant among the writers, and the media pays much more attention to politicians, starlets and comedians—one and the same—than to intellectuals.

INTERVIEWER: Having lived for many years outside of Argentina, what is your conception of home?

VALENZUELA: I lived for over three years in France, one in Normandy and then in Paris. Practically a year in Barcelona. And ten glorious years in New York, from where I moved back and forth to Mexico and, at least once a year, with trepidation, home to Buenos Aires. I don't miss anything anymore, neither people nor places.

Many writers say that language is their real home. I am all for that notion. During the last military dictatorship it was said that the writers who had left the country would progressively distance themselves from their roots until one day they would no longer be Argentine writers. It was a way of dismissing those voices, the only ones capable of being critical and objective about the regime. I, for one, don't need my roots deep in the ground; I carry them with me—like the aerial roots of our local *clavel del aire*.

Anyhow, you can never really return home. Buenos Aires has changed so much that it is no longer my city. It is a good place to clam-in and write, and the mother tongue is crucial. One thing I discovered in coming back is the importance of your own intonations as background noise. I left New York when I started dreaming in English, talking to myself in English, thinking in English. The Argentine language is a home I don't want to lose.

INTERVIEWER: How has your identity as a writer been influenced by having homes in both New York and Argentina?

VALENZUELA: I always have written on that bridge between two places. For me, it is a necessary position: the displacement and decentering of a single perspective. I often write about Buenos Aires when I am away from it. I know for sure that *Clara* came to life because I was missing Buenos Aires so much. That novel is so Buenos Aires of the 1940s—the lowlifes, prostitutes and pimps, the carnivals. Being away gives me a good perspective. Now I am elated writing about New York in Buenos Aires. It's a way of being in two places at the same time, ubiquity being one of my big dreams in life.

INTERVIEWER: When you lived in New York in the eighties, you taught creative writing at New York University. What was that experience like, considering the fact that you were teaching in your second language?

VALENZUELA: I enjoyed my classes in New York precisely because of the strangeness with the language. It was good both for me and for the students, since we were sharing a frontier. We were breaking boundaries together.

INTERVIEWER: Would you say that Argentine writers—Latin American writers in general—have a different way of writing fiction than their American counterparts?

VALENZUELA: Oh, yes. I always am quite disturbed when American reviewers call my fiction surrealist. I consider it realist in excess. Latin American writers think of reality as having a wider span, that's all—we explore the shadow side of it.

But the real difference has to do mostly with the origins of language. Spanish grammar is different from English grammar. This means that we have a different approach not only to the world, but to the word. At times it is something very subtle, a more daring immersion into the unknown. "*Un día sorprendente*," to give a very specific example, doesn't mean exactly the same as "*un sorprendente día*." In English, you cannot even turn around a phrase or leave a dangling participle. Joyce needed to explode the English language to allow its occult meaning to emerge; Cortázar just plays around with Spanish words and grammar for the same purpose. Ours is a much more elastic grammar. English is onomatopoeic, beautifully strict, clear cut. Spanish, on the other hand, is more baroque and allows for ambiguity and metaphor. Does it have to do with the speaker's character; or is character, as we may surmise, a construction of language?

INTERVIEWER: What do you think about the idea of women's language?

VALENZUELA: I openly fight for it. I think there is a different charge in the words—women come from the badlands of language. Women know a lot about ambivalence and ambiguity—which is why, I think, good, subtle political writing by women novelists is dismissed in Argentina. Women are expected to console, not disturb the readers.

INTERVIEWER: Do you consider yourself a feminist?

VALENZUELA: I think of myself as somebody who is a born feminist but doesn't like any *isms*. I don't want to be obliged to anything. I hate labels. But ever since I was a little girl, I fought my way as a woman; I saw the oppression too clearly. I think of myself as a casualty of that war and I bear my wounds with pride, though I avoid banner waving.

INTERVIEWER: Going back to your time at NYU: What do you think a writer who teaches can offer to a writer in a creative-writing class?

VALENZUELA: You cannot make a writer—it is an innate way of seeing the world, and a love of language, and a lifetime commitment. But the students in those classes already had a writer's mind, so you could teach them to see what they didn't see in their own work and move them beyond their own limitations—force them, push them inside the darkest corridors of their imagination, and also motivate them.

INTERVIEWER: Have you ever taken a creative-writing class?

VALENZUELA: Never. The streets, journalism and travel were my classes. I love to roam on my own in the bad neighborhoods of foreign cities. But who knows, a good writer's workshop could become the equivalent of that, and it might even put you on the right path when you are blocked. Though I'm too proud, too old and too lazy to even consider such a thing.

INTERVIEWER: You started out as a journalist. Do you think journalism has contributed to your fiction?

VALENZUELA: Not necessarily. Both worlds run parallel for me, but never—as yet—converge. Journalism taught me to be very precise and brief, very attentive to language. At *La Nación* my boss, Ambrosio Vecino, was a very literary man, a real teacher. He had been Cortázar's best friend during their college years together. But journalism requires a horizontal gaze; it is absolutely factual. On the other hand, fiction requires a vertical gaze—delving deeper into the non-facts, the unconscious, the realm of the imaginary. These are two very different ways of seeing the world.

Fiction, for me at least, is the best way to say things. I can be much more clear-minded if I allow my imagination to take the lead—never loosing the reins, of course, but at full gallop. I also believe that, if you are fortunate, you can access the unconscious through fiction; in my case, elaborate ideas emerge in a very organized manner. Fiction for me is a way of "writing what you don't know about what you know," to quote Grace Paley.

Borges has this wonderful phrase in a short story: "*La falta de imaginación los movió a ser crueles*" (the lack of imagination moved them to cruelty). Though cruelty with imagination can be the worst of all—just think of certain torturers in our respective countries. As a tool, imagination should only be used by writers, in their writing.

INTERVIEWER: What was Cortázar like?

VALENZUELA: I saw Julio Cortázar for the last time in December 1983. We spent a long afternoon together, and he confessed a strong need to write a novel. I asked him if he had any idea about the plot of his future novel. No, he didn't, but he had a recurrent dream in which the publisher handed him the printed book, and he glanced through it and found it perfect—he finally had been able to say what he had wanted to say all his life. And it didn't surprise him at all that the book was written not in letters, but with geometrical figures. He died the next year, on February 14. I remember thinking that the writers who had been honored with his friendship should bring his book into existence—one writer could write the triangle, another the cube, the circle or sphere, and so on.

INTERVIEWER: How does the writing process work for you? Do you know, for example, when you are starting a novel as opposed to a short story?

VALENZUELA: Yes, absolutely. Well, except for my first novel, *Clara*. Back then, I never thought I would be able to write a novel, and suddenly the idea I had for a short story needed to branch and develop.

Otherwise the division is clear. You inhabit another realm when you are writing a novel. It's like being in love—being "in novel." At times, the need is unbearable. During those periods, I don't want to write short stories. On the other hand, I might get a spark or an idea for a story; then I need a certain willpower to start pulling the thread, with the exact tension and patience so as to discover what lies behind the glimpse. Cortázar said that when the moment came he had to go to the typewriter and pull the story out of himself as if he were pulling out some kind of creepy creature, *una alimaña*. It sometimes feels like that.

INTERVIEWER: Do you have a writing schedule?

VALENZUELA: Each work finds its own time. For many years I wrote at night. Then I became scared of writing at night, probably on account of the ghosts that you call to mind when you are writing, mostly when dealing with the subject of torture and other dark political issues. I've returned to the night shift just recently, and am rediscovering the pleasure of total silence. But I still enjoy jumping out of bed and onto the computer—from dream to word, with no time to repent.

INTERVIEWER: You don't have any rituals or routines that prepare you for writing?

VALENZUELA: I don't have a ritual, but I like them a lot. With this postmodern contraption, the PC, I just do a few hands of solitaire as a warm-up. I wish I could play the piano instead.

INTERVIEWER: Do you write straight through from beginning to end?

VALENZUELA: In general, yes. When I don't write straight from beginning to end, even if doing so takes a couple of years, I know I'm in deep trouble.

INTERVIEWER: Do you revise much?

VALENZUELA: This last novel had many versions. It probably has to do with the fact that I write on a computer now. I find it quite degrading, but times are changing. Before, I wrote by hand with a soft fountain pen—I still regret the loss of my old Parker 51, a gift from my father when I turned thirteen. If I needed a certain rhythm, I went to the typewriter. Writing by hand forced me to retype each page at least three times, and each time I retyped it I would hear the pound of the words, and polish them until they reached the perfect intonation.

INTERVIEWER: How does a book start?

VALENZUELA: *El gato eficaz,* for example, just started pouring out of me. It was a very intense experience. I was a writer-in-residence at the International Writing Program at the University of Iowa and, after a couple of blank months, this strange text came into being—

and with such unusual language, so wicked and crazy. The words I used in telling that story were so unfamiliar to me that I had to write them down the minute they came. I was writing in elevators, I was writing in the streets, I was writing all over the place, on little notebooks and pieces of paper, trying to get hold of every phrase.

INTERVIEWER: What about *Black Novel with Argentines*? How did that start?

VALENZUELA: I was in New York and I thought I wanted to write a detective novel à la Chandler, but by the second page my intentions had flopped. I already knew who the killer was and who the victim was and how he had killed her. I knew, and I couldn't lie to the reader. I realized then that the real, and only, search had to be for the motive of the crime. I went on writing, and not getting any wiser about it. Many times I thought I would have to throw the whole thing away. All the while, these flashes about repression in Argentina kept popping into the mind of my Argentine protagonist, Agustín Palant. Finally, I saw the complete picture—the return of the repressed—and knew I had to be very careful not to spell it out bluntly. Since the story deals with repression it is also about what cannot easily be said. Argentina, like Agustín, needs to know, but doesn't want to hear.

INTERVIEWER: How do you deal with politics in your writing?

VALENZUELA: When I was young and all of those literary discussions were taking place in my home, the idea of politics in writing was anathema. Only Ernesto Sábato insisted that you could use politics in fiction. For Borges and the people around him, *politics* was a dirty word. You know: art for art's sake. So back then I thought that you shouldn't put politics where your mind was, where your writing was.

Now I know differently. Although the only way to deal with politics in literature is to avoid the message at all costs, without being self-righteous or judgmental. I learned that lesson inadvertently in the process of writing *Strange Things Happen Here*, in 1975.

Returning from two years of travel, I was faced with such a violent Buenos Aires that I didn't recognize my city anymore. I decided that the only way I could understand—or at least have a feeling of belonging—was by writing; I decided to write a story a day, somewhat like an AA program. So I went to the local cafés, where the paranoid feelings were so palpable that any phrase I could pick up triggered a story. Often the phrases I would overhear had nothing to do with what people were actually saying.

INTERVIEWER: Do you mean that you misheard them, or that their speech was codified in some way?

VALENZUELA: Both. The basic idea was to work around what goes unsaid yet is there, throbbing. To grasp the underlying paranoia. Usually, I misheard the phrases—but it is true that everything more or less political was said elliptically or in a coded manner. Anyway, what was important to me then were random words that would trigger my imagination. Using black humor, the grotesque, the exasperation of language, I managed to depict the horror of oppression and torture, and reintegrate myself into the reality we were living then. I wrote thirty stories in one month. In the process, I learned how to write politics without giving a message.

INTERVIEWER: Is it important to avoid the message because it makes for better fiction, or because it more easily eludes censorship?

VALENZUELA: I don't have a real message to give; I don't know the solution. But if I believed I did, I would write an essay, a column, even a pamphlet—and never contaminate fiction with a message. On the contrary, I believe fiction is a search shared with the reader.

INTERVIEWER: Has your work ever been censored? I'm thinking of "Page Zero," from your novel *He Who Searches.*

VALENZUELA: "Page Zero" was a censored page from the Spanish original. In 1979, I was correcting the proofs. The military had

taken over in March, and my editor, Enrique Pezzoni, was coura-
geous enough to go ahead with the publication but asked for cau-
tion. In "Page Zero," an introduction that is really an epilogue, the
main protagonist is interrogated and tortured. His confession is
supposed to be the text of the novel. I agreed with the publisher to
pull out "Page Zero," but we forgot to take it off the table of contents. No one noticed anything; the novel was experimental enough.

Those were bad times for publication. We had to play around
the margins of a very diffuse, random but lethal censorship. The
publishers of a distinguished house that specialized in psychology
and sociology—two very threatened disciplines at that time—
went to see the colonel who was in charge of education and culture
and asked him for guidelines that could be followed. The colonel
was outraged. "How can you ask that? You can publish whatever
you want. This is a free country, with a free press and freedom of
speech. Of course," he added, "if some madman or other decided to
plant a bomb in your publishing house, there is nothing we can do
about it."

INTERVIEWER: What do you think about Joseph Brodsky's claim
that good poetry can only be written under political repression?

VALENZUELA: I used to quarrel with Brodsky over that claim.
Brodsky would say, with his deep voice, that censorship was bad for
the writer but good for literature. That upset me to no end—it may
be true in places like the former Soviet Union, where censorship
was regulated, but not in countries like Argentina, where censorship was completely random. You had no idea what would not
please some military or other, and if something happened to upset
them they would go for the kill—your parents, your children, even
your friends. I might be ready to put my life at stake for my
thoughts, but not everybody else's. Brodsky would say that a writer
who cannot put everybody's life at risk is not worth the name, and
that censorship pushed you to produce tighter metaphors. I think
that a writer who cannot find the right metaphor is not worth the
name, neither under a dictatorship nor a democracy.

INTERVIEWER: Have you ever experienced exile?

VALENZUELA: Once, for a month and a half—it wasn't much, yet it was difficult to bear. In 1976, I went to New York for the launching of my second book in English, *Strange Things Happen Here.* Two days after I left Buenos Aires, the police raided my apartment, where my daughter was alone with her boyfriend—they were in their teens— and searched everything. They were looking for me. I had been fighting for human rights, hiding people who were in danger, getting crucial information out of the country. Fortunately, it was the police who came and not the paramilitary; they were threatening but they didn't take the kids away or harm them. I was advised not to come back. I remember spending a whole night with a Rubik's Cube, trying unsuccessfully to solve it, as if that would put my life back in place. Eventually, I managed to return to Buenos Aires, only to leave it again—but this time it was my decision. I became an expatriate, not an exile.

INTERVIEWER: A similar scene appears in "Fourth Version," when the character Bella goes abroad to perform her one-person show.

VALENZUELA: Yes, I do steal from my life at times! In that scene, Bella receives a phone call and is informed that some people are looking for her and that she should not come back. Her attitude and outlook change—she finally acknowledges the weight of her work—and she decides to return to a violent Buenos Aires and fight, with her own weapons, not allowing fear to paralyze her as it paralyzed others.

INTERVIEWER: Conversely, characters and events that originate in your fiction at times transgress their limits, literally invading reality; your novel *Bedside Manner,* for example, which unwittingly foretold a true military insurrection.

VALENZUELA: That was an ugly coincidence. An uprising of the rebel military took place the day after the book was launched.

Since the novel speaks about just such an uprising, my friends claimed I was overdoing it with the promotion of the book.

The novel takes a very pataphysic—you know, never take serious things seriously—approach to reality. The uprisings were very real—the insurgent officers called themselves the *Carapintadas,* since they smothered their faces with camouflage grease. Everything in *Bedside Manner* is real—the hyper-hyper inflation, raids for food, the shantytown—except the overlapping of ridiculous situations. There are many other examples. I believe narrative knows better than we all do.

INTERVIEWER: You yourself appear as a character in *The Lizard's Tail.* Why?

VALENZUELA: While I was writing *The Lizard's Tail* I realized that the Sorcerer was taking over the novel. This had to do with his choice of words—I had given him the first person, and with it the power over language. I couldn't fight with him from the outside— it would have been a form of literary cheating—so my only possibility was to get in the novel myself.

INTERVIEWER: What do you mean by "literary cheating"?

VALENZUELA: I was playing a difficult, two-sided game. Not that I was writing an historical novel, but very recent history was at my doorstep, and the novel goes back and forth between the first-person character of the Sorcerer and the omniscient I. But the real person, José López Rega, on whom the character was based was very much alive then, and I just couldn't distort the facts and kill him in fiction for my convenience. It would have been too easy, and would have spoiled the whole project.

INTERVIEWER: Have you ever thought about writing your memoirs?

VALENZUELA: Of sorts. Not literary memoirs. But I've written diaries on and off, except for the last ten years or so. I always fantasize about writing travel logs, but then traveling gets the best of me and I don't write. Also, I'm afraid that writing diaries is a way of avoiding fiction, so when I'm into a novel or a sequence of stories, I forgo the diaries.

But I think my life is literary and adventuresome in many ways, and I would love to tell it—if I could just pass the stage of direct narrative, which bores me to no end, especially because, in this case, I already know the outcome. There is no surprise left. Sticking to facts, however interesting, doesn't allow me to delve into metaphor, to understand the deeper implications.

The novel I just finished, *La travesía*, at first was intended to be a kind of apocryphal autobiography. After a couple of versions, I moved the whole thing from the first to the third person—the protagonist sounded too savvy for my taste, so I abandoned the autobiographical pretense.

INTERVIEWER: May I ask what the new novel is about?

VALENZUELA: *La travesía* has to do with secrets. What are the secrets that we want to keep from others and what happens when we try to keep them from ourselves. It's a bildungsroman of adulthood. This is the first time I've dealt with reality, and it was hard for me. The whole plot is invented, but the people surrounding the protagonist are not. I played with those disquieting feelings I used to get from Jerzy Kosinski's novels: where does autobiography stop and invention start?

INTERVIEWER: Your complete short stories were published recently. How did it feel to see your stories all under one roof?

VALENZUELA: I was very excited to get in touch with my first stories again. Each story has its own independence. Each story is like its own individual, grown up and on its own. When I saw them all together, like a family, I could see the thread connecting them.

INTERVIEWER: Do you regret anything you've published?

VALENZUELA: There are so many writers who have burned or disclaimed their first books. Borges, for example. What a nuisance. I am very irreverent; I know no shame in that sense. It would mean some kind of censorship, wouldn't it? Of course, there are some books I like better than others—some books still surprise me now, as if someone else had written them. On the other hand, I often regret what I haven't written because I was too lazy or too cowardly. Writing takes real courage and commitment.

—*Ksenija Bilbija*

# NOTES ON CONTRIBUTORS

KSENIJA BILBIJA (Luisa Valenzuela interview) is an associate professor of Spanish and Portuguese at the University of Wisconsin at Madison. She is the author of *Metaphors of Narrative Genius in Twentieth-Century Latin American Literature* and the editor of the journal *Letras Femininas*.

RONALD CHRIST (Jorge Luis Borges interview; translator, Pablo Neruda interview) is the publisher of Lumen Books and won the Kayden National Translation Award for Diamela Eltit's *E. Luminata*.

RITA GUIBERT (Pablo Neruda interview) is a Spanish translator and editor. She has been a member of the PEN American Association since 1972.

SUSANNAH HUNNEWELL (translator, Mario Vargas Llosa interview) is a contributing editor at *George* magazine.

SARAH LEE (Luisa Valenzuela introduction) works at Random House and is an advisory editor of *The Paris Review*. She lives in New York City.

ALFRED MACADAM (Guillermo Cabrera Infante, Carlos Fuentes, Octavio Paz interviews) teaches Latin American literature at Barnard College–Columbia University. He has translated novels by Carlos Fuentes, Julio Cortázar, José Donoso, and Juan Carlos Onetti as well as Fernando Pessoa's poetic diary *The Book of Disquiet*.

SILVANA PATERNOSTRO (Gabriel García Márquez feature) works at the World Policy Institute and is the author of several books, including *In the Land of God and Man: A Latin Woman's Journey*.

CHARLES E. RUAS (Carlos Fuentes interview) is the author of *Conversations with American Writers* and the editor of Marguerite Young's *Harp Song for a Radical: The Life and Times of Eugene Victor Debs*. He is currently a visiting professor at Stendhal University in Grenoble, France.

RICARDO A. SETTI (Mario Vargas Llosa interview) lives in São Paulo, Brazil, where he is the editorial director of the women's magazine division in Editora Abril, the largest publisher in Latin America. The interview that appears in this book is a condensed version of a longer interview with Vargas Llosa, published in book form in Portuguese, Spanish, and French.

PETER H. STONE (Gabriel García Márquez interview) has worked at various magazines throughout New York, including *Ramparts*.

JASON WEISS (Julio Cortázar interview) recently completed a book on Latin American writers in Paris. He has translated Luisa Futoransky's *The Duration of the Voyage: Selected Poems* and Marcel Cohen's *Mirrors*, and edited *Back in No Time: The Brion Gysin Reader*. He is currently at work on a novel.

KATHLEEN WHEATON (Manuel Puig interview) has worked as a journalist and travel writer in Madrid, Buenos Aires, Rio de Janeiro, and Mexico City. She is currently based in Chicago and is working on a collection of short fiction.

A NOTE ON THE TYPE

The principal text of this Modern Library edition
was set in a digitized version of Janson,
a typeface that dates from about 1690 and was cut by Nicholas Kis,
a Hungarian working in Amsterdam. The original matrices have
survived and are held by the Stempel foundry in Germany.
Hermann Zapf redesigned some of the weights and sizes for Stempel,
basing his revisions on the original design.

# MODERN LIBRARY IS ONLINE AT
## WWW.MODERNLIBRARY.COM

---

## MODERN LIBRARY ONLINE IS YOUR GUIDE TO CLASSIC LITERATURE ON THE WEB

### THE MODERN LIBRARY E-NEWSLETTER

Our free e-mail newsletter is sent to subscribers, and features sample chapters, interviews with and essays by our authors, upcoming books, special promotions, announcements, and news.

To subscribe to the Modern Library e-newsletter, send a blank e-mail to: **join-modernlibrary@list.randomhouse.com** or visit **www.modernlibrary.com**

### THE MODERN LIBRARY WEBSITE

Check out the Modern Library website at
**www.modernlibrary.com** for:

- The Modern Library e-newsletter
- A list of our current and upcoming titles and series
- Reading Group Guides and exclusive author spotlights
- Special features with information on the classics and other paperback series
- Excerpts from new releases and other titles
- A list of our e-books and information on where to buy them
- The Modern Library Editorial Board's 100 Best Novels and 100 Best Nonfiction Books of the Twentieth Century written in the English language
- News and announcements

Questions? E-mail us at **modernlibrary@randomhouse.com**
For questions about examination or desk copies, please visit
the Random House Academic Resources site at
**www.randomhouse.com/academic**